D. H. LAWRENCE AND THE IDEA OF THE NOVEL

D. H. LAWRENCE AND THE IDEA OF THE NOVEL

John Worthen

First published 1979 by
THE MACMILLAN PRESS LTD
London and Basingstoke
Associated companies in Delhi
Dublin Hong Kong Johannesburg Lagos
Melbourne New York Singapore Tokyo

Typeset in Great Britain by
PREFACE LTD
Salisbury, Wilts
and printed by
Billing & Sons Limited,
Guildford, London and
Worcester

British Library Cataloguing in Publication Data

Worthen, John
D.H. Lawrence and the Idea of the Novel
  1. Lawrence, David Herbert —Criticism and
interpretation
  I. Title
823´.9´12   PR6023.A93Z/

ISBN 0–333–21706–3

Contents

Preface

This is not a book of novel theory. It is a book about the changing way in which Lawrence saw his novels; it is a history of his changing relationship with his audience. There is a widespread belief that, after *The Rainbow* and *Women in Love*, Lawrence ceased to write his novels with very much care. I suggest that, on the contrary, he always knew what he wanted to do in them, even if we do not value the result as highly as we do those earlier books.

I am frequently concerned with the composition and the publication of Lawrence's novels. Novels are always the productions of a society, never simply the eruptions of genius. I work through the history of each book's composition to establish its identity as Lawrence himself discovered, and modified, it.

I would have liked to have discussed the novel *Mr Noon*, but the full text has not yet been published.[1] Remarks on the published section will be found in Chapters 6 and 7. I have not discussed *The Boy in the Bush*—the novel by Mollie Skinner which Lawrence rewrote in 1923. Although he may have made it his own by rewriting it, it was not his original conception; and I have chosen to work through from conception to publication.

I have often quoted from Lawrence's letters; they were for him what poems, essays and a diary might have been for another man—only, characteristically, he addressed himself to a reader when he wrote them.

I hope that this book, however inadequately, shows the truth of Terry Eagleton's remark that the task of criticism is 'to show the text as it cannot know itself, to manifest those conditions of its making (inscribed in its very letter) about which it is necessarily silent'.[2]

Speke's Valley, 1978   J.W.

Acknowledgments

I wish to thank the University College of Swansea for granting me leave of absence to write this book; the librarians, staff and secretaries of the Humanities Research Center, University of Texas; the staff of the Houghton Library, Harvard, the British Library, and the Boston Center for Criminal Justice; F. M. and D. G. Worthen; Lesley Brooksmith, Andrew Brown, 'Tricia Davis, Keith Sagar and Anne Serafin. I am especially grateful to Pat O'Connor and John Turner for their advice.

For permission to reprint copyright material, the publisher and I are indebted to the following:

Laurence Pollinger Ltd on behalf of the Estate of the late Mrs Frieda Lawrence Ravagli, and Viking Penguin Inc. for the extracts from the works of D. H. Lawrence.
The University of Wisconsin Press for the extracts from *D. H. Lawrence: A Composite Biography*, 3 Vols, edited by Edward Nehls.
Mrs C. Wood and Jonathan Cape Ltd for extracts from *D. H. Lawrence: A Personal Record*.

The following Libraries, and Cambridge University Press, have kindly co-operated in allowing the use of extracts from previously unpublished material:
Humanities Research Center, The University of Texas at Austin, for extracts from manuscripts.
The Houghton Library, Cambridge, Massachusetts, for a quotation from a D. H. Lawrence manuscript.
The Provost and Fellows of King's College, Cambridge, for a quotation from a letter written by D. H. Lawrence to E. M. Forster.
Yale University Library for extracts from a letter written by D. H. Lawrence to Catherine Carswell, 31 March 1920, now in the Beinecke Rare Book and Manuscript Library.

J.W.

Abbreviations

WP	*The White Peacock* (1911; rpt. Harmondsworth: Penguin Books, 1950)
T	*The Trespasser* (1912; rpt. Harmondsworth: Penguin Books, 1960)
SL	*Sons and Lovers* (1913; rpt. Harmondsworth: Penguin Books, 1948)
R	*The Rainbow* (1915; rpt. Harmondsworth: Penguin Books, 1949)
WL	*Women in Love* (1920; rpt. Harmondsworth: Penguin Books, 1960)
LG	*The Lost Girl* (1920; rpt. Harmondsworth: Penguin Books, 1950)
AR	*Aaron's Rod* (1922; rpt. Harmondsworth: Penguin Books, 1950)
K	*Kangaroo* (1923; rpt. Harmondsworth: Penguin Books, 1950)
PS	*The Plumed Serpent* (1926; rpt. Harmondsworth: Penguin Books, 1950)
FLC	*The First Lady Chatterley* (1944; rpt. Harmondsworth: Penguin Books, 1973)
JTLJ	*John Thomas and Lady Jane* (1972; rpt. Harmondsworth: Penguin Books, 1973)
LCL	*Lady Chatterley's Lover* (1928; rpt. Harmondsworth: Penguin Books, 1960)
Fantasia	*Fantasia of the Unconscious and Psychoanalysis and the Unconscious* (1922 and 1921; rpt. Harmondsworth: Penguin Books, 1971)
Phx	*Phoenix*, ed. E. McDonald (London: Heinemann, 1936)
Phx II	*Phoenix| II*, ed. W. Roberts and H. T. Moore (London: Heinemann, 1968)
Poems	*The Complete Poems of D. H. Lawrence*, ed. V. de S. Pinto and W. Roberts, 2 vols., 2nd ed. (London: Heinemann, 1967)
Delavenay	Emile Delavenay, *D. H. Lawrence: L'Homme et la Genèse de Son Oeuvre, Les Années de Formation 1885—1919*, 2 vols. (Paris: Klincksieck, 1969)
ET	E. T. [Jessie Chambers], *D. H. Lawrence, A Personal Record* (London: Cape, 1935)

Frieda   Frieda Lawrence, *The Memoirs and Correspondence*, ed. E. W.
              Tedlock (London: Heinemann, 1961)
Nehls   Edward Nehls (ed.), *D. H. Lawrence: A Composite Biography*,
              3 vols. (Madison: Univ. of Wisconsin Press, 1957–9)
Tedlock   E. W. Tedlock, *The Frieda Lawrence Collection of D. H.
              Lawrence Manuscripts* (Albuquerque: Univ. of New Mexico
              Press, 1948)
Roberts   Warren Roberts, *A Bibliography of D. H. Lawrence* (London:
              Hart-Davis, 1963)

Note on the text

Quotations followed by a date are from Lawrence's letters; followed by an abbreviation, are taken from the edition cited in the list of Abbreviations; followed by a superior number, from the edition cited in the Notes.

1 *The White Peacock*

Why did D. H. Lawrence become a writer and a novelist? And why did he start by writing *The White Peacock*? I ask the unanswerable questions simply to stress how being a writer is a matter of choice, of situation, of need and compulsion, rather than of destiny. The psychology of a writer is only one element among many; his background, upbringing and early experience of the world can help us to understand those choices, such needs and compulsions.

Biographers have pointed out that Lawrence's maternal grandfather was a noted hymn-writer, and that his mother is known to have written poetry. Such things probably matter rather less than the importance which his upbringing gave to the written and printed word. In Lawrence's case, reading and writing were activities valued particularly by his mother for the chance they provided of an escape from the life she herself had known—the chance of getting out of the working class. Lawrence's father could barely read, and when a copy of *The White Peacock* arrived at the family home he 'struggled through half a page, and it might as well have been Hottentot'. What struck him most forcibly was the money his son was getting paid for it. 'Fifty pounds! An' tha's niver done a day's hard work in thy life' (*Phx* 232). It was a shrewd thrust at the son whose education had freed him from the world his father inhabited.

But Lawrence was not the first in his family to make headway with books. His elder brother Ernest had been locally famous for his love of books as well as for his striking ability to 'get on' in life; part of the obituary for him in the local paper made that very clear.

> At the Eastwood library there was no more familiar figure than his, he was a great reader from a boy, and in his early teens he had become acquainted with most of the present day writers and many of the past. . . . His knowledge for a young man was considerable, London's gaiety could not wrest from him his love for work and his keen desire to get on.[1]

We tend to link the young Bert Lawrence's passion for reading with his friendship for Jessie Chambers, because it was she who recorded the books they read together, and his enthusiasms. But when she and Lawrence chose books together at the Mechanics' Institute Library in Eastwood, they were getting books for their own families as well as for themselves. Lawrence's mother read a good deal; her son's rather unflattering memory of her reaction to *East Lynne* and *Diana of the Crossways* (*Phx II* 593) should be balanced by our knowledge of her reading Flaubert's *Sentimental Education*, albeit with 'a severe look of disapproval' as Lawrence told Grace Crawford (04 viii 1910). On the evidence of *Sons and Lovers*, which can probably be trusted on such a point, she also wrote the occasional paper to be given at meetings of the Womens' Guild: 'It seemed queer to the children to see their mother, who was always busy about the house, sitting writing in her rapid fashion, thinking, referring to books and writing again. They felt for her on such occasions the deepest respect' (*SL* 68). Serious attention to reading and books was a natural interest for a son who was not only academically clever, but who was particularly encouraged by his mother to better himself and 'get on' as Ernest had done; it obviously fell to Lawrence to take up, in some measure, the role of Ernest in the Lawrence household after 1901.

But the young Lawrence was also haunted, even obsessed, by that other family out at the Haggs farm. For the Chambers family, literature was not an instrument to self-improvement, but as natural an interest as farming. Books and reading in the Lawrence household inevitably became a focus of the division between the mother and the father, exactly as the spoken word was, with the children caught between the 'King's English' of the mother, and the dialect of the community which they spoke outdoors but of which she could never speak so much as a sentence (*Phx II* 592). At the Haggs farm, no such tensions existed. Mr Chambers would read out loud the serialisation of *Tess of the D'Urbervilles* in the newspaper, for the benefit of his wife and any of the children old enough to appreciate it. As a family, they not only read but talked about their reading. When Mrs Lawrence and her son visited the farm, what she had in common with the Haggs' household quickly emerged. Jessie Chambers remembered how 'the conversation had turned upon books';

> My parents adored Barrie, *The Little Minister* and *A Window in Thrums*. The talk was lively and Mrs Lawrence seemed to be the pivot upon which the liveliness centred. . . .
> 'Who likes Scott?' I asked.
> '*I* do,' Mrs Lawrence replied, beaming encouragement upon me.
> (*ET* 24–5)

In that 'book-loving household' (*ET* 25), the whole family would take part in charades and play-readings; Jessie remembered her father playing Macduff and stopping in horror over his final speech to Macbeth: 'Oh dear, oh dear! How awful!' (*ET* 108). Friends of the family would sometimes gather for charades and sing-songs at the Lawrence home, but they were never family activities in the same way—and they were not literary, either. At the Haggs farm, literature and books could haunt Lawrence like a passion; in the Lawrence homes in Walker Street and Lynn Croft, they were inevitably complicated by the divisions and ambitions of the family.

So it is significant that the first things we can regard Lawrence as writing—the first items discussed by Jessie Chambers in her chapter 'Literary Formation'—were the long letters Lawrence sent the Chambers family while he was convalescing after pneumonia, in the winter of 1901–1902. 'They were accounts of what he had been doing or reading, bits of himself put down on paper, often very amusingly' (*ET* 91). It is worth comparing those with his habit, also noted by Jessie Chambers, of incorporating the events of everyday life directly into his fiction, particularly in his first novel; a novel as record of landscape and observation was one of the ways in which he first conceived of it. And, again, the events of daily life were those of the Haggs' household and the fields and woods round about; that was the material he chose for a novel.

But he did not start that novel for another four years; the passion he took to the Haggs was for reading and for talk about reading. The Chambers family were bombarded with books they 'must' read, and with the talk of them. However, with the men of the family working on the farm, and the only other adolescent (May Chambers) rather hostile to him, it was natural that Jessie should have become his partner in literature. As Lawrence wryly and unforgiveably summed it up in later life, in the shape of Mellors' disdainful account of his boyhood:

> I read and I thought like a house on fire, for her. . . . And about *everything* I talked to her: but everything. We talked ourselves into Persepolis and Timbuctoo. We were the most literary-cultured couple in ten counties.
>
> (*LCL* 208–9)

For both of them, that discussion became an escape from their respective families; and for Lawrence it was an escape into a world without the tensions and ambitions of home. His interest in books was not, in any case, something that the other children of the Lawrence family would have had much sympathy with. Ernest had died in 1901, George and Emily had no interest in books (and both left home early), and Ada's attitude both to literature and to Jessie Chambers can be gauged from an exchange with the latter over *The Tempest* when they were both studying at the Pupil-Teacher Centre. 'Miranda's noble speeches fired my spirit, and I murmured to A., "That's just what I believe." "Humph, I think its's rubbish," was her whispered rejoinder' (*ET* 47).

In 1928, Lawrence summed up what he then saw as his family's attitude to his writing in those early days:

> He wrote for Miriam, the girl on the farm, who was herself becoming a school-teacher. She thought it all wonderful—else, probably, he would never have written—His own family strictly 'natural' looked upon such performance as writing as 'affectation.' Therefore wrote in secret at home.
>
> (*Phx II* 300)

In 1928 he was being careful to distinguish the 'natural' from the bourgeois in his early experience, and to stress that he rejected the bourgeois in favour of the natural. But that conclusion is in complete contradiction with the start of his writing career; and accordingly, in 1928, he made writing a 'performance' and landed a lot of the responsibility for it on to Jessie Chambers. What the passage is trying to say is, I believe, quite untrue to what actually happened in 1906, though its outlines may be true: he did keep his writing secret, and it was done for Jessie to read. As late as 1909 he was distinctly embarrassed at being thought an author, and refused to let his poems be sent to the *English Review* without a *nom de plume*: 'I don't want folk in Croydon to know I write poetry' (*ET* 157). When the poems were in print, 'people read them and told me so, to my embarrassment and anger. I hated being an author, in people's eyes' (*Phx II* 594). But that was not because he, like his family, regarded writing as an 'affectation'; we can see how his writing, from the start, provoked a contradiction in his own nature and circumstances, not just in his family. Even when an intimate friend like George Neville called for Lawrence at the Haggs, he would as like as not find him and Jessie 'with their heads close together and the crumpled papers spread out in front of them; but the papers soon disappeared with my arrival' (*Nehls* i 46). The earliest writing was secret, almost embarrassing; but when Jessie had a letter from the *English Review* showing interest in Lawrence's poems, Lawrence's reaction was to say: 'Let me take it to show mother' (*ET* 159). This despite the fact that, in 1928, he wrote that 'his mother, whom he loved best on earth, he never spoke to, about his writing. It would have been a kind of "showing off," or affectation' (*Phx II* 301). Success was a different matter. We know how hard Lawrence tried to get a copy of *The White Peacock* into his mother's hands before she died; but it was not that he wanted her to read it. It was a proof of success. He later summed up her attitude towards success: 'you had to be clever & rise in the world, step by step' (*Phx II* 301).

It seems clear that, at moments anyway, writing seemed to offer such a future; Jessie Chambers remembered him exclaiming 'I'll make two thousand a year!' (*ET* 168). But writing was ordinarily a particularly

vivid focus of his own contradictory distance from the class and community he knew best. As he remarked, feelingly, to Jessie on another
occasion: 'What will the others say? That I'm a fool. A collier's son a
poet!' (*ET* 57). She saw no problem: 'What does your father's occupa-
tion matter?' But to Lawrence, caught in loyalty between the miner's
kitchen and the woods round Strelley Mill, it certainly did. When his
father eventually struggled through that half page of *The White
Peacock*—'and it might as well have been Hottentot'—in some ways it
was more foreign than any foreign language could be, with its narrator
fancying the trees 'too dark and sober to dally with the sun' (*WP* 13),
with the 'whole place . . . gathered in the musing of old age'. The novel
was written in the language of the highly educated and artistic person
with literary aspirations whom Lawrence had in part become between
1901 and 1910, and that language was utterly foreign to the life of the
collier or the general life of the community. With the sarcasm of years
at his disposal, Lawrence recalled in 1928

> the slightly self-conscious Sunday afternoon, when I was nineteen,
> and I 'composed' my first two 'poems.' One was to *Guelder-roses*, and
> one to *Campions*, and most young ladies would have done better: at
> least I hope so. But I thought the effusions very nice, and so did
> Miriam.
>
> (*Poems* ii 849)

By 1928 he could afford to be sarcastic about his passion for books and
his girlish enthusiasms, and he could be witty about his 'affectation'|of
writing; but between 1904 and 1910, his self-conscious and secretive
efforts represented a claim on a life utterly different from that of the
Eastwood community he knew. And it was a claim staked with all his
intelligence and all his aspiration.

The idea of writing fiction, as it first possessed him, was inevitably
and inherently alien to working-class life. It meant a rejection of the
industrial town and the desolated landscape for the life of art and the
deep country. Before, apparently, he wrote a word, Lawrence knew
that 'It will be *poetry*'—eliciting from Jessie Chambers the response
'Well, isn't that the very greatest thing?' (*ET* 57). It would be poetry
and poetic fiction; poetry like that of Meredith in the appropriately
named 'Love in the Valley' they both liked so much, poetic fiction like
The White Peacock, set in the woods and fields immediately surrounding
the Haggs farm. Lawrence explained how he could not, anyway, do
very much to control it: 'I'm afraid it will be a mosaic. My time's so
broken up . . . I don't see how there can be any continuity about it. It
will have to be a mosaic, a mosaic of moods' (*ET* 104). None of this
version survives, but judging by surviving fragments of the second
version, its 'moods' were primarily melancholic and self-conscious; its

mosaic would have been a mixture of natural description and romance between 'an upright young farmer' and a 'superior young lady' who was seduced by a superior young man and then abandoned. Its Hardy-like plot was narrated by the sensitive Cyril (who was to remain in all four drafts of the book), not primarily as a narrative device—for the convention of having him observe all the scenes he describes is quickly dropped, even in the last version—but as a kind of tragic chorus, a necessary peg to hang the fine and moody writing on. Lawrence had remarked that 'I don't want a plot, I should be bored with it', and he was happy simply to follow through two contrasting relationships (*ET* 103), and use Cyril's monologues in the intervals.

But he seems immediately to have realised at least some of its weaknesses: 'he immediately started to rewrite it' (*ET* 117). We also, interestingly, know a little about what his mother thought of it. Apparently she came across part of it by accident, and would 'say nothing except "I wish you had written on another line"' (04 v 1908), as Lawrence told Blanche Jennings. 'To think that *my* son should have written such a story' (*ET* 117) was how Jessie Chambers heard her react; she must have read the part about Lettie's seduction. Later still, Lawrence told May Chambers that 'she doesn't like what I write. Perhaps if it had been romance. . . . But I couldn't write that' (*Nehls* iii 618). Romance would be both safe and saleworthy, and remained in Lawrence's mind as an alternative to his kind of serious fiction: he planned to write it after 'Paul Morel' (the early *Sons and Lovers*) as a way of making money. The other alternative, of course, was to give up fiction for qualifications; Lawrence could have gone on to take his degree at Nottingham University College, after his two years' course leading to the teacher's certificate—and the maternal advice was always '*Be good, and you'll get on in life*' (*Phx II* 260). But he decided to go on with his writing, as he told Blanche Jennings:

> I have pretty well decided to give up study, and to comfort my poor soap-bubble of a soul with writing . . . I dread your giving me more maternal advice—in this vein: 'Get on—take your degree—then you can hope to leave the elementary teaching that you hate.'
>
> (26 x 1908)

Lawrence did not become a full-time writer until he went to Germany in May 1912; and even that trip had been planned to put him in touch with his uncle Fritz Krenkow, who might have been able to help him become a Lektor at a German university. He remained in his teaching job till November 1911, and it took a severe illness to get him out of it. While his mother was alive he felt obliged to send money home, out of his secure teacher's income; and no sooner had his mother died than Lawrence found himself trying to finance a marriage to Louie Burrows.

The years 1908 to 1911 obviously frustrated Lawrence because he could not find time to write; but they also show his commitment to earning a decent living. In the words of Ford Madox Ford,[2] 'He wasn't at any rate going to take any material chances without weighing them very carefully' (*Nehls* i 117). He had been brought up to be a reliable salary-earner, and he wanted to be sure that his kind of writing could support him. Until 1912, he had no evidence that it could.

Consequently he wrestled with *The White Peacock* throughout his college career and during the first part of his time in Croydon, hoping to turn it into a book which would prove that he was a writer. 'I must have written most of it five or six times' (*Phx II* 593); he used to write 'patches' of it during lectures at college (*Phx II* 300). And although he was also writing poems and the occasional short story, it is clear that the novel was not only the biggest of his tasks, but occupied the largest place in his ambitions. It was the only one of his earliest works he was prepared to let people see, and ask their advice about; Jessie Chambers read it, as she read everything, but it was also read by Alice Dax, Blanche Jennings, a friend of hers, Lawrence's mother, and A. W. McLeod. And of course it was shown to Ford in 1909. When the latter launched Lawrence's career by printing his poems in the *English Review*, Lawrence told Louie Burrows that 'I never thought of myself blossoming out as a poet—I had planted my beliefs in my prose' (11 ix 1909). On the five occasions he mentioned to Blanche Jennings his hopes of becoming a writer, during 1908, it was to his novel and to literary journalism that he looked in every case.

But even there, we find a significant complexity. In 1908 Lawrence had nothing with which to support his belief in himself as a writer except unpublished poems and a sprawling unfinished novel. When he talked about a career as a writer, he made the idea banal so that it should not be bathetic. His letters to Blanche Jennings are crucial documents in our understanding of his ambition to be a writer; they are designed to dazzle with literary wit, they are full of the contradictions implicit in his actual situation. For instance:

> And I am poor—and my mother looks to me—and I shall either have to wear motley all my days and be an elementary school teacher, or be an elementary school teacher without motley—a lamentable figure I should cut—unless I can do something with that damned damnation of a Laetitia . . .
>
> (04 v 1908)

If writing to her was an opportunity to show off a little of his brilliance, it was also an opportunity to demonstrate how that brilliance floated clear of the family he knew and the way of life he had been brought up to; the brilliance was that of literary aspiration, and as such had nothing to do with Eastwood. We can see Lawrence making a few spasmodic attempts to become a published writer in 1908 and 1909, but it is clear that he was not very serious in them. There was too much at stake, as that rather despairing brilliance to Blanche Jennings suggests. 'Being a writer' was something both dangerously attractive, and also alien; for all his exhibitions of style and artistry, it was clearly a contradictory matter.

And *The White Peacock* was gradually dug out 'in inchoate bits, from the underground of my consciousness' (*Phx II* 593). It was less a divine labour than a matter of proving to himself and to others that he was a writer, and that he knew what a novel could be. In his aesthetic declaration of 1908, the essay 'Art and the Individual', the 'mission of art' is to

> bring us into sympathy with as many men, as many objects, as many phenomena, as possible. To be in sympathy with things is to some extent to acquiesce in their purpose, to help on that purpose. We want, we are for ever trying to unite ourselves with the whole universe. . . .
>
> (*Phx II* 226)

The idea is obviously similar to the famous remark in *Lady Chatterley's Lover* that the novel 'can inform and lead into new places the flow of our sympathetic consciousness' (*LCL* 104). But to judge by its surviving fragments, the 'purpose' in which the 1908 *White Peacock* would like to acquiesce is a sympathy with nature and the natural (as against the seducing gentilities of a Leslie); and the sympathy it demonstrates hardly aims to unite 'with the whole universe': it is on the side of the angels and the educated public. Being a literary artist, for Lawrence in 1908, meant demonstrating fine and metaphorical expression—meant being demonstrably cultured. *The White Peacock* never stopped being a work of art which anyone could recognise as such. If we compare a passage from this 1908 version with the same passage as published in 1911, it is remarkable how little it is fundamentally changed, for all the cuts:

> There the daffodils were lifting their glorious heads and throwing back their wanton yellow curls to sport with the sun. At the foot of each sloping, grey old tree a family of these healthy, happy flowers stood, some bursten with overfulness of splendour, some raising their heads slightly, modestly showing a sweet countenance, others still hiding their faces, leaning forward from the jaunty cluster of grey green spears; many were just venturing timidly out of their sheaths, peeping about. I felt inclined to hug them, I wanted desperately to know their language perfectly so that I might talk out my heart to them. They had a rich perfume as of oranges; they laughed

to me, and tried to reassure me. So I looked up, feeling my spirit triumph again, and I saw betwixt me and the sky the trees with lifted fingers shaking out their hair to the sun, decking themselves with buds as white and cool as a water-nymph's breasts. Why should I not be glad? For even where the ground was hard by the paths the colts foot discs glowed in merry company. . . .[3]

(Tedlock 5)

There the daffodils were lifting their heads and throwing back their yellow curls. At the foot of each sloping, grey old tree stood a family of flowers, some bursten with golden fullness, some lifting their heads slightly, to show a modest, sweet countenance, others still hiding their faces, leaning forward pensively from their jaunty grey-green spears; I wished I had their language, to talk to them distinctly.

Overhead, the trees with lifted fingers shook out their hair to the sun, decking themselves with buds as white and cool as a water-nymph's breasts.

I began to be very glad. The colts-foot discs glowed and laughed in a merry company down the path. . . .

(WP 185)

The cuts are all good ones. The fact that Cyril feels like hugging the daffodils is of no interest to anyone but himself; likewise with the daffodils' attempt to reassure him. Adjectives and adverbs suffer the heaviest cuts, and when they are changed the replacements are more precise: 'distinctively', 'pensively'. But the most carefully designed metaphors are retained: the water-nymph's breasts remain white and cool, the countenances of the daffodils remain sweet, the coltsfoot discs remain a merry company. The language remains both wistful and exotic; the scene's primary function is still to display sensitivity to nature. The crucial thing is that Lawrence himself knew very well what was wrong with this kind of writing, and knew it as early as 1908. He remains unsurpassed as a critic of the novel, telling Blanche Jennings that it was 'all about love—and rhapsodies on spring scattered here and there—heroines galore—no plot—nine-tenths adjectives—every colour in the spectrum descanted upon—a poem or two—scraps of Latin and French—altogether a sloppy, spicy mess' (15 iv 1908).

In 1910, he summed it up as 'a decorated idyll running to seed in realism' (18 x 1910). Our conclusion must be that he did not suddenly mature into an aversion to this kind of writing around the years 1911–12; he knew what he was doing, as early as 1908. He told Blanche Jennings that it was 'cloyed with metaphoric fancy' (11 xi 1908), which is absolutely right, and that 'the theme is abominable—I blush for myself': but the book's basic concerns and manner did not change through all the subsequent revision. If Lawrence really dug the novel out of the 'underground of my consciousness', as he claimed in 1928, we should ask why that underground was so pastoral, why it was so empty of the things he had known before the cultural explosion of his adolescence, and why it was so damnably conscious of literary style.

Again, in 1908 Lawrence understood what was wrong with his use of Cyril as a narrator; he told Blanche Jennings that 'I will . . . stop up the mouth of Cyril—I will kick him out—I hate the fellow' (30 vii 1908). But just as the gamekeeper Annable was necessary to the novel because—otherwise—'it's too much one thing, too much *me*' (*ET* 117), so Cyril appears to have been necessary to the novel in order to be 'me'. He is akin to those other sophisticated travellers Bernard Coutts (in 'The Witch *à la Mode*'), Cyril Mersham (in 'A Modern Lover') and John Adderley Syson (in 'The Shades of Spring'); Coutts and Cyril both return mysteriously from France, in a well-bred way, and the others both go back to the country of their hearts to find their old girlfriends in the arms of other men. But none are as mysterious and unrealistic as Cyril, wandering alone in Nethermere, feeling 'the anguish of the bracken fallen face-down in defeat' (*WP* 347). Cyril is necessary to *The White Peacock* as tragic chorus, as commentator and sensitive observer; Lawrence does not risk letting the story tell itself, or the people make their own lives without commentary; it is not that kind of book. From its gesturing chapter titles (the last chapter being 'A Prospect Among the Marshes of Lethe') to the monologues delivered by all the characters in their moments of self-revelation, it is a book dedicated to a demonstration of the poignancy and pain of suffering and defeat. All three main male characters end up defeated (and Annable has been killed); Lettie and Meg are also miserable. Only Emily, Cyril's erstwhile sweetheart—he forgets her simply by failing to remember her—ends happily; and in so literary a book the contrast is explicit between her Happy Ending and George's tragic fate. It is a book that cannot, that does not dare to, leave itself alone; all the characters speak with Lawrence's own voice and insight at moments, and the very bracken takes up a significant pose when Cyril looks at it. Even Annable, who dominates the action the moment he appears, is obliged to sum up his philosophy for us: 'Be a good animal, true to your animal instinct' (*WP* 173), and is packed into a single chapter of significance. *The White Peacock* is a book which, over four years, Lawrence wrote and rewrote with something rising to obsession. A great deal had come to depend on it; it was a sustained exercise in literary culture, its themes were made (as he knew) terribly obvious, and some of its over-writing is perhaps exactly that—something done once too often.

But as if to confirm his success at the literary mode, the majority of the book's reviewers made a point of its stress on suffering—it was something they knew how to cope with; and they registered its exqui-

siteness too. The *English Review* found the book 'a work of artistic and
literary excellence, as the writing of a man who knows he will achieve
both fame and distinction',[4] and the *Manchester Guardian* noted that 'Mr
Lawrence can write. There are some fine rhapsodies in the book. . . .'[5]
Some objected to what they saw as its brutality and over-explicitness,
but in general the book was accepted for what it was: a rather odd
pastoral and rhapsodic novel, finely written. Lawrence may have been
'very young when I wrote the *Peacock*—I began it at twenty. Let that be
my apology' (20 ii 1911), but the book tells us more about how he saw
literature between 1906 and 1910 than about his immaturity.

It has, again, become a standard critical charge against the novel
that it elevates its version of the Lawrence family to the middle class,
conveniently disposing of the unwanted father as it does so. It is true
that the family is most unconvincing, but I would suggest that Lawrence had other reasons than snobbery for making the change. The
death of the absent father is seized as an opportunity for mystery and
romance, and the family is created without the particular—and inevitable—tensions of his own; the obstacles in Lettie's way are made those
of temperament and uninspired moments, rather than those of class;
the issue between her and Leslie is not a class issue, and even more
surprisingly, the issue between her and the young farmer George is not
allowed to be, either. We can see the same kind of transposition happening between the first and third versions of *Lady Chatterley's Lover*,
when the working-class Parkin is transmuted into the *déclassé* Mellors.
Lawrence wanted, obviously, to create effects with the fictional family
of *The White Peacock* that would not have been possible with his own.
Not only is the Beardsall father turned into a tragic romance—we can
be glad that Mr Lawrence got no further than page one of the book—he
is, significantly, referred to as 'the Father', not 'our father'. He is an
exhibit rather than a character. The decent and commercial marriages
of Lawrence's elder brother and sister are also eschewed, as are the
succession of family houses in Eastwood. The Beardsall cottage (again,
a significant word) on the edge of Moorgreen reservoir (itself revamped
as Nethermere) is that of people with a private income; the novel has
other functions for the working class than letting them occupy the
natural foreground. It presents them rather as Flemish genre-painting
presents the rowdy individuals in its taverns; as fascinating examples of
vitality and depravity; grotesque, charming—or both. Annable's teem-
ing family, also doing duty as animal vitality, stands in for the working
class, and when Cyril and Lettie meet two young colliers on the road,
we have a description of them as curiosities rather than people. But to
the readers of such novels, colliers *are* curiosities. Cyril and Lettie, in
their carriage with 'John' the coachman, and the collier lads shouting
'ooray!' (*WP* 123) as 'Christmas came in with their acclamations', are
equally unreal; they are the stock figures of the nineteenth-century

society novel, and all of them vanish like spirits at cock-crow with the ending of the chapter.

If we put beside them something Jessie Chambers once wrote about Lawrence and Eastwood, we can see the extent to which they are fictional.

> Lawrence belonged absolutely to the stock from which he sprang; bone of their bone. There was no distance between him and the people amongst whom he lived; when he talked to them he spoke out of the same heritage of thought and feeling; he was like them, only greater, in a sense he contained them in himself. He had a marvellous understanding of collier folk, men and women; he knew just how they felt about things and what their reactions were, and how their thinking was not so much of the mind as, to use his own phrase, of the blood. He was quite at home with them and they with him, whereas I always felt, and was, an outsider, a 'foreigner' as they would say. But Lawrence was not a 'foreigner', he was one of them in an extremely close and subtle relationship.
>
> *(Delavenay* ii 665)

The author who created the interesting curiosities on the road simply was not concerned with the people whom the man knew; and he was also a different author from the creator of stories like 'The Christening' and even the earliest 'Odour of Chrysanthemums'. We can see why Ford Madox Ford seized on Lawrence as a potential writer of 'workingman novels' but was to be disappointed (*Nehls* i 116). The author of *The White Peacock* was not trying to deny his roots; he was simply creating what he felt a novel should be. When the novel does concern itself with class distinctions, in the gross parody of the upper classes at play in 'Pastorals and Peonies', all the girls cry over a sentimental little story Cyril tells. They, too, are the stock figures of a novel; rather pretentious but soft-centred aristocrats.

Even George, who has moments of physical actuality, is more interesting in the novel as an example of something—at first, physical ease, and later on, spiritual decline—than *as* something. This is also true of Leslie. He is a highly-strung and enervated anti-hero long before he is a coal-owner or coal-owner's son. In the first chapter, he even acts as a Regency rake, sprawling in his garden chair thinking of women—'These girls are so daft with a fellow!' (*WP* 22). It is made of secondary importance that his feeling of superiority to George would be, in large part, a class superiority; it is presented as that of the mind's presumption over the body, of the fine-souled and nervous man's response to one who is, by nature, less refined. What goes wrong between George and Lettie, too, is made a matter of a finer nature rejecting a coarser. The actual or potential barriers between a capital-less farmworker and the girl with a fortune of a couple of thousand pounds are precisely what the novel is not concerned with; the novel offers a clash of character and temperament and destiny, not of class. Lettie is eventually given to Leslie, with a kind of tired irony, because the novel is presenting a study of George's tragic decline.

What I suggest all this means is Lawrence's problem with finding a public voice as a novelist. As the figure of Annable shows, Lawrence can offer more than Cyril's sensitivities; but the transformation of the personal insight into the public statement, in this novel, means that Lawrence changes his knowledge of people into images of them appropriate for a novel. Cyril then fills in the gaps with patches of fine feeling which occasionally rise to the level of a tragic chorus. Again, Lawrence was aware of the danger of a novel like this as early as 1908, when he voiced to Blanche Jennings his fear that 'folk talk about themes too much' (11 xi 1908); but even if he rectified that fault, he could not (and did not want to) stop them representing themes. I suggest that the same failure to be confident of a public voice lies behind the cloying metaphorical habit, too. In his private letters we can see Lawrence playing attractive games with words, but without the context of the personal relationship, the novel's metaphors are frequently only tedious. He could write to Louie Burrows, for instance—after a paragraph of gentle banter—that 'After much nibbling of bad cake you come to the almond paste at last: I'm coming to Leicester on Wednesday . . . ' (12 ix 1908). The joke is small-scale, self-mocking, rather attractive. But that same voice in a novel, constructing ingenious metaphors, is hugely amplified; it loses all traces of its self-mockery and can sound simply precious. But Lawrence obviously wants a public voice, wants to transform the private into the public—wants to be a novelist.

And so, for instance, he can insert a prose poem like 'I was born in September, and love it best of all the months' (*WP* 74) into Chapter VI; the private tone is wrenched into that of public declamation, and becomes unbearably portentous. It was not until much later in life that Lawrence managed to find a public voice suitable for direct communication with his audience—one that could be direct and personal without being embarrassing. His use of the first person in his fiction was nearly always a failure, and none of his other novels employ it. *The White Peacock* shows how hard it was for an intensely intelligent and sensitive and well-read young man to write a novel; how much the complexities of his own upbringing affected the kind of novels he would write; how much the literary explosion of his adolescence, although vital in creating in him a desire to write independently of his family —and, indeed, independently of his mother's ambition for him— actually interfered with his capacity to write a novel. I suspect that Lawrence had to write a novel like *The White Peacock* to start freeing himself from the contradictions that inhibited his attempts at a public voice—to free himself a little from his idea of what a novel should be. He had to learn a way of making a novel that, without being a copy of other novels, could actually address itself to an audience. He also had to learn, by trying, whether the audience whose appreciation he aimed for in *The White Peacock* was really the audience he wanted. But it is, too, important to register that he had the ambition of writing for an audience from the start.

2 *The Trespasser*

There is general critical sorrow over *The Trespasser*. 'It need not detain us long';[1] 'little needs to be said';[2] 'the less said the better'.[3] But although it is perhaps the worst novel Lawrence wrote, it is all the same a remarkably revealing book. It shows us the kind of novelist Lawrence was between 1910 and 1912, and could have gone on being. And we cannot simply dismiss it as youthful or immature. Its composition was curiously intertwined with that of *Sons and Lovers*—the novel generally thought to mark Lawrence's maturity as a writer.

He wrote the first version of *The Trespasser*—then called 'The Saga of Siegmund'—between April and the start of August 1910. He began 'Paul Morel'—the first version of *Sons and Lovers*—at the start of October 1910. He was then involved with 'Paul Morel' until November 1911, when he was ill for a month. As soon as he was well, he took up the 'Saga' and revised it as *The Trespasser*. Within ten days of finishing it, however, he had started work on 'Paul Morel' again, which he was to finish in mid-April. But by then he was making considerable proof corrections to *The Trespasser*. We can link the work he did on 'Paul Morel' in the summer of 1911 with his simultaneous reading of Stendhal's *Le Rouge et Le Noir* (hero—Julien Sorel). In January 1912 he compared his personal involvement with *The Trespasser* to Stendhal's involvement with Julien Sorel (21 i 1912). *Sons and Lovers* as we have it dates, in most respects, from the period September–November 1912, so that it was actually finished less than ten months after *The Trespasser*. We cannot say that the work of January 1912 was startlingly immature while the work of September–November 1912 was startlingly mature. I suggest that, if the novels are different, it must partly be because Lawrence wanted *The Trespasser* to be as it is; and that is what makes it such an interesting case.

'The Saga' was orginally provoked by Helen Corke's tragic experience in the Isle of Wight in 1909; the man with whom she had gone on holiday committed suicide on his return. Lawrence had known her before that event, but not well; having learned what had happened, he was one of those who helped her through the autumn and winter 1909–10. In the spring of 1910 he showed her the MS of *The White Peacock*, then awaiting final revision; she agreed to read it and comment on it. This led naturally to her showing him what she was writing; she had completed a retrospective diary of her days on the Island, and was writing a long 'letter' to the dead man. By the spring of 1910 she trusted him enough to let him see the five-days journal.

He reminded her how, according to her own record, she had suggested to 'Siegmund' that he should try and write of their experience in musical form. Might he, Lawrence, take her poems [e.g. journal—'prose poems'] and base upon them his own conception of Siegmund's story. 'Let it be a saga, as it cannot be a symphony,' he begged.[4]

In 1968 she remembered that remark as 'it shall be a poem as it can't be a symphony'.[5] Lawrence's original motive for taking up the story seems to have been a compound of practical sympathy—the best way of helping her through the experience being to understand it completely, himself—sympathy with her which bordered on love, and fascination with the subject. But he also needed another novel. *The White Peacock*, having drawn into itself almost everything he had thought and felt for the past four years, was at last almost finished. He must sometimes have wondered where another novel could come from, and had told Jessie Chambers at Easter that 'he would write a "bright" story' with her brother Hubert as hero (*ET* 181), to be set 'within the familiar Midland environment'. That obviously was not 'Paul Morel'; the 'bright' story sounds more like the 'romance' he said he would dedicate himself to after 'Paul Morel' was finished (06 xii 1910). But Helen Corke's material was very striking. Lawrence's sense of the tragic in literature at this time contained a strong element of the suicidal. George Saxton in *The White Peacock* in effect kills himself; Paul Morel was to contemplate suicide; Baxter Dawes in the final *Sons and Lovers* is a man who gives up and nearly dies; Mr Morel in the 1911 'Paul Morel' gives up and dies after coming out of prison. The suicidal in literature is the ultimate assertion of the individual's alienation from society, from family, finally from the body itself. Suicide is a natural preoccupation of a culture which is particularly concerned with the moral integrity of the individual. Lawrence's own fascination with the subject is clear, and the first-hand creation of the subject in the 'Saga' was compelling in its own right. It is notable that Lawrence wrote the 'Saga' to create, and do justice to, the man involved; the woman, after all, survived, and had her own understanding of the affair. He wrote the novel in a little over three months, while engaged full-time in teaching; he told Helen Corke that 'I don't think I do Siegmund injustice' (12 v 1910), for all the speed of composition.

What was more, he began to have sympathies with Siegmund that put him, too, in the role of potential—and angry—lover of Helen Corke.

You are part of his immortality. That is what would make me go wild, if I woke up. You see, I know Siegmund is there all the time. I know you would go back to him, after me, and disclaim me. I know it very deeply. I know I could not bear it. I feel often inclined, when I think of you, to put my thumbs on your throat.

(12 v 1910)

Siegmund, too, looks at Helena almost in hatred as they leave the island, and feels 'tortured with the problem of her till it became acute, and he felt as if his heart would burst inside him' (*T* 132). It seems undeniable that the first writing of the 'Saga' took Lawrence bodily into that relationship with Helena. He told Jessie Chambers, just as he started to write, 'not to attempt to hold him. He told me most impressively the story of the Shirt of Nessus. Something of that, he said, something fatal, perhaps, might happen if I insisted on holding him' (*ET* 181–2). From the start, the novel was a challenge Lawrence felt impelled to accept; a challenge to identify with the man who kills himself, the fascination of a man sucked by passion 'down into a vortex' (*ET* 190). Writing the novel was a way of experiencing that sensation himself.

But why, then, did he write it like this?

The sun grew stronger. Slower and more slowly went the hawks of Siegmund's mind, after the quarry of conclusion. . . .
'If I had her more, I should understand her through and through. If we were side by side we should grow together. If we could stay here, I should get stronger and more upright.'
This was the poor heron of quarry the hawks of his mind had struck.
Another hour fell like a foxglove bell from the stalk. There were only two red blossoms left. Then the stem would have set to seed.

(*T* 123–5)

The artist who was fascinated by the vortex chose to express it through such metaphors of hawks, herons and foxgloves; we cannot separate our understanding of his approach to that compelling subject from the way in which he created it. Large portions of *The Trespasser* are written in a style even more untiringly metaphorical than that of *The White Peacock*. Helena looks out of a window: 'The moon was wading deliciously through shallows of white cloud. Beyond the trees and the few houses was the great concave of darkness, the sea, and the moonlight. The moon was there to put a cool hand of absolution on her brow' (*T* 36). At such a point we can make a precise check on Helen Corke's influence on Lawrence's novel; the provocation for that passage came from the following passage in her Freshwater Diary: 'I look out at eleven oclock. The moon is wading through shallows into a clear depth of blue.'[7] So the 'wading' was her idea, not Lawrence's. But the 'deliciously' is his, and so is the moon's cool hand of absolution. For all the deliberate beauty of the Freshwater Diary's prose-poems, the novel is far more extravagant in its search for significance. One diary entry—'The way home lies across country. We pass a little Catholic church in the fields: a carved Christ looks down from his cross over the mounds of the dead'[8]—turns into this:

> The way home lay across country, through deep little lanes where the late foxgloves sat seriously, like sad hounds; over open downlands, rough with gorse and ling, and through pocketed hollows of bracken and trees.
>
> They came to a small Roman Catholic church in the fields. There the carved Christ looked down on the dead whose sleeping forms made mounds under the coverlet. Helena's heart was swelling with emotion. All the yearning and pathos of Christianity filled her again.
>
> (*T* 55)

The human feelings are curiously muffled: the only vivid things are the metaphors—sad hounds and coverlet—and the sad hounds are more sad than serious. The metaphorical style was one Lawrence had developed long before meeting Helen Corke, and one he was very aware of. 'What a beastly habit of metaphor I have,' he wrote to Blanche Jennings (08 v 1909), but that did not stop him spinning the most outrageous ones in letters to her.

> You see there are so many lees, so much mud at the bottom of the wine of me (wine, I say!)—that after any little shaking of change I am turbid. Every time I have been poured from the bowl of circumstance and environment into a fresh vessel, then have the clouds come up from the bottom of me, and for some time the sunshine can find no road in me.
>
> (20 i 1909)

It is important to stress that he only used this style to certain correspondents; there is no trace of it in his letters to May Chambers, or (in 1911) to his sister Ada. But we can hear the exact note of *The Trespasser* in the letters he wrote to Grace Crawford in 1909 and 1910; she was an artist, and he made sure that she registered the fact that he was, too:

> Here is the 'morceau' of Francis Thompson: no hound but an exquisite little thing written as most of Thompson's on a dim sad day when the dew stays grey on the grass. Poor Thompson! Poor me and my rhetorics!
>
> . . . It is a shame to break the moment from its stalk, to wither in the vase of memory, by thanking you.
>
> (21 xi 1909)

The self-conscious little apologies serve to draw attention to the wit and artistry, not to conceal them. Here, and in the novel, the insights of a genuinely sensitive observer—who feels that such insights have no artistic significance unless they are displayed—serve the taste of a supposedly genteel audience.

What is more, the style was extremely attractive to his contemporaries; *The Trespasser* (even more than *The White Peacock*) showed that Lawrence had gauged his effects accurately. Reviewers who found the book morbid, or even immoral, praised its style as a saving virtue. Of the twelve reviews I know, no fewer than ten singled out the style for special praise. (Of the other two, one ignored the style in its condemnation of the book's immorality, and the other attacked the style violently: 'We thought we had left this kind of prose behind us.')[9] But these are representative comments: 'A great deal might be said in favour of Mr Lawrence's prose. There are here descriptions . . . that must rank in any anthology amongst the prose writings of our time.'[10] 'Full of exquisite perceptions, and would be worth reading for those alone.'[11] The *English Review* even quoted the paragraph in which the foxgloves sit like sad hounds, and commented: 'That is admirable. Here is a writer with style.'[12] Three reviewers singled out the description of the sunrise watched by Siegmund at the end of the book, and gave it special praise: 'one of the most memorable pieces of writing known to us,' said the *Westminster Gazette*.[13] It runs, in part:

> The day was pushing aside the boughs of darkness, hunting. The poor moon would be caught when the net was flung. Siegmund went out on the balcony to look at it. There it was, like a poor white mouse, a half-moon, crouching on the mound of its course. It would run nimbly over to the western slope, then it would be caught in the net, and the sun would laugh, like a great yellow cat, as it stalked behind playing with its prey, flashing out its bright paws. . . . Siegmund sat watching the last morning blowing in across the mown darkness, till the whole field of the world was exposed, till the moon was like a dead mouse which floats on water.
>
> (*T* 184)

The analogy with Siegmund's situation is oppressive, and the natural event is swamped with significance. The word used by two reviewers—'exquisite'—seems perfectly appropriate; and, like most exquisite things, it also seems self-regarding.

We cannot blame Helen Corke for this, however dangerous her prose-poems may have been as a starting-point for Lawrence. The description of the sunrise, for instance, is Lawrence's own creation. We know that the penultimate chapter, describing Beatrice's life after the suicide, was only conceived during the final revision of the book in

January–February 1912, when Helen Corke was far away; yet its very first paragraph contains one of those amazingly extended metaphors which more than anything else make the prose precious; they are a kind of challenge to the reader's credulity, the work of a literary high-wire artist.

> Beatrice was careful not to let the blow of Siegmund's death fall with full impact upon her. As it were, she dodged it. She was afraid to meet the accusation of the dead Siegmund, with the sacred jury of memories. When the event summoned her to stand before the bench of her own soul's understanding, she fled, leaving the verdict upon herself eternally suspended.
>
> (*T* 202)

And even when Lawrence rewrote his early version at the start of 1912, and expressed his pleasure with the improvement—'done the first chapter—heaps, heaps better. There was room for improvement, by Jove!' (03 i 1912)—he still left an amazingly mannered prose. There are twenty-nine descriptive adverbs in four pages, in that chapter, as the prose struggles for deft and delicate touches. Lawrence told Helen Corke that all he was doing, in this revision, was 're-cast the paragraphs, and attend to the style' (01 ii 1912); so to a great extent it was a stylistic revision; and he knew, while he was doing it, what was wrong with the book: it was 'too florid, too *chargé*' (29 i 1912).

But even though he may have known what he was trying to correct, the character of the book had been formed in the writing of the 'Saga': 'it can't be anything else—it is itself. I must let it stand' (29 i 1912). However critical he may have been of the book in the early months of 1912, he did not want to embark on either an entirely new book, or a complete rewriting. He not only 'let it stand', he actually added to its 'literary' quality; the style had its own safety and certainty. As his reviewers confirmed in the summer, the majority of his readers would be at home with that style.

This is the more interesting because the 'Saga' had, at one stage, come under very serious criticism—from Ford Madox Ford. Ford had arranged for Heinemann to see *The White Peacock* MS (which had been accepted immediately), and though Lawrence saw much less of him after the winter of 1909, he was still Lawrence's major contact with the literary world in the summer of 1910; and he saw the 'Saga' MS almost as soon as it was finished, in August. Heinemann had first claim on the book, but Lawrence still wanted Ford's advice. By the start of September, he had it: 'Hueffer abused me roundly,' he told Grace Crawford (12 x 1910). 'He says it's a rotten work of genius, one fourth of which is the stuff of masterpiece . . . he says prose *must* be impersonal' (09 ix 1910). Lawrence later reported Ford's actual words, in a letter to Garnett: 'It has no construction or form—it is execrably bad art, being all variations on a theme. Also it is erotic—not that I, personally, mind that, but an erotic work *must* be good art, which this is not' (18 xii 1911). Later in life, Ford wrote his own account of the matter, and described Lawrence bringing him, one day,

> half the ms. of *The Trespassers*[*sic*]—and that was the end. It was a *Trespassers* much—oh, but much!—more phallic than is the book as it stands and much more moral in the inverted-puritanic sense. That last was inevitable in that day, and Lawrence had come under the subterranean-fashionable influences that made for Free Love as a social and moral arcanum. So that the whole effect was the rather dreary one of a schoolboy larking among placket holes, dialoguing with a Wesleyan minister who has been converted to Ibsen . . . it had the making of a thoroughly bad hybrid book and I told him so.
>
> (*Nehls* i 121)

As usual with Ford, the details of that account are quite untrustworthy; what is surely accurate is the perception that the novel was 'hybrid' and that Lawrence had come under 'subterranean-fashionable influences' in London. Ford had picked Lawrence out, in 1909, because 'He knows the life he is writing about in a landscape just sufficiently constructed with a casual word here and there' (*Nehls* i 109)—thinking there of a story like 'Odour of Chrysanthemums'. *The White Peacock* had overlaid its conscious artistry on such a talent; but at least Lawrence was capable of escaping 'the tiresome thing called descriptive writing, of which the English writer is as a rule so lugubriously lavish' (*Nehls* i 109). And in both his short stories and his first novel, Lawrence had been concerned with 'what we used to call "the other half"'—though we might as well have said the other ninety-nine hundredths'; however genteel his novel had been, it had also been resolutely provincial. In the 'Saga', for Ford, Lawrence had not only abandoned any account of the life he knew; he had blossomed into exactly the kind of descriptiveness Ford had counted him saved from. The descriptiveness of *The White Peacock* had been obsessive enough for a recent researcher to count '145 different trees and shrubs, 51 animals and 40 different birds',[14] but that of *The Trespasser* was a welter of vague impressionism. Ford advised Lawrence not to publish the book at all, and when Lawrence wrote to say that he did not intend to, remarked that *The Trespasser* 'would damage your reputation perhaps permanently' (18 xii 1911). Ford undoubtedly meant that the charge of eroticism would damage Lawrence; but he also believed that the eroticism only achieved its prominence because of *The Trespasser*'s faults.

For fourteen months Lawrence left the book unpublished and uncorrected; according to Helen Corke, 'his faith in the work dropped to zero point'.[15] It seems probable that if Lawrence had not become friendly with Edward Garnett in the autumn of 1911, the novel would never have been published. Lawrence and Helen Corke had, anyway, made an agreement that the novel 'should remain unpublished for five years',[16] and though Heinemann were prepared to publish it, they showed no keenness for it. But when Edward Garnett read it in December 1911, he wrote Lawrence a 'very exciting' letter about it (18 xii 1911); even if Heinemann showed no desire for it, as reader for Duckworth Garnett was prepared to recommend it. He also made various comments on the MS. The crucial thing was that Garnett's sudden keenness coincided with Lawrence's sudden need; after his illness of December 1911, Lawrence was determined not to go back into school-teaching, and if he could get the 'Saga' into print as well as the novel 'Paul Morel' promised to Heinemann, he had some chance of being able to make a living as a writer. If Garnett's enthusiasm had come even three months earlier, it is doubtful whether it would have weaned Lawrence away from 'Paul Morel', which was proving enough trouble as it was. But with a month's convalescence to work in, and Garnett's advice and encouragement to sustain him—and with Heinemann obviously prepared to wait a little longer for 'Paul Morel', because of Lawrence's illness—then Lawrence could spend his month revising the 'Saga'. Garnett later wrote that he thought *The Trespasser* an advance over *The White Peacock* because it was less immature and sprawling; his main criticism of it was for its 'occasional commonness both of language and tone'[17] which suggests that he, too, found it over-written. But he certainly wanted to attract Lawrence to Duckworth and away from Heinemann—and succeeded: six of Lawrence's next seven books were published by Duckworth. Still, he found the 'commonness' only 'occasional', and the advice we know he gave was limited to specific details. He certainly encouraged Lawrence to 'wage war on my adjectives. *Culpa mea!*' (05 iv 1912) while proof-correcting. But so far as Lawrence was concerned, criticism of the book was less important than commercial backing; and we know from his experience with Garnett over *The Rainbow* that the latter was far more opposed to his experiments than to his conventionalities.

The finished *Trespasser*, then, is something of a living fossil; a chance survivor of an earlier epoch, not a novel which Lawrence ever very much wanted to publish; not, indeed, a novel which he would have wanted to rewrite or to have published at any earlier or later date. On the other hand, it is for those reasons a particularly well-preserved fossil; it demonstrates what an artistic novel built around a tragic hero looked like to a man between two worlds, like Lawrence in 1910. It marks the apex of his capacity to write brilliantly and poetically in a void of his own choosing between the world he knew and the world he rected; according to Helen Corke, 'his faith in the work dropped to zero point'.[15] It seems probable that if Lawrence had not become friendly with Edward Garnett in the autumn of 1911, the novel would never have been published. Lawrence and Helen Corke had, anyway, made an agreement that the novel 'should remain unpublished for five years',[16] and though Heinemann were prepared to publish it, they showed no keenness for it. But when Edward Garnett read it in December 1911, he wrote Lawrence a 'very exciting' letter about it (18 xii 1911); even if Heinemann showed no desire for it, as reader for Duckworth Garnett was prepared to recommend it. He also made various comments on the MS. The crucial thing was that Garnett's sudden keenness coincided with Lawrence's sudden need; after his illness of December 1911, Lawrence was determined not to go back into school-teaching, and if he could get the 'Saga' into print as well as the novel 'Paul Morel' promised to Heinemann, he had some chance of being able to make a living as a writer. If Garnett's enthusiasm had come even three months earlier, it is doubtful whether it would have weaned Lawrence away from 'Paul Morel', which was proving enough trouble as it was. But with a month's convalescence to work in, and Garnett's advice and encouragement to sustain him—and with Heinemann obviously prepared to wait a little longer for 'Paul Morel', because of Lawrence's illness—then Lawrence could spend his month revising the 'Saga'. Garnett later wrote that he thought *The Trespasser* an advance over *The White Peacock* because it was less immature and sprawling; his main criticism of it was for its 'occasional commonness both of language and tone'[17] which suggests that he, too, found it over-written. But he certainly wanted to attract Lawrence to Duckworth and away from Heinemann—and succeeded: six of Lawrence's next seven books were published by Duckworth. Still, he found the 'commonness' only 'occasional', and the advice we know he gave was limited to specific details. He certainly encouraged Lawrence to 'wage war on my adjectives. *Culpa mea!*' (05 iv 1912) while proof-correcting. But so far as Lawrence was concerned, criticism of the book was less important than commercial backing; and we know from his experience with Garnett over *The Rainbow* that the latter was far more opposed to his experiments than to his conventionalities.

The finished *Trespasser*, then, is something of a living fossil; a chance survivor of an earlier epoch, not a novel which Lawrence ever very much wanted to publish; not, indeed, a novel which he would have wanted to rewrite or to have published at any earlier or later date. On the other hand, it is for those reasons a particularly well-preserved fossil; it demonstrates what an artistic novel built around a tragic hero looked like to a man between two worlds, like Lawrence in 1910. It marks the apex of his capacity to write brilliantly and poetically in a void of his own choosing between the world he knew and the world he aspired to. It shows what kind of novelist he might have been if he had stayed in London and written to impress, if he had continued to think of a novel as an opportunity for brilliant display, as a timeless and unlocated art. By the start of 1912, his short stories had on one or two occasions been allowed to draw fully on the complexity of his Midlands life; pieces like 'The Miner at Home', 'Strike Pay' and 'Her Turn', which he wrote shortly after finishing *The Trespasser*, described vividly both a world and feelings which he had kept resolutely out of both his novels up to then. He had written dialect poems, too, with Garnett's particular encouragement. But he had reserved his novels for another world, and showed in them a determination to meet the novel-reading public on its own ground, and in a language he thought appropriate.

And if we compare the style and pressure of *The Trespasser* with a short story like 'The Witch *à la Mode*', written in Croydon during 1911 and creating an antagonistic (and sexually highly-charged) relationship between a hero distinctively autobiographical, and a woman recognisably the Helena of *The Trespasser*, we can see how a story which is not even set in the Midlands is both far less over-written than the novel, and more complex in its version of human relationships because unconcerned to make a saga-tragedy out of them. The two works are nicely parallel, in fact, because Garnett saw them both and gave advice about them. The story presents another of those revealing self-projections of Lawrence as the bloodless, elegant, sophisticated cosmopolitan intellectual who, like Cyril in *The White Peacock* and Cecil Byrne in *The Trespasser*, observes others from the point of artistic detachment which plagues both novels. But at least his relationship with Winifred/Helena steers clear of the novel's over-laden significances; and Bernard can be direct even when metaphorical.

'Exactly! That's what you want me for. I am to be your crystal, your "genius". My length of blood and bone you don't care a rap for. Ah, yes, you like me for a crystal-glass, to see things in: to hold up to the light. I'm a blessed Lady-of-Shalott looking-glass for you.'
'You talk to *me*,' she said, dashing his fervour, 'of my fog of symbols!'[18]

In *The Trespasser* we find the autobiographical Stranger, Hampson, using the same metaphor, but the self-consciousness of his words, and the self-deprecating apology at the end, mark it out as a different kind of production altogether:

'Fools—the fools, these women!' he said. 'Either they smash their own crystal, or it revolts, turns opaque, and leaps out of their hands. Look at me, I am whittled down to the quick; but your neck

is thick with compressed life; it is a stem so tense with life that it will
hold up by itself. I am very sorry.'

All at once he stopped. The bitter despair in his tone was the voice
of a heavy feeling of which Siegmund had been vaguely aware for
some weeks. Siegmund felt a sense of doom. He laughed, trying to
shake it off.

'I wish I didn't go on like this,' said Hampson piteously. . . .

(*T* 85–6)

In the novel, Lawrence uses a style and an approach he does not use in
the story; the *Doppelgänger* figure of Hampson is a pretentious and
unfleshed idea.

In general, too, *The Trespasser* is written with the language and man-
nerisms of Lawrence's poetry of the period; it is significant that there
should be extant two poems working out situation and character for the
novel—'Red' and 'A Love-Passage' (*Poems* ii 889 and 876). No other
extant poems relate so directly to any of the novels. And *The Trespasser*
is also a poetic novel because it aspires to be a tragic one. Throughout
the period 1909–11, Lawrence insisted on his friends reading the Greek
tragedies which were impressing him so much. *Oedipus Tyrannus* was
'the finest drama of *all* times. It is terrible in its accumulation—like a
great big wave coming up—and then crash! *Bacchae* I like exceedingly
for its flashing poetry' (26 iv 1911). He and Helen Corke read *Alcestis*
and *The Trojan Women* together in the winter of 1909, and she associated
the latter play with her own state of mind after the Island tragedy. *The
Trespasser* aims precisely at those poetic qualities of tragedy which
Lawrence admired so much, and surprised him 'by its steady progres-
siveness' (19 i 1912); its sense of impending disaster is very carefully
worked out. And, of course, all three of Lawrence's first novels are
different kinds of tragedy—'all great works are,' he told his sister: 'the
tragic is the most holding, the most vital thing in life' (26 iv 1911). But
The Trespasser is the most self-consciously literary of the three, the most
deliberately made according to a pattern. Its strength lies in other
things altogether, like the creation of the MacNair children, and the
moment when Beatrice gets a window-cleaner to find what her husband has done—which creates the fact of death far better than does the
tragic sense of doom. The man peers into the room:

'I believe 'e's 'anged 'imself from the door-'ooks!'
'No!' cried Beatrice. 'No, no, no!'
'I believe 'e 'as!' repeated the man.
'Go in and see if he's dead!' cried Beatrice.
The man remained in the doorway, peering fixedly.
'I believe he is,' he said doubtfully.
'No—go and see!' screamed Beatrice.

(*T* 192)

Intense feeling—'No, no no!'—is answered only by the language of native caution; the novel stops trying to impress us, and creates a human situation, caught between disaster and comedy. And we forget, for a moment, the controlling hand of the author.

For that is, perhaps, the most significant weakness of the novel: Lawrence's authorial presence as aesthete, psychologist and tragedian. Not only does Siegmund speak with the voice of his creator; so does the *Doppelgänger* Hampson, and there is a third authorial presence in Cecil Byrne.

An omniscient narrator, too, continually makes remarks such as 'The heart of life is implacable in its kindness. It may not be moved to fluttering of pity; it swings on uninterrupted by cries of anguish or of hate' (*T* 186–7). Lawrence certainly knew how self-involved he was with the book; it was

> so much oneself, one's naked self. I give myself away so much, and write what is my most palpitant, sensitive self, that I loathe the book because it will betray me to a parcel of fools. Which is what any deeply personal or lyrical writer feels, I guess.
>
> (21 i 1912)

The Trespasser marked the end of the road for Lawrence as a 'personal or lyrical writer'; 'Paul Morel', though autobiographical, would be mostly far less personal, and would hardly be lyrical at all.

The Trespasser's final link with *Sons and Lovers*, however, was to finance it; it made Lawrence the money which enabled him to stay abroad in 1912 and write. As he told Violet Hunt, the money 'carried him through the winter and one must publish to live' (*Nehls* i 128).

3 Sons and Lovers

Sons and Lovers is not only clearly an autobiographical novel—something a number of its first readers realised without any knowledge of Lawrence's private life—it is a book written out of a situation and a dilemma which seeks a form transforming that situation and dilemma into a novel. Its author also sees the situation as 'the tragedy of thousands of young men in England' (19 xi 1912). He could label it, quite casually, as '*Sons and Lovers*—autobiography' (23 xii 1912); but in a letter to the man who had once been the closest of his male friends, A. W. McLeod, he wrote that 'I felt you had gone off from me a bit, because of *Sons and Lovers*. But one sheds one's sicknesses in books—repeats and presents again one's emotions, to be master of them' (26 x 1913). That suggests rather more of what was involved, even if (with the awareness of hindsight) Lawrence's first word for the novel's contents was 'sicknesses'. As befits a book written so much out of his own life, it is the only one of his novels which we find him rethinking later. When, for instance, he read *The White Peacock* in Mexico in 1924, for the first time in fifteen years, it seemed simply 'strange and far off and as if written by somebody else' (*Nehls* ii 414); but *Sons and Lovers* was a book which, in 1922, he 'felt like rewriting' because 'he had not done justice to his father' (*Nehls* ii 126); and *Aaron's Rod* (completed the previous year) arguably demonstrates an attempt, in part, to recreate the figure of his father with a good deal more sympathy.

Given all this, it is strange to realise that not only did he find *Sons and Lovers* a difficult book to write: he found it hard to make it autobiographical. If I interpret the evidence correctly, it seems (as much as any of his novels) to have changed in direction while being written, and to have become a different kind of novel in the process. The final version may have amounted to a liberation, a shedding of sicknesses; but like most liberations it seems to have been less a clean break with the past than a compulsive, final, recreation of it. I suggest, and will argue, that *Sons and Lovers* is a book which bears the imprints of sickness and surgery as much as of health.

It took, in all, just over two years to write; in that time we can detect at least four versions which seem to differ a good deal. But those particular years, after all, contained perhaps the greatest changes ever to happen in Lawrence's life as a man and as a writer. When he started the novel, sometime around October 1910, he had been a schoolteacher in a London suburb for two years, with a home in the Midlands to help support and his own living to make. His few published writings offered little chance of his being able to do more than teach for the foreseeable future. He had had two groups of poems and one short story (not altogether his own work)[1] published in a magazine of reputation, and that was all. His first novel had been accepted by Heinemann, and he had the draft of a second—but the latter he had been advised not to publish. His mother was alive, though seriously ill, and 'home' was as securely Eastwood as it had been all his life; even if the language and style of his first two novels had shown his aspirations for another world, the Midlands community was where he actually belonged. He had, too, just broken his four-year unofficial engagement to Jessie Chambers.

But when he finished *Sons and Lovers* in November 1912, he was living in Italy with another man's wife—a German aristocrat: his mother had been dead for nearly two years. He had in the interval been engaged for a year to a 'nice' girl, of whom his mother had approved;[2] he had tried for a job as the headmaster of a small country school, he had hoped that his writing might make him enough capital (£100 minimum) to marry on, provided that he also had £120 a year income. He was on the verge of settling down to the respectable middle-class life of the professional teacher. But he abandoned hopes of the job, the income, the marriage, the home—even the country—in a flight from respectability and any secure financial prospects when he eloped in May 1912. But by November 1912 he had had two novels published, with some good reviews, a good deal more poetry and quite a lot of prose. He was an expatriate professional writer, for better or worse, with every prospect of staying one. As I suggested in Chapter 2, we can gauge the extent to which his writing changed, and his sense of a novel changed, between January 1912 and November—the dates when he completed *The Tres-passer* and *Sons and Lovers* respectively; the final writing of *Sons and Lovers* released Lawrence as a writer who could go on to create *The Rainbow* and *Women in Love*.

Yet, autobiography as *Sons and Lovers* was, it chose to demonstrate a hero almost irretrievably caught in his past; its last chapter is called 'Derelict', and shows Paul Morel tragically unable to do anything with his life except, finally, cling to the fact that he is alive: 'at the core a nothingness, and yet not nothing' (*SL* 510). The tragedies of which Lawrence had had personal experience by the end of 1912 had been those of his parents' unhappy marriage, and the break-up of Frieda Weekley's marriage (and her loss of her children) when she came away with him. But *Sons and Lovers* sets out very firmly not to deal with the second of those; it is the psychological tragedy of an individual, an unmarried individual. Every autobiography, of course, has to impro-vise its ending; but we can see Lawrence deliberately excluding any future possibilities for Paul's life except the 'quickness' of which the last sentence of the book speaks. Those other possibilities were, indeed, to be quickly developed in the sequence of novels started between December 1912 and March 1913, finally in 'The Sisters'. But Paul's final loneliness is both empty and wholly individual; he remains unmarried, with no possibility of an 'insurrection' like that of Alvina Houghton in the novel started in January 1913: in England, despite his vague ideas of going abroad—and the characters of 'The Sisters' all travel in their pursuit of fulfilment in marriage: still tied to his mother, limited to the unceasing to-and-fro of an emotional life which has been on the rocks for the past ten years. It is not surprising that, in comparison with the description of the Morels' marriage, Paul's final experiences have seemed thin—perhaps arbitrary. The lives of his parents, for all their disasters, have shown how people have to live, and go on living, not how they choose to die. But Paul, at the end, is relieved of those imperatives of life, and we can see that process starting to happen when Mrs Morel looks at her son, and feels that she fights 'for his very life against his own will to die . . . at this rate she knew he would not live' (*SL* 315). Paul's destiny is being placed on a different footing from that of the other characters; I would suggest that Lawrence's way of making Paul's life into a tragedy is by isolating him as a psychologically damaged individual. In a book where our sense of the adjustments people make to each other is so strong, that isolation of the hero for a particularly internal struggle is very striking, and tells us a good deal about what Lawrence's conception of tragedy was at that date. One of the few points of contact between *The Trespasser* and *Sons and Lovers*, in fact, is in this isolating of the tragic hero from everything except the torture of his own thoughts. I shall return to the matter.

The novel was first conceived in the autumn of 1910; but, interestingly, neither of the people who knew his writing best at the time seem to have known that he had started it: both Helen Corke and Jessie Chambers assert that he began it in 1911. The reason, I suspect, is contained in a remark he made just before Mrs Lawrence died in December 1910:

> You see mother has had a devilish married life, for nearly forty years—and this is the conclusion—no relief. What ever I wrote, it could not be so awful as to write a biography of my mother. But after this—which is enough—I am going to write romance—when I have finished Paul Morel, which belongs to this.
>
> (06 xii 1910)

The novel 'Paul Morel' 'belongs to this'—to this autumn, this death. It seems almost certain that Lawrence began to write the book only after he had learned of his mother's fatal illness. And though he saw a good deal of Helen Corke that autumn, and showed her manuscripts, he was actually in the Midlands that autumn more than at any time since

1908. Helen Corke noticed how, when he returned to Croydon in January 1911, he had 'reverted to his Eastwood self so fully that we meet almost as strangers'.³ His time in Eastwood culminated in the death of his mother and his own engagement to Louie Burrows; but it produced a number of remarkable letters about his mother's life and marriage, all of which read like passages from that 'awful' biography of her which must have lain behind the first 'Paul Morel'.

My mother was a clever, ironical delicately moulded woman of good, old burgher descent. She married below her. My father was dark, ruddy, with a fine laugh. He is a coal miner. He was one of the sanguine temperament, warm and hearty, but unstable: he lacked principle, as my mother would have said. He deceived her and lied to her. She despised him—he drank.

Their marriage life has been one carnal, bloody fight. I was born hating my father: as early as ever I can remember, I shivered with horror when he touched me. He was very bad before I was born.

(03 xii 1910)

If 'Paul Morel' was begun while Lawrence was in that frame of mind, it would have amounted to a panegyric of his mother and a damning of his father. Interestingly, he had told his publisher in October that he intended it to be 'a restrained, somewhat impersonal novel' (18 x 1910). He was trying to persuade Heinemann not to publish the 'Saga', but to take this new novel instead; if the 'Saga' had been a 'florid prose poem', the new book (he promised) would be different. Not for the first time, Lawrence was getting caught between what a publisher expected, and what he actually wanted to produce.

We do not know how much of this first version was actually written: 'one-eighth' by mid-October, apparently (18 x 1910), but it probably came to a halt quite soon after that. The second version started in March 1911, and would, he told Helen Corke, make the British Public 'stone me if ever it catches sight . . . glory, you should see it' (14 iii 1911). But he was not referring to the novel's explicit sexuality, which caused so much trouble with Heinemann in 1912; it was apparently the realism—what the *Daily News* review of *The White Peacock* called its 'brutality'—which would be found offensive. 'I am afraid it will be a terrible novel. But, if I can keep it to my idea & feeling, it will be a great one' (13 iii 1911). It sounds very much, still, like the novel prefigured in the December 1910 letter: 'it is very terrible, mis-marriage,' he had then remarked. But he found it extremely hard to write. The previous year had seen him producing the 'Saga' at amazing speed; but in April 1911, 'Paul Morel' was 'that great, terrible but unwritten novel, I am afraid it will die a mere conception' (12 iv 1911). The word 'conception' suggests that Lawrence had a particular sense of the novel from the start, unlike those novels which overtook him in mid-flight (like 'The Sisters'); as he had written to Heinemann back in October, the novel was 'plotted out very interestingly (to me)' (18 x 1910). I suspect that this is a unique reference in Lawrence to a novel being 'plotted out' before being written; and even allowing for the fact that it was designed to convince Heinemann of his reliability as an author, the remark corresponds too closely to what we later hear of the book's 'idea & feeling' to be ignored. 'Paul Morel' existed as an idea before it existed as a novel: an idea of mis-marriage, of tragic waste. I have already quoted his remark of April 1911 about all great art being tragic: but that remark was made in the context of a description of his own family, and the fact that Lawrence's fiancée Louie had no conception of what they had all been through; 'she's seen nothing whatever of the horror of life, and we've been bred up in its presence: with father' (26 iv 1911). 'Paul Morel' must have tried to show 'how relentlessly tragic life is' in an account of a ruined marriage, a horrific father and a beatified mother.

This version of the book occupied Lawrence fitfully throughout the summer of 1911; it took on the proportions of an imposed task. 1911 was the year for Lawrence when 'everything collapsed' (*Poems* ii 851), and the novel which was going to be 'great' finally ran into the sand. Lawrence kept writing it partly because he had a novel promised to Heinemann, partly because if he were to do anything in life except be a school-master, it had to be with his writing; partly because it still seemed an important thing to be doing; partly because (ironically), engaged to Louie Burrows, he had at least to make the effort to earn money on which to marry. So the tragic novel, growing out of an experience of which she could have no conception, became a means to an end, and something of which Lawrence would send her dutiful progress reports. At one stage he must have promised her to write a steady ten pages a week (or weekend): 'at your behest I wrote yester-day fourteen pages of Paul Morel' (01 v 1911); 'I have managed my ten pages of Paul' (07 v 1911). But he gave up in July; and, significantly, eventually sent it to Jessie Chambers for her comments, as he always used to. He had been mostly out of touch with her during 1911, but—knowing the family, knowing him, knowing Miriam—she could be turned to. It was not just an ending which would fit it for Heinemann|which the novel needed; it seemed, wrote Jessie Chambers 'to have come to a standstill. The whole thing was somehow tied up.'

He was telling the story of his mother's married life, but the telling seemed to be at second hand, and lacked the living touch. I could not help feeling that his treatment of the theme was far behind the reality in vividness and dramatic strength. Now and again he seemed to strike a curious, half-apologetic note, bordering on the sentimental. . . . A nonconformist minister whose sermons the mother helped to compose was the foil to the brutal husband. He gave the boy Paul a box of paints, and the mother's heart glowed with pride as she saw her son's budding power. . . . It was story-bookish. The elder brother Ernest, whose short career had always seemed to me most moving and dramatic, was not there at all.

(*ET* 190–1)

Part of what seems to be this draft survives, and bears out Jessie Chambers' opinion of it.[4] There are memorable things in it which she forgot, and she has some details wrong, but the lack of direction in the surviving sections—which read like a compulsive recreation of memories—and the story-bookish quality of the whole are terribly obvious. Memories are occasionally supported by melodrama; as when Mr Morel confronts his son Arthur (who plays something of the roles of both Paul and William in the final version), throws the carving steel at him, and kills him. Mr Morel is jailed, and dies soon after being released. The book's invention, if it can be called that, is mostly on that level; Mr Morel's brutality is thus exaggerated, tragedy is wrung from it, and Mrs Morel is exculpated. The brutality of the miner's kitchen is emphasised by making Miriam the daughter of a well-to-do shop-keeping family; Paul goes there for his music lessons from Miriam's governess, and is able to compare his life at home with the Staynes' household. Tea is

> served in the morning room, where Mrs Staynes sat. Paul thought it very beautiful to sit perfectly at peace, in a quiet room, taking tea with people of refined manners: no dinner boiling on the hob, no miner eating dinner noisily while other folk had tea, no jumping up and down to serve vegetables and puddings, no discord, no hopeless scotch in the conversation, no spots on the cloth. The boy looked at the fine linen and china, at the glisten of silver and of flowers; he noticed the quiet, refined accent of everybody. . . .[5]

Above all, what remains of this version lacks the tension between Mrs Morel and her sons which becomes the very centre of interest in the final version: the tension is between animality and sophistication, and the mother's culture is something her sons can properly aim for. The novel which 'belongs to this' was in danger of turning into its own kind of romance—as Jessie Chambers pointed out: 'I thought what had really happened was much more poignant and interesting than the situations he had invented' (*ET* 192). Rather as with *The White Peacock* and *The Trespasser*, Lawrence's sense of the kind of conflicts suitable for a novel—ones which he would also like to have been part of his own childhood—dominated his knowledge of the real tensions of that community and upbringing.

Jessie agreed with Lawrence to write notes about her memories of their shared adolescence, to help him recreate 'what had really happened' (*ET* 192), and Lawrence apparently started a new version of the novel in November 1911 (presumably under threat of the March deadline for Heinemann); but after his illness that winter, and the hasty revision of *The Trespasser*, he could not return to 'Paul Morel' until February 1912. It is perhaps significant, too, that he broke his engagement to Louie Burrows at the start of February: an engagement symbolic of his mother's hopes for his 'getting-on' in life, to the girl his mother approved of. For the first time, perhaps, Lawrence was able to stand back and estimate the damage his mother's hopes and her love had done to him; the new 'Paul Morel' could be more that the tragedy of her wasted marriage—it could also create the conflict between mother and son over the women in his life.

Lawrence certainly seemed to find this version of the novel a breakthrough into the novel he had always hoped he could write; he was also freed from full-time education or employment for the first time since 1906, and wrote it extremely fast—between mid-February and mid-April 'at a white heat of concentration' (*ET* 201). It was at this point that Jessie Chambers recoiled from what she had helped Lawrence do; she found this version of the book betraying everything she felt she had been to Lawrence for the previous ten years. She saw him glorifying the figure of his mother, at her own expense: she felt that he was grossly unfair to their own 'desperate search for a right relationship' (*ET* 203); and he totally omitted the thing which had kept them together in spite of everything—her 'devotion to the development of his genius' (*ET* 203). According to her later recollection, the part of the novel devoted to Miriam, as written early in 1912, was unchanged in the final version of the novel: 'I found the proof-sheets tallied word for word with the Ms I had read' (*Delavenay* ii 709). This suggests that the treatment of Miriam in *Sons and Lovers* was worked out in this third version of the novel; and, too, that Lawrence knew what he was going to do with Paul. He was making Paul's art painting, not writing like his own; which meant that there could be no literary discussion with Miriam. The amazing intellectual pursuits recorded in Jessie Chambers' memoir are, therefore, ignored; and Miriam is a less impressive character in the novel than we may suspect Jessie Chambers of being in real life; she is conceived of as someone for Paul to abandon, not as someone he can love. So far as the real-life Jessie Chambers was concerned, Lawrence had 'handed his mother the laurels of victory' (*ET* 202), in showing Paul abandoning Miriam partly in response to his mother's pressure on him; but what Lawrence seems to have been doing was weakening the relationship of Paul and Miriam to demonstrate the particular (and in a way *peculiar*) love of Paul for his mother. Doubtless it was desperately cruel to Jessie Chambers to make the real-life situation into this kind of demonstration. But in that 'white heat of concentration' Lawrence obviously conceived a new idea for his novel: not simply the tragedy of a brutal, even murderous, father, and a wronged mother, but the tragedy of a damaged child. We know nothing about the experiences of Paul after his relationship with Miriam in this version, apart from Jessie Chambers' remark that 'the Clara of the second half of the story was a clever adaptation of elements from three people, and her creation arose as a complement to Lawrence's mood of failure and defeat' (*ET* 202). It is vital that we should read 'Paul' in that sentence, not 'Lawrence': it is Paul whose life is being made a subject for failure and defeat. That was probably the discovery and advance made in this version of the novel.

When Lawrence went to Germany in May 1912, he took the MS with him for what he hoped would be a final revision. We know almost nothing about what he did to the novel, except that—given the strength of Heinemann's reaction to the novel in June—he may well have made the love scenes more explicit. Anyway, 'it's rather great,' (02 vi 1912), Lawrence remarked cheerfully as he sent it off to Heinemann.

As with the submission of *The Rainbow* to Methuen in the summer of 1914, this was an occasion when a publisher's return of an apparently completed MS provoked still another, significant, rewriting. At the start of July, Lawrence heard that Heinemann refused to publish the novel: 'William Heinemann said he thought *Sons and Lovers* one of the dirtiest books he had ever read' (*Phx* 233). Lawrence was outraged, insulted, in a way amused; he would have been in a difficult position if Duckworth had not been prepared to accept the novel. He was also made aware of a growing contradiction between what he wanted to do, and what was possible in a commercial novel. 'Heinemann, I can see, is quite right, as a business man,' (03 vii 1912) he told Garnett. But in July 1912 Lawrence wrote two letters which hint at a new attitude towards his public, and towards novels. Frieda's ex-husband had given him a·strange sense of courage:

> What the English *can* be if they are hauled by the neck into it, is something rather great. I should like to bludgeon them into realising their own selves. Curse you, my countrymen, you have put the halters round your necks, and pull tighter and tighter from day to day. You are strangling yourselves, you blasted fools. Oh my countrymen!
>
> (08 vii 1912)

There is a good deal of self-mockery in those reflections. But Lawrence is also viewing England, and his role as a writer for England, in a wholly new light; he deliberately assumes a role (and mocks it) in order to see how it feels.

Why, why and why was I born an Englishman!—my cursed,
rotten-boned, pappy hearted countrymen, *why* was I sent to *them*.
Christ on the cross must have hated his countrymen. 'Crucify me,
you swine,' he must have said through his teeth. . . .
   They deserve it that every great man should drown himself. But
not I (I am a bit great).

(03 vii 1912)

Behind the self-parody, the inflation, the combination of anger and
malice and amusement, there is a voice of a writer considering his role
as the voice of his country; as if he, an artist abroad, both impatient and
concerned, should properly take on the task of bludgeoning them 'into
realising their own selves'. This is a new voice for Lawrence—obviously a development of that feeling he had had even before he started to
write: 'I feel I have something to say . . . I think it will be didactic' (*ET*
102). Even in 1912, it is only a passing tone, and made in both jest and
anger; but it corresponds to a note that grew stronger the following
year. And, significantly, it is a role as writer for 'my countrymen' which
he first understands; not for 'my people of the Midlands'—'my folk'.
He writes like a man who feels drawn to assist the destiny of a race. To
assert 'England' like this, even as a joke, means the adoption of a stance
along with seers and prophets, on the one hand, and with the intel-
ligentsia on the other.
   This is, perhaps, an odd conclusion for a man who had been writing
that very personal, autobiographical novel 'Paul Morel'—a novel he
continually referred to as his 'colliery novel' in the spring of 1912. It
suggests a distance between the author and the idea of his art: a new
sense of how, as an artist, he could use his art to *do* things. Ford Madox
Ford had wanted Lawrence to write novels of the working-
class—'workingman novels' (*Nehls* i 116)—but Lawrence had chosen,
and here newly affirms that choice, to write for the people of England.
It was both a larger and a looser aim, both more deliberate and more
dangerous; it inevitably casts the author in the role of seer and prophet
and intellectual. The next time we hear it clearly is, significantly, just
after Lawrence finished *Sons and Lovers*: 'It is a great tragedy, and I tell
you I have written a great book. It's the tragedy of thousands of young
men in England—it may even be Bunny's tragedy. I think it was
Ruskin's, and men like him' (19 xi 1912). And he also wrote to McLeod
that 'It's quite a great work. I only hope the English nation won't rend
me for having given them anything so good' (02 xii 1912). If *Sons and
Lovers* shows us Lawrence maturing as an artist, it also shows him
newly aware of the kind of artist he could be.
   Garnett performed the same service for the rejected 'Paul Morel' as
he had for the 'Saga', and supplied comments and notes; Lawrence
began to rewrite the novel in September 1912. It was at this point that

Frieda Lawrence first influenced the book; Lawrence, she told Garnett, 'is writing P. M. again, reads bits to me and we fight like blazes over it, he is so often beside the point, "but 'I'll learn him to be a toad' as the boy said as he stamped on the toad"' (*Frieda* 185). By then she had obviously read the previous draft: 'I think L. quite missed the point in "Paul Morel". He really loved his mother more than anybody, even with his other women, real love, sort of Oedipus; his mother must have been adorable' (*Frieda* 185). The idea that Mrs Lawrence was simply 'adorable' was one that she was soon to change; but we can see that Frieda is seizing on a particular thread in the book—the unaturally loving son—as the 'point' of it. This was something which had obviously been in Lawrence's own mind ever since the very first version; a letter to Rachel Annand Taylor in December 1910 remarked that he and his mother 'have loved each other, almost with a husband and wife love, as well as filial and maternal. . . . It has been rather terrible and has made me, in some respects, abnormal' (03 xii 1910). There is nothing, at least, in what survives of the second version to compare with this, and the fact that Frieda seized on the idea as something missing from the previous version suggests that the September 1912 version of the novel was the first to make it prominent. However, the creation of a Miriam figure who *could* not win her Paul, in any circumstances, opened the way for a mother whose role became dominant; and the latter created the novel's ambivalent attitude towards a Clara who offers Paul so much, and who yet has to be rejected. The advance made by this last version of the book seems to have been that of making the mother not just the central figure, but a destructive and creative centre too.

Whether Lawrence had read any Freud for himself by 1912 is both unimportant and unlikely; Frieda's phrase 'sort of Oedipus' reveals how her knowledge of Freud, coming through her conversations with Otto Gross (and with the café circle surrounding him), allowed her to argue a case with an exciting freshness. For Lawrence, working for two years at a novel which had never found a satisfactory centre, her ideas came just when he needed them. We know that he responded gratefully both from the contents of the finished novel, and from the summary of it he sent to Garnett as soon as he had finished it; this states a new idea for the book which, despite its familiarity, must be examined:

I tell you it has got form—*form*: haven't I made it patiently, out of sweat as well as blood. It follows this idea: a woman of character and refinement goes into the lower class, and has no satisfaction in her own life. She has had a passion for her husband, so the children are born of passion, and have heaps of vitality. But as her sons grow up she selects them as lovers—first the eldest, then the second. These sons are *urged* into life by their reciprocal love of their

mother—urged on and on. But when they come to manhood, they
can't love, because their mother is the strongest power in their lives,
and holds them. It's rather like Goethe and his mother and Frau von
Stein and Christiana—As soon as the young men come into contact
with women, there's a split. William gives his sex to a fribble, and
his mother holds his soul. But the split kills him, because he doesn't
know where he is. The next son gets a woman who fights for his
soul—fights his mother. The son loves the mother—all the sons hate
and are jealous of the father. The battle goes on between the mother
and the girl, with the son as object. The mother gradually proves
stronger, because of the tie of blood. The son decides to leave his
soul in his mother's hands, and, like his elder brother go for passion.
He gets passion. Then the split begins to tell again. But, almost
unconsciously, the mother realises what is the matter, and begins to
die. The son casts off his mistress, attends to his mother dying. He is
left in the end naked of everything, with the drift towards death.

(19 xi 1912)

The insistence 'form—*form*' is obviously designed to persuade Garnett
(now a publisher's reader upon whose advice Lawrence depended, as
well as a friend) that *Sons and Lovers* had a shape of its own: and so is the
plot outline, with its particular emphasis. The 'idea' expressed here, in
fact, sounds like a realisation about the book which Lawrence could
only have come to after writing it. Frieda herself wrote to Garnett about
'form': Lawrence's early reviewers had tended to criticise the construction of his books, and Garnett must have been critical too. 'I also feel',
wrote Frieda, 'as if I ought to say something about L's formlessness. I
don't think he has no form. I used to. But now I think anybody must
see in "Paul Morel" the hang of it. The mother is really the thread, the
domineering note' (*Frieda* 185). 'Domineering' must be an appropriately Freudian slip for 'dominant': so far as Frieda was concerned (and
I think she is putting simply what Lawrence said in his summary) the
new focus for the book was its demonstration of the power of possessive
mother-love. So that William, for instance, was not only in the novel for
the sake of his tragic life-story (which was something Jessie Chambers
had suggested should be included): he could be made to conform to the
dominant idea. At least, in recollection he could. As many critics have
pointed out, the novel itself does not properly support the summary.
But neither is it innocent of the idea; as so often with Lawrence's novels
from *Sons and Lovers* onwards, a new idea of what he wanted his novel to
say and be had overtaken Lawrence in the course of writing it; and the
idea appears throughout, not fully worked out; I suspect it was not fully
articulated until the summary itself was written.

So that although William may not be quite what the summary says
he is, there is evidence at points in the novel of the deliberate realisation

of the 'idea'. One scene of particular interest in the novel is the last part of Chapter 8—the sequence in which Paul burns the bread because he is talking to Miriam and Beatrice, and comes back to confront his mother; there is a quarrel with his father, and a final conversation between Paul and his mother. There is an earlier version of this scene, untouched by the ideas developed by the last version and explicit in the summary, extant in the play *A Collier's Friday Night*. This was written first in 1909, and may have been revised in 1910; but it was out of Lawrence's possession after April 1912 and he never handled it again. It can stand very usefully as an example of the naturalism characteristic of parts of the early versions of the novel. Even in details, parts of the scene are identical in the two versions, and this is particularly interesting because the whole sequence, according to Jessie Chambers (who was in a position to know), was an amalgamation of three different incidents occurring on three different evenings (*Delavenay* ii 676). The scene had a certain coherence for Lawrence, obviously, that he should use it in such a similar form on two different occasions.

The first crucial difference between the two versions comes when, in the play, the quarrel between the son and the father *precedes* the conversation between the mother and the son about his love for her and for his girl-friend. The quarrel between father and son in the play is a result of the father's drunken bad temper, and his jealousy of the little delicacies which his wife buys the children. After he has left, the son reassures his mother that, in spite of his girl-friend, he really loves her best, and the scene (and the play) ends with their reconciliation.

In the novel, however, we have some of this conversation before the father enters; and it ends with something very like a love scene between the mother and her son. '"And I've never—you know, Paul—I've never had a husband—not really—" He stroked his mother's hair, and his mouth was on her throat' (*SL* 262). Kisses on the throat are particularly evocative of passion in *Sons and Lovers*: we see Paul kiss Clara on the throat just before they make love beside the river Trent in Chapter 12, and just after they make love in Chapter 13. A few lines later, after Paul has again—'trembling'—kissed his mother, Morel comes in. It has often been pointed out how his first words to Paul establish a note of jealous challenge: 'At your mischief again?' (*SL* 262) Then comes the quarrel, and then the final scene between Paul and his mother in which the proto-Hamlet tells the actual Gertrude 'Don't sleep with him, Mother' (*SL* 264). The chapter ends with deliberate flatness after the drama: 'Everybody tried to forget the scene.'

The scene in the play has the kisses of the son and mother interrupted by their anticipation of the return of the daughter Nellie:

> *He takes her in his arms, and she kisses him, and he hides his face in her shoulder. She holds him closely for a moment; then she kisses him and gently*

releases him. He kisses her. She gently draws away, saying, very tenderly:
MOTHER; There!—Nellie will be coming in.
ERNEST *(after a pause)*: And you do understand, don't you, Master?
MOTHER *(with great gentleness, having decided not to torment him)*: Yes, I
understand now. *(She bluffs him.)*
ERNEST *takes her hand and strokes it a moment. Then he bends down and
continues to unfasten his boots. It is very silent.*
I'm sure that hussy ought to be in—just look at the time!
ERNEST: Ay, it's scandalous![6]

Ernest strokes his mother's hand, not her face (as in *Sons and Lovers*):
and the kind of subtle drama of nuance at which the play aims (*'having
decided not to torment him'*) is quite different from the raging melodrama of
the novel, in which Mrs Morel not only pants with exhaustion after
walking uphill (as in the play) but sits 'bluish round the mouth', with a
weak heart; then has her passionate scene with Paul; then moans and
faints away during the quarrel between father and son. Paul, too, goes
to bed 'in a fury of misery' (*SL* 264) in the novel; Ernest and his mother
have a final tender parting with 'a dangerous gentleness'[7] in their tones;
but it is dangerous only to the kind of life they have to lead in the
miner's kitchen. The passions of *Sons and Lovers* belong to another creation.

In such a scene, the novel is asserting the jealousy of the father, and
the son's feelings for his girl-friend, only in so far as they relate to the
son's mother-love: that is the primary impact of the scene. It is, I
suggest, significant that the title *Sons and Lovers* only came to Lawrence
in the course of writing this last draft of the novel. At the start of
October, when it was more than half written, he was saying 'I shall
alter the title' from 'Paul Morel' (06 x 1912); but not until he had
written 400 pages of it, out of 500, did he ask Garnett 'Will *Sons and
Lovers* do for a title? I've made the book *heaps* better—a million times'
(30 x 1912). So he would seem to have invented the title sometime
between half and three-quarters of his way through the book. (The
scene I have been discussing is almost exactly half-way through.) And,
above all, he was conscious of how much he had changed it, in this last
writing; it was not only 'a million times' better, 'I've got a heap of
warmth and blood and tissue into that fuliginous novel of mine' (05 xi
1912). 'Fuliginous' means dusky or sooty: the novel's obscurity was
being cleared, and its warm life reasserted. 'F[rieda]. says it's her—it
would be'; but if she helped Lawrence make clear the 'domineering
note' then it was a fair claim.

I do not wish to imply that the novel is deeply damaged by the
expression of ideas explicit in the summary. As the tone of that summary suggests, Lawrence seized on the 'idea' excitedly; it gave some
passages of the book a coherence which they almost certainly lacked in

previous drafts. In very few places is it as crudely expressed as at the end of the 'Strife in Love' chapter. One of its effects, however, is to make the rejection of Miriam more complicated; because though the novel starts to express a new 'idea' of Paul being caught between his love for his mother—'real Oedipus'—and his love for Miriam, that is not something it can express with any clarity. The presentation of Miriam has almost completely failed to create the kind of love between her and Paul which the latter's feelings for his mother could actually interfere with. All the way through the novel there are reminders of Paul's need of Miriam, of his intimacy with her—as when she feels that Paul 'understood the slightest quiver of her innermost soul' (*SL* 204), or the novel refers to 'their old rare harmony' (*SL* 279). And yet the chapter 'Lad and Girl Love' is remarkable for its almost complete refusal to show Paul's love for Miriam. Miriam loves Paul, of course, but long before Mrs Morel can ever interfere with the young couple, Paul is independently reacting against Miriam; and not as a youth whose real love belongs elsewhere, but because (in part) Miriam is so difficult to relate to, is so spiritually demanding; and because, in part, Paul's own sexuality is so inhibited. The whole chapter 'Lad and Girl Love' shows Paul going to Miriam for reasons he does not understand; but knowing very well the strength of his reaction against her. When, a little later, Paul feels torn between Miriam and his mother, and is angry with Miriam because she 'caused his mother suffering', we are told that 'he hated her—and he easily hated her' (*SL* 238). That ease of hatred and anger is something that the whole novel demonstrates; and in the first instance, at any rate, it has nothing to do with Paul's feelings for his mother. We can be sure that our perception of this anger with Miriam has nothing to do with our knowledge of the real-life situation of Lawrence and Jessie Chambers: one of the most perceptive early reviewers put a finger on the oddity of the presentation of Miriam with great acuteness, and without any knowledge of the biographical situation:

Many men, and perhaps most women, will say to themselves as they read: 'Yes, this is how Miriam seemed to Paul, but this is not what Miriam was.' We suspect—and it is a tribute to the strength of the illusion created—that, if the girl's story had been written, we should have found her by no means so abnormal a person as represented, and her wayward lover considerably more comprehensible.[8]

The chapter 'Strife in Love' offers us a slightly later version of events, in general, and shows Paul's anger with Miriam resulting from his love for his mother; to that extent, it is a refinement of the earlier analysis, and does make the 'wayward lover considerably more comprehensible'. But—with its explicitly Oedipal situation at its close—'Strife in Love' is perhaps the novel's turning-point, too; it shows Lawrence at grips with his new 'domineering' idea.

The whole of William's career, of course, had taken place earlier in the book, and though the November 1912 summary places William in the same dilemma as Paul, it has to rewrite the novel to do so. In the novel, the most that happens between William and Mrs Morel over William's girl Lily is 'a conflict between them'; but this is caused by Mrs Morel's very natural sense of her son wasting himself, not by a possessive mother-love. William says: 'I can't give her up now; it's gone too far. . . . And, besides, for *some* things I couldn't do without her' (*SL* 164). William is clearly trying to live by a social code which sees engagement as obligation; and just as clearly he feels sexually responsible to her, too: 'for *some* things I couldn't do without her'. Far from being possessive, Mrs Morel is actually sympathetic and understanding. She goes out of her way to be nice to the girl, and she gives William utterly sensible advice: 'remember there are worse wrongs than breaking off an engagement' (*SL* 164). She sees 'the despair on his face', and she wants to help. The November 1912 summary is quite different: 'As soon as the young men come into contact with women, there's a split. William gives his sex to a fribble, and his mother holds his soul. But the split kills him, because he doesn't know where he is' (19 xi 1912). There is no soul-holding in the novel; the split we see in William is between two (or more) ways of life. He is stuck in the new obligations that come with the limited advance to economic freedom that he has made; we see in him the limitations of 'getting on' in life (as Mrs Morel hopes her sons will). Lily has, appropriately, pretensions to being a lady; and William is both proud of that, and hates her for it, when he sees her with his family. No split with his mother kills him; he overworks himself trying to make enough money to have a decent middle-class wedding and marriage, and he dies of a creeping skin disease that starts from the chafing of his clerk's collar. It is certainly true that William 'doesn't know where he is', but not in the sense of the summary; breaking from the life he knows at home, striving to better himself—to fulfil his mother's ambitions for her sons—he destroys himself. He is thoroughly rooted in the novel's sense of code and class, and that is the strength of its creation of him. When the summary makes a psychological tragedy out of his career, it goes hopelessly wrong.

On the other hand, we need to ask why Paul's affair with Clara ends as it does. Two pages before the novel ends, when he sees Miriam for the last time, Paul feels how he 'wanted her to hold him and say, with joy and authority: "Stop all this restlessness and beating against death. You are mine for a mate." She had not the strength' (*SL* 508). And like *The Rainbow*, *Sons and Lovers* ends before the main character finds 'a mate'. But unlike the later novel, it makes that character's position tragic—'Derelict', as the last chapter title calls him: unable to cope with himself, still restless and 'beating against death'. The two novels Lawrence wrote after *Sons and Lovers* would be most concerned with the way individuals found their partners; the first three novels were much more concerned with the failure of relationship. And of the three, *Sons and Lovers* has the closest and most nearly vital relationships for its hero, and the greatest sense of desolation at the end—with just a spark of hope. The relationship with Miriam, for all its intensity, had been doomed from the beginning; but Clara succeeds in giving Paul (and achieving herself) that sense of 'joy and authority' he wants. And when they make love as the peewits call, in the chapter 'Baxter Dawes', there is a strong sense of a next step for Paul after his state of being 'derelict'. *Sons and Lovers* here starts to create a new way of looking at human beings; as both less and more than individuals. Paul and Clara feel themselves part of the larger movement of the cosmos; we start to see them as we see Tom Brangwen, and Lydia, and Will, in *The Rainbow*, as inhabitants of another world beside 'the world of life' (*R* 81).

But *Sons and Lovers* is a novel concerned with·creating a tragically damaged hero; it relegates such experiences to the class of 'passion', simply, and they are not allowed to stand between Paul and his tragedy. The novel's structure and argument demand that such a next step be denied almost as soon as created. So the experience, and the way of looking at people, lead to nothing because Clara demands too much: 'Something great was there, she knew; something great enveloped her. But it did not keep her . . . she had not got him; she was not satisfied' (*SL* 431). The women thus ruins the new creation (they have been Adam and Eve in the previous paragraph), and Paul has to go back to his mother, his final break with Miriam, and his final loneliness. Clara and Baxter Dawes are, rather unconvincingly, re-united; Paul reconciles them as if they were the warring adults his own parents are, and he their caring son. Their loose end of the plot is tied up, and Paul moves into 'Derelict' by himself.

Given the importance of that experience with Clara, it is striking that Paul's relationship with her should not prosper or, at least, develop. We are further told that Clara finds 'Some part, big and vital in him, she had no hold over; nor did she ever try to get it, or even to realise what is was' (*SL* 439). I suspect that we readers do not know what it is, either. Is it Paul's independence? His artistic talent? His feeling for Mrs Morel? When, however, Paul says to his mother that he cannot give himself to his women—'And I never shall meet the right woman while you live' (*SL* 427)—then we are being offered something akin to an explanation of his conduct and feelings. For a man who can be taken into another cosmos by the woman he loves, Paul is also presented as an extraordinarily casual and patronising lover. 'He knew that she was dreary every evening she did not see him, so he gave her a good deal of his time' (*SL* 428). The whole affair with Clara presents a far more complex case of the failure of a relationship—and, I would suggest, a far more contradictory one—than can be explained by Paul's being unable to love anyone except his mother. In the end, even Clara's return to Baxter Dawes is made simply psychologically fulfilling: she turns to him again 'to be self-sacrificial. . . . She wanted to do penance' (*SL* 466). I would argue that such explanations are simple and arbitrary; Clara is being pushed into the wings so that the greater action of Mrs Morel's death and Paul's continuing love for her can be staged. I cannot help feeling that Mrs Morel's hold over Paul is, in fact, being used in the cases of both Miriam and Clara to provide explanations of the failure of relationships where the reality of the relationship is rather different, and too complicated simply to be met by such an explanation.

But the 'idea' which in the autumn of 1912 came to Lawrence apparently allowed him to cut through the emotional tangles of the book which he had been trying to write his way out of for the previous two years—even if, in so doing, he had to weaken the book's characteristic strength: its creation of the Morel family understood not simply in psychological or moral terms, but as it existed in a community. Mrs Morel is not simply a mother who loves her sons because of the badness of her own marriage, but a mother who is possessed by an idea of their excape from the world she feels condemned to; her ideas of success and of 'getting on' are as dangerous as her love. A slight weakness in the novel is its failure to create much sense of the adult Paul's day-to-day work at Jordan's: like Mrs Morel, the novel is more concerned with his success as an artist. And yet even that is significantly unlike the success of the novelist who wrote *Sons and Lovers*. The apex of Paul's achievement as an artist is in exhibiting pictures at Nottingham Castle (and getting them bought by the local gentry), and designing embroideries 'for altar-cloths and similar things'. Liberty's take several of his designs, but it is hard to see how the novel can justify the remark 'He was gradually making it possible to earn a livelihood by his art' (*SL* 367). We are not taken close to him as an artist—only as one who successfully sells his work. The novel makes him a painter and designer rather as it endorses Mrs Morel's attitude towards her husband; while on the one hand it offers an exceptional account of the difficulties of growing up and living in this community, on the other hand it is prepared to moralise Walter Morel out of serious existence, and to see Paul's success as a painter simply from the point of view of his success in the middle-class world. Following Paul's success in selling his painting to Major Moreton, Mrs Morel starts to dress a little more stylishly; Paul declares that 'she looked a lady . . . as much as Mrs Major Moreton, and far, far nicer'. And the novel comments: 'The family was coming on. Only Morel remained unchanged, or rather, lapsed slowly' (*SL* 313). Like its earlier comment that Morel 'had denied the God in him' (*SL* 82), it assumes Mrs Morel's attitude without having the same reasons to do so. But within a page, it is offering a fine contrast between Paul's assertion that one gets 'life itself, warmth' from the common people, and Mrs Morel's awkward question: 'But, then, why don't you go and talk to your father's pals?' (*SL* 313). We see both her sense of class and superiority—'She frankly *wanted* him to climb into the middle class' (*SL* 314)—and the reasons for it: it also creates Paul's kind of idealism and youthfulness and rootlessness. Another son might well have gone and talked to Morel's 'pals'; Paul never would. The novel, that is, creates the life and tensions of a community; but parts of it need to be understood as reflections of the particular needs and predilections and 'sicknesses' of its author; its structure is not organic but internally divided. The 'idea' of obsessive, 'domineering' mother-love is simply the final divisive and cohesive force in the book: cohesive in drawing together the various stages of Paul's emotional life under a common influence, and divisive because it operates in the book with the force of a prejudice, breaking up the social complexity of the novel in favour of moralised respectability and social ambition.

It is particularly appropriate that, of all his novels, *Sons and Lovers* should have acquired still another diversifying element after its composition, when Edward Garnett advised (and made) extensive cuts in it before publication, thus modifying its structure and its meaning still further; it was made to fit the idea of how long a novel should be according to a publisher's reader. To complete this diversifying history, Lawrence himself wrote a 'Foreward' in January 1913 which has hardly anything to do with the novel itself. He did not write it to be published—'I should die of shame if that Foreword were printed' (01 ii 1913) he told Garnett—but because 'I wanted to *write* a Foreword': he still had more to say. Like one of the little faces high up in Lincoln Cathedral in *The Rainbow*, the 'Foreword' suggests 'However much there is inside here, there's a good deal they haven't got in' (*R* 204). It is the first of Lawrence's sparrings with prose exposition of 'philosophy'; it eventually gets round to the concept of the 'Son-lover', but its approach is abstract and its language Biblical-metaphorical. It investigates relationships in terms of 'Word' and 'Flesh' (though it gets entangled in its terminology so that 'the Father' is 'more properly, the Mother');[9] it is the first full expression of Lawrence's developing dualism. Its significance is that it shows him looking forward beyond *Sons and Lovers* to novels which are not naturalistic, and (in particular) suggests how a special language will be necessary for him on the unfamiliar and unexplored ground of such a novel. It also, of course, looks forward to novels of successful relationships between men and women—for 'if a son-lover take a wife, then is she not his wife, she is only his bed':[10] but 'in the woman is the eternal continuance, and from the man, in the human race, comes the exclamation of joy and astonishment at new self-revelation, revelation of that which is Woman to a man'.[11] That 'joy and authority' to which Paul could have responded—and which the real-life original of the autobiographical hero had himself known in the last few months of writing the book, but chose not to include in it—that 'joy' could be a new subject for a novel.

When Frieda Lawrence looked back at *Sons and Lovers* from the standpoint of February 1914, when Lawrence was writing the penultimate version of *The Rainbow*, she remarked: 'You see, I don't really believe in *Sons and Lovers*; it feels as if there were nothing *behind* all those happenings as if there were no *"Hinterland der Seele,"* only intensely felt fugitive things' (*Frieda* 202). The way in which Lawrence started work so excitedly on so many different projects in the months after *Sons and Lovers* suggests that the novel had indeed been a successful exorcism of many ghosts, and that some at least of its intenser feelings were both personal and 'fugitive'.

4 The Rainbow

Lawrence knew, even before he finished *Sons and Lovers*, that he would be starting another novel almost immediately. But that novel was not, as it turned out, to be his next important project; it took him several months to find out what that was. He had told Garnett at the end of October that he would be starting '*Scargill Street* . . . in a fortnight' (30 x 1912); Garnett had obviously heard of the idea before—it may well have been that novel 'purely of the common people' (04 viii 1912) which Lawrence told him about in August. The novel with the best claim to be 'Scargill Street' is the co-called 'Burns Novel' which Lawrence in fact started in mid-December; it tells us a good deal about the kind of book Lawrence was turning to after *Sons and Lovers*. He wrote to Garnett:

> I shall make him live near home, as a Derbyshire man and shall fictionise the circumstances. I think I can do him almost like an autobiography . . . I've only got Lockhart's *Life*. I should like to know more about the Highland Mary episode. Do you think it's interesting?
>
> (17 xii 1912)

In the first meeting of 'Jack' with 'Mary Renshaw' (changed from 'Burns' in the MS)[1] we can perhaps see a version of Burns' own meeting with Mary Campbell. Jack is a small-time farmer, educating himself in the evenings, when he meets Mary; Burns was a small-time farmer, educating himself in the evenings, when he met Mary. Burns wrote songs and sang them; Jack 'knows more songs than any lad i' th' country' (*Nehls* i 188). Jack has none of the bashfulness of a Paul Morel; the first evening that he meets Mary, he takes her in his arms and persuades her to stay outside the house with him. Lockhart's *Life* of Burns describes his 'facility in addressing the fair sex, [entering] into conversation with them with the greatest ease and freedom'.[2] But, as Lawrence said, he did not intend to limit himself to the 'circumstances' of Burns' life; he meant to treat the book as an 'autobiography'. Coming so soon after the completion of *Sons and Lovers*, this is particularly interesting. Paul Morel is an artist, but only an amateur (and his art is for the gentry); before Lawrence himself, Burns was the greatest British writer from the working, or peasant, class—and Lawrence had 'always been fond of him, as a sort of brother' (19 xii 1912). And in

Burns' problems with his contemporaries' proprieties, Lawrence would
naturally have seen a mirror of his own escapes from conventionality,
culminating in his elopement with Frieda Weekley.[3] There remains too
little of the 'Burns Novel' for us to know how it would have developed,
but it is significant that the three other novels Lawrence started during
the next three months all have women as their central characters, and
in no sense were 'like an autobiography'. The 'Burns Novel' would
perhaps have been another step along the same road as *Sons and Lovers*,
with a new honesty in its autobiographical element—it could have
suggested the growth of the working-class poet's mind in a hostile
culture. But it would also have been another story set in England, while
'The Sisters' and probably 'The Insurrection of Miss Houghton' took
their heroines out of England into social and intellectual worlds that
challenged their Englishness. Their sexual experiences, too, were to be
a long way from those of Paul Morel or any potential 'Burns' character;
they would not just be the significant start of experience, but would
redirect their energies and transform their lives. The 'Highland Mary'
episode, of love, lost love, and life without love, would have been far
more the conventional material of a novel; and however much the
'Burns Novel' had updated the love story of Jack and Mary, it would
have been a novel about the past, in so far as it limited itself to the
social and emotional experiences possible in one small community; and
Lawrence's sense of history as he would discover and explore it in the
final *Rainbow* was concerned with the past's development into the modern world—something far harder to do in the life of a single hero and
heroine. Lawrence gave the novel the setting he knew from the hills and
villages round Gargnano; but the old England he created from those
elements could well have been a nostalgic recreation.

After working at the novel around Christmas 1912, he gave it up; but
within a fortnight was 'simmering a new work' he refused to tell Garnett about 'because it may not come off. But the thought of it fills me
with a curious pleasure—venomous, almost. I want to get it off my
chest' (12 i 1913). It sounds very different from the 'Burns Novel': it
was the novel Lawrence came to call 'The Insurrection of Miss Houghton'. It was a book which 'will give most folk extreme annoyance to
read, if it doesn't bore them' (17 i 1913); and getting it 'off his chest'
sounds as if this attack on his contemporaries' sensibilities was also an
attack on small-town England as he had known it. We can postulate a
novel about the revolt and (probably) sexual 'insurrection' of a girl in
such a community. It was not an autobiographical novel, about either
Lawrence or Frieda (11 iii 1913), but it *was* about a woman and
that in itself is important. It is striking how much of Lawrence's fiction
after *Sons and Lovers* is primarily about the experience of women; of his
remaining seven completed novels, five have women as their protagonists (*The Rainbow, Women in Love, The Lost Girl, The Plumed Serpent, Lady*

Chatterley's Lover). And the abortive novel he had apparently just given up for the 'Insurrection', 'Elsa Culverwell',[4] had—like 'The Sisters'— been a woman's first-person narrative. The women Lawrence had known best in England—Jessie Chambers, Helen Corke, Louie Burrows, Alice Dax—were intelligent women who in three cases out of four had made careers for themselves in the man's world as school-teachers. To that extent they had successfully broken with the traditionally house-bound lives of working-class and middle-class women. Lawrence's own mother, too, had been a teacher who followed her instincts into marriage with a coal-miner and thus broke with the respectability of her family. Alice Dax, Jessie Chambers and Helen Corke were all prepared to follow their instincts and sexual loyalties rather than the pattern of conventional behaviour. And all three participated in extra-marital affairs. Louie Burrows, though more conventional, was deeply involved in the suffrage moment.

Yet Lawrence was not prepared to make these women the heroines of his time. The novel about Helen Corke's affair—*The Trespasser*—is more about the man than the woman. For the sake of *Sons and Lovers* in its final manifestation, Lawrence was prepared to ignore Jessie Chambers' individual stand and rebellion (and only makes Miriam a teacher right at the end of the book), though he makes Clara (partly drawn from Alice Dax) something of a liberated woman. Yet in the end Paul returns her to her husband, and the novel consigns her to conventionality. The end of the novel is dominated by the man's fate and the man's struggle. What perhaps made the difference between the conception of *Sons and Lovers* and the conception of 'The Insurrection' was Lawrence's experience of the von Richthofen family; we can assume that the experiences of Miss Houghton were not those which any of the women Lawrence knew in England could have had. It is, too, striking that Ursula's experiences as a school-teacher in *The Rainbow* were apparently drawn in part from the experiences of Else von Richthofen, and not from any of the women teachers Lawrence had known in England; and *The Rainbow*, primarily the experience which gave rise to the modern woman growing up in England, was dedicated 'Zu Else' by Lawrence's particular wish (31 v 1915). Frieda, Else and Joanna von Richthofen were women of a different calibre from those he had known before. Frieda had been prepared to give up her marriage, her security, her reputation and (in the end) her children, to live with this unemployed young Englishman; for the previous ten years she had, through letters and visits to Germany, escaped her Nottingham domesticity to move in the circles of some of the leading German intellectuals and revolutionary thinkers. Her sister Else had married one intellectual, Edgar Jaffe, but was close to Max Weber and his wife Marianne. Only Alice Dax, perhaps, of the women Lawrence knew in England, was prepared to act as unconventionally as Else and Frieda; and only out of

anger and frustration, not from conviction. And however advanced
Eastwood and Shirebrook had been, they did not compare with the
intellectual café circles of Munich. Lawrence told Garnett about the
von Richthofen sisters in May 1912:

> the eldest, a professor of psychology and economics—left her hus-
> band, gone with two other men (in succession—yet *really*
> good—good, the sort of woman one reverences). Then there's
> Frieda. Then the youngest sister, very beautiful, married to a brute
> of a swanky officer in Berlin—and, in a large, splendid way—*cocotte*.
> Lord what a family. I've never seen anything like it.
>
> (09 v 1912)

And Lawrence wrote to Else in 1913:

> Do write about the women—their aims and ideals—and a bit about
> them personally, any you know and how they'd rather paint pictures
> than nurse children, because any motherly body can do the latter,
> while it needs a fine and wonderful woman to speak a message.
>
> (10 ii 1913)

The independent woman was a character who, from now on, would
recur in his fiction; and the life-choices he had seen in the von Richthofen sisters came to matter far more than those he had seen in Jessie
Chambers, Helen Corke, or Alice Dax. And, as Frank Kermode has
pointed out, the novel's depiction of the situation of women in a society
has become one of the best roads to understanding a society or a
period.[5]

But not only did the 'Insurrection' have a new sense of subject; very
quickly it became 'quite different in manner from my other stuff', so
that Lawrence had to think, even at this stage, of rewriting so that it
would appeal to an existing public: he began to find himself out on his
own, with a new subject, a new style, and an increasingly unpublishable book. When rewritten, he told Garnett, 'it might find a good
public amongst the Meredithy public' (01 ii 1913), but in this unmod-
ified form it was increasingly what he wanted to do as a novelist—because it made him feel

> I think, do you know, I have inside me a sort of answer to the *want* of
> today: to the real, deep want of the English people, not to just what
> they fancy they want. And gradually, I shall get my hold on them.
> And this novel is perhaps not such good art, but it is what they want,
> need, more or less.
>
> (01 ii 1913)

That sense of the book as an answer to need; not as an aesthetic object for an existing public (as *The White Peacock* and *The Trespasser* had pre-eminently been), but as a means of both changing and remaking its audience—this was a vital change in Lawrence's sense of the novel and what he wanted to do with it. He wrote to McLeod in April that 'I do so break my heart over England when I read *The New Machievelli*. And I am so sure that only through a readjustment between men and women, and a making free and healthy of this sex, will she get out of her present atrophy' (23 iv 1913). The 'Insurrection' was obviously taking on the job of working for that 'readjustment', and was making sex 'free and healthy':

> . . . nobody will ever dare to publish it. I feel I could knock my head against the wall. Yet I love and adore this new book . It's all crude as yet, like one of Tony's clumsy prehistorical beasts—most cumbersome and floundering—but I think it's great—so new, so really a stratum deeper than I think anybody has ever gone, in a novel. . . . But nobody will publish it. I wish I had never been born. But I'm going to stick at it, get it done, and then write another, shorter, absolutely impeccable—as far as morals go—novel . . . or else what am I going to live on, and keep Frieda on withal.
>
> (11 iii 1913)

Lawrence simultaneously had to write publishable novels for a precarious living, and to write as he wanted, too: 'I think, do you know, I have inside me a sort of answer to the *want* of today . . .' (01 ii 1913). His first two novels, addressed to a limited and specific public, were behind him, and *Sons and Lovers* had thrown him forward into creating a novel truly of the modern woman, not of the tragic man; the 'Insurrection' made him aware of his audience, and how 'gradually, I shall get my hold on them' (01 ii 1913). A novel could be one of the growing points of society; it could create and lead an advance in consciousness; people could come to realise their own true feelings through it, and could realise what it meant to belong to their generation. Following Lawrence's sense that his 'life work' was 'sticking up for the love between men and women' (25 xii 1912), this new novel marked still another advance: the novel could be 'an answer to the *want* of today'.

But it seemed, too, that 'The Insurrection' had to stop; it had become commercially impossible. Lawrence abandoned it for 'a new, lighter novel' which would be 'quite decent (D.V.)' (22 iii 1913). His prayer was not answered: 'The pot-boiler is at page 110, and has developed into an earnest and painful work' (05 iv 1913). But that development of the pot-boiler into seriousness cannot have been much of a surprise: 'I have to write what I can write,' he told Garnett a month later. 'I *know* I can write bigger stuff than any man in England

Harold ... and I write for men like David [Garnett] and [Hobson]—they will read me, soon' (09 v 1913). The new novel was called 'The Sisters', and takes us directly back to Lawrence's experience of the von Richthofen family.

Significantly, Else von Richthofen visited the Lawrences exactly at the time he was starting the new novel, but later on Frieda took both sisters to be, in this first version, herself: 'they are *me*, these beastly, superior, arrogant females!' (*Frieda* 195). It was certainly a light-hearted, at times a 'flippant' book (22 iv 1914), but it quickly became an attempt to do something which sounds exactly like 'The Insurrection':

> I can only write what I feel pretty strongly about: and that, at present, is the relation between men and women. After all, it is *the* problem of today, the establishment of a new relation, or the readjustment of the old one between men and women.
>
> (09 v 1913)

In one sense, he would never get away from that subject again; it would certainly occupy him through to the end of *Women in Love*, four years later.

We are less in the dark about 'The Sisters' than we are about 'The Insurrection'; a five-page fragment of it survives.[6] It is very near the end of the novel, is perhaps the end itself; Gerald confronts Gudrun—with whom he has had an affair—and Loerke, a German sculptor who has also been her lover. Gudrun is pregnant, and Loerke has come to London. But Gerald asks Gudrun to marry him. Gudrun fires up: '"And I want to know why—why now—and not before?" . . . "I didn't know before," Gerald interrupted, lamely, but doggedly.'[7] And Loerke taunts Gerald so that the latter 'seemed choked in the mud of his shame. Suddenly he flung up his face blindly, crying stubborn with misery: "I didn't know."'[8] Loerke leaves, and Gerald remarks that '"he is a decent fellow, really."' '"Ha!" she cried. "Decent! He is decent. I loved him."'[9] But, all the same, she agrees to marry Gerald, though—as he knows—

> she came to him as the father of her child, not as to a lover, a husband. Well, he had had a chance, and lost it. He had been a fool. Now he must make the best of it, and get her again. But it hurt that she did not seem to want him very much. It hurt keenly.
>   Then while he was thinking, with his forehead hard with pain, she kissed him, drawing him to her, murmuring 'My love!'[10]

Things will never again be as they were; too much love has been killed and gone dead. Yet Gudrun and Gerald can accept each other, can be tender to each other still, and can finally trust each other too: that can be their love. What happened to Birkin and Ella (later to become Ursula) in this version, we cannot tell; but the Gudrun-Gerald relationship certainly shows that love is not the 'end of experience' (to use the language of the first page of *Women in Love*), and that passion is not the end in itself which it had seemed to be for Paul at times towards the end of *Sons and Lovers*. Gerald and Gudrun may well lose that sense of each other which originally created the relationship; but they can re-establish the ground of their love. Lawrence is deliberately going beyond the habit of the conventional novel, that when a man and a women are in love with each other, then the relationship is somehow settled. In 'The Sisters', the women demand as much as the men demand; their equality is marked, and their needs as great.

One other thing suggested by this surviving fragment is that the Crich family is obviously in the novel, and yet it appears to be without the tragic resonances of the Crich family of *Women in Love*. Mrs Crich is an aristocratic eccentric, not a woman whose family is fated because of its relationship with social England. It appears likely, in fact, that 'The Sisters' was not a novel about England as both *The Rainbow* and *Women in Love* were to be; and a letter Lawrence sent Garnett in May 1913 perhaps suggests why: 'I can only write what I feel pretty strongly about: and that, at present, is the relation between men and women' (09 v 1913). Both *The Rainbow* and *Women in Love* tried to do a good deal more than that.

Lawrence finished the first 'Sisters' in the early summer of 1913, before going to England; and restarted it when he got back to the Continent in August. The novel's relationship with a Continental erotic movement and with the experience, in particular, of Frieda's sisters rather than of women he knew in England is perhaps emphasised by the way Lawrence resolutely wrote the novel out of England. This time it proved far harder to write: '*The Sisters* is the devil—I've made two false starts already—but it'll go—' (24 viii 1913). It soon acquired 'a new basis altogether' (04 ix 1913): 'so different from anything I have yet written, that I do nothing but wonder what it is like' (06 x 1913). It took him three and a half months longer than he had anticipated to reach the end, and even then he never quite finished it. Garnett saw the first half only, in January 1914.

Throughout the composition of this novel—which he told Garnett he 'should rather call *The Wedding Ring*' (30 xii 1913)—Lawrence insisted how different it was from his other novels, in particular from *Sons and Lovers*; in the changing of the style we can see him changing his idea of the book.

It is *very* different from *Sons and Lovers*: written in another language almost. I shall be sorry if you don't like it, but am prepared. I shan't write in the same manner as *Sons and Lovers* again, I think—in that hard, violent style full of sensation and presentation. You must see what you think of the new style.

(30 xii 1913)

What Lawrence wanted to do, now, was write a novel without a 'moral scheme', without the revelations of character typical of *Sons and Lovers*, without placing the characters in hard-edged psychological opposition to each other. He was consciously committing himself to an experimental method, in fact, and it proved the end of his working relationship with Edward Garnett. We need to remember that Garnett was not only a friend, but the reader and adviser for the firm most likely to publish Lawrence's work; and Lawrence knew that he 'must write to live' (29 i 1914); but he ended up no longer trusting Garnett's instinct for his work as either critic or publisher's adviser. He felt that Garnett was trying to push him back into an outmoded manner: 'you should understand, and help me to the new thing, not get angry and say it is *common*, and send me back to the tone of the old *Sisters*' (22 iv 1914). The new book was written with what Lawrence elsewhere called 'the exhaustive method' (29 i 1914), and we can perhaps see what he meant by examining a surviving fragment of 'The Wedding Ring'.[11]

This consists of an extraordinary episode fairly early in the relationship of Birkin and Ella, when Ella is still suffering the after-effects of her relationship with Ben Templeman. Birkin comes to see her; she breaks down and falls to her knees, crying. Birkin watches her, and finally says 'I love you'. This is perhaps exactly the kind of thing Garnett would have found '*common*', not to say melodramatic. But Lawrence is doing something quite new for him. Before Ella 'caught him to her', Birkin has been characterised by 'the steady hardness of the eyes . . . his voice had a hard, vibrating quality'.[12] We are not meant to see him—Lawrence wants us closer to him than that, and stresses Birkin's strangeness, his immediate impact on Ella (and hers on him). She cries out 'do you love me?' but the question is beside the point; something from the past is breaking in her, and 'she slid away to the floor at his feet, unable to stand, unable to hold her body erect'.[13] It is not that her feeling for Birkin is so overwhelming, but that it is forcing her into agonising physical reaction against the self which is ordinarily in control. 'She must double up.'[14] And that happens twice. Realisation has attacked her like a blow in the stomach; it must be acknowledged, and this stranger must be acknowledged, though the person she *has* been reacts violently against such an acknowledgement. Birkin, too, suffers; he loses himself, but not in love. In spite of himself, he is forced to act instinctively and responsively; but his awareness grows more slowly than Ella's and by the time he is asking 'do you really care for me?' she is withdrawing into coldness and self-possession. ' "I don't know," she said. "Don't ask me now. You'd better go and leave me." '[15] But again she is overwhelmed—'the hurt, the grief, was rising again'. Not, I think, simply grief for her 'earlier love affair' as Mark Kinkead-Weekes suggests,[16] but grief that feeling has again broken her open. And this time Birkin too is forced agonisingly into response: '"I," he stammered, blanched with the struggle to speak—"I love you." '[17] Lawrence is using the word 'love' quite differently from *Sons and Lovers*, where Paul could 'love' Miriam, and be quite unchanged by her. 'The Wedding Ring' is attempting to deal with the almost unexplored depths of human feelings, so that Birkin walks away 'feeling as if the heavens had fallen, and he were not himself, he were somebody else, walking in a different life. In one crash, the whole form of his life, the whole conception of himself, which he had, was gone. . . .'[18] Ella, too, 'felt a responsibility coming upon her, that almost silenced her . . . something was taking place, implicating her with him, which she could never revoke or escape. And blindly, almost shrinking, she lapsed forward.'[19]

We can see why Lawrence insisted that it was so different from *Sons and Lovers*; but it is, too, a difficult kind of fiction for its reader; it depends upon his feeling its mood and its vital undercurrents almost personally—he has to be totally involved. When Ella sees Ben Templeman again, at the end of the fragment, 'She knew him without looking: his peculiar, straying walk, the odd, separate look about him which filled her with dread. He had still power over her: he was still Man to her.'[20] It is not, I suggest, simply our ignorance of the rest of the novel which makes such passages so difficult. 'He was still Man to her', in particular, sounds like popular magazine cliché, and suggests what Garnett found *'common'*. The point seems to be that Ben Templeman's 'separate' look is very different from Birkin's otherness, and that the way it forces her into relationship is also different. But it is easy for us readers not to realise the force of such distinctions.

Lawrence may have realised the strangeness of what he was doing; this version of the novel came to a halt at the start of February 1914.

> I had nearly finished it. It was full of beautiful things, but it missed—I knew that it just missed being itself. So here I am, must sit down and write it out again. I know it is quite a lovely novel really—you know that the perfect statue is in the marble, the kernel of it. But the thing is the getting it out clean.
>
> (09 ii 1914)

What he sat down and wrote was the first 'Rainbow',[21] which was probably the first of his attempts at this elusive novel which fully developed a sense of the Brangwen family's past. The relationship 'between men and women' which Lawrence had set himself to write in

March 1913 was taking on complications which in the final *Rainbow* were historical and spiritual. The very titles of the early versions, in fact, give us a clue to the kind of novels they were; 'The Sisters' had been a study of contrasted individuals—'woman becoming individual, self-responsible, taking her own initiative' (22 iv 1914); 'The Wedding Ring' presumably made the marriages of those women its primary concern; 'The Rainbow' (a title suggested by Frieda Lawrence) suggests for the first time a metaphysical dimension.

To Lawrence it seemed that this new version of the novel was an advance because he had stopped struggling with Frieda and 'the work is of both of us' (22 iv 1914). But other factors were probably just as important. It was in the late spring of 1914, just a fortnight after finishing the novel, that Lawrence wrote his famous letter about Marinetti, the futurists, and 'what the woman *is*—what she IS' (05 vi 1914) in his new version of the book. But we can tell that this was not an isolated insight, or even necessarily provoked by the futurists, by the way it develops an idea suggested the previous winter in a letter to Henry Savage. The letter is not as widely quoted as the letter about futurism, and has the advantage of being somewhat clearer, and untouched by the violent language of futurism; it describes very well the kind of fiction Lawrence was coming to wish to write.

> There is something in the Greek sculpture that any soul is hungry for—something of the eternal stillness that lies under all movement, under all life, like a source, incorruptible and inexhaustible. It is deeper than change, and struggling. So long I have acknowledged only the struggle, the stream, the change. And now I begin to feel something of the source, the great impersonal which never changes and out of which all change comes . . . there is behind every woman who walks, and who eats her meal, a Venus of Melos, still, unseeing, unchanging, and inexhaustible. And there is a glimpse of it everywhere, in somebody, at some moment—a glimpse of the eternal and unchangeable that they are.
>
> (24 xi 1913)

This passage is developing the language which Walter Pater had used in *The Renaissance* (1873) to discuss Greek sculpture, and Lawrence thanks Savage for the loan of a book by Pater in the same letter. Lawrence had clearly been reading the essay on Winckelmann, which actually uses the example of the 'Venus of Melos' to make some of its points. Pater finds Greek sculpture revealing 'not what is accidental in man, but the tranquil godship in him, as opposed to the restless accidents of life';[22] the Hellenic ideal 'allows passion to play lightly over the surface of the individual form, losing thereby nothing of its central impassivity, its depth and repose'.[23] Greek sculpture is, too, 'characterless, so far as character involves subjection to the accidental influences of life'.[24] Lawrence had been trying to get beyond the 'certain moral scheme' he wrote of in June 1914 ever since completing *Sons and Lovers*; and what he saw in the futurists, Pater had helped him see first in his own writing. Miriam and Mrs Morel had both been damaged by being forced into that 'moral scheme': there had been no 'eternal and unchangeable that they are'; they had been locally presented and provincially judged. That was what Frieda Lawrence obviously had in mind when she said that 'to me it seems an irreligious book' (*Frieda* 202). Once he was clear of its emotional entanglements, that came to be Lawrence's reaction too. The first 'Rainbow', he insisted, was different because he could get his 'soul into it' (22 iv 1914), meaning not simply that he could work harder at it, but that he could pursue the reality of relationships at a deeper level than the personal; the lives it described were not to be judged morally but as responding to the 'eternal and unchangeable that they are'.

So that when, for instance, Ursula in the finished book escapes from the horses at the end, it is to lie

> as if unconscious upon the bed of the stream, like a stone, unconscious, unchanging, unchangeable, whilst everything rolled by in transience, leaving her there, a stone at rest on the bed of the stream, unalterable and passive, sunk to the bottom of all change.
>
> (*R* 490)

The unchangeable self which had almost disappeared in her during her attempt to subdue herself, marry Skrebensky and be conventional, here re-possesses her. This is the new area of feeling to which Lawrence wished to carry the action of his novel; and to call people's selves 'eternal' or 'a phenomenon', and to examine their lives as 'states' of being, meant that a radically new sense of what a novel could and should do was developing in Lawrence. He had begun to write a novel which we can only describe as religious in its attitude to the things it found most worth describing; the point of it was to suggest a new idea of self. Such a conception meant that Lawrence was not only making greater demands on his readers; he was actually trying to change them, to change their attitude to the selves they believed in and found important.

The final extraordinary thing about this first 'Rainbow' is that, so far as Lawrence was concerned in mid-1914, it marked the *end* of his attempt to write such a novel. But for the first World War, it would almost certainly have been published as the finished and final novel. We should never have known *The Rainbow* and *Women in Love* as distinct novels, in fact; because the first 'Rainbow' was accepted for publication in the summer of 1914, and Lawrence had no intention of ever going back to it.

The first 'Rainbow' was accepted by Methuen, not by Duckworth; this was to be important for its subsequent fate. Garnett was obviously unhappy about the book, and when Methuen offered Lawrence one of their regular three-novel contracts (with the promise of £300 advance on royalties) he let them have it. And then he immediately started planning his next novel, for which he felt he needed to do some reading in the British Museum (16 v 1914).[25]

What changed everything was the War; in common with a number of other publishers, Methuen immediately suspended the payment of advance royalties, and returned unpublished MSS.[26] So in the middle of August 1914 Lawrence found himself impoverished again, with the novel MS back on his hands. He could not return to Italy, as he had planned; he rented a cottage in Buckinghamshire.

What interested him as a writer in the subsequent months was neither his old novel nor any new one, but a book he had been thinking about since June, on the characters in Hardy. Edward Marsh had sent him a complete set of the novels as a wedding present, and 'out of sheer rage' (05 ix 1914)—with the world, with the War—he started the book. It was unlike anything he had written before, and it was not published in his lifetime, but we can see in it the same change in attitude towards what writing could, and should, do for its readers as had been becoming clear in his novel-writing since *Sons and Lovers*. And the rereading of Hardy which provoked it confirmed him in his growing certainty about the kind of novel he did *not* wish to write. When he actually discusses Hardy's novels in the 'Study', he makes them the novels he would have written if he had been Hardy; so, for instance, he makes Arabella in *Jude the Obscure* understand Jude and his situation, and leave him 'the stronger and completer' (*Phx* 495), when Hardy's feeling about her is exactly the opposite. Hardy's books provoke some ideas which are important if we are to understand the new direction of Lawrence's fiction, but mostly the 'Study' is important for ideas that Lawrence brought to Hardy in reaction against him. He tended to rewrite Hardy's books so as to make them conform to the ideas he felt Hardy had instinctively grasped but which his own novels could fully demonstrate.

The ideas which dominate the 'Study' are those of impersonal forces existing in and through and behind human beings, in terms of which we can understand ourselves and our history. Lawrence sometimes calls them Law and Love, sometimes the Male and Female principles; and he uses such words to construct complex structures of meaning in which Raphael, Wordsworth and Michelangelo suddenly find themselves sharing the same sentence as examples of a similar tendency;

only for the next paragraph to make careful distinctions between them. It is a kind of writing which is very difficult to respond to; either it makes perfect sense, brilliantly, or it leaves us cold. It needs us to share the writer's point of view implicitly. It also shows, strikingly, how much these ideas needed a less self-indulgent form, and more real context, one which would offer opposites and problems.

The second thing the 'study' offers is a kind of writing very different, again, from anything Lawrence had done before. The 'Foreword' to *Sons and Lovers* had, at least, prefigured the kind of ideas dealt with in the 'Study'; but the writing of the latter is allegorical, whimsical, capable of being serious (or going sour) in a second; and, as popular writing, different from anything in the novels before *Mr Noon* and *Aaron's Rod*. The second chapter title gives an idea of it: 'Still Introductory: About Women's Suffrage, and Laws, and the War, and the Poor, with Some Fanciful Moralising' (*Phx* 404). The 'Study' suggests how controlled a writer Lawrence was in the work he prepared for publication; he did not allow himself such rhetorical flourishes and sideways leaps in work he offered an audience. For example:

> But law is a very, very clumsy and mechanical instrument, and we people are very, very delicate and subtle beings. Therefore I only ask that the law shall leave me alone as much as possible. I insist that no law shall have immediate power over me, either for my good or for my ill. And I would wish that many laws be unmade, and no more laws made. Let there be a parliament of men and women for the careful and gradual unmaking of laws.
>
> (*Phx* 405)

For all its commonsense, this is marked by an uneasy combination of tones. One of the things Lawrence was working for in the 'Study' was a voice in which he could discuss the things that mattered to him most, in a way that would really engage people's attention. And this, too, was something far more controlled and successful in *The Rainbow*, except at moments which I shall discuss.

But the 'Study', primarily, developed one of the insights which lay behind the advances of 'The Wedding Ring' and the first 'Rainbow'—the Paterian idea of the 'eternal and unchangeable behind the woman'. Lawrence expressed the idea, in the terms it takes on in the 'Study', in a letter to Gordon Campbell:

> I went to the British Museum—and I know, from the Egyptian and Assyrian sculpture—what we are after. We want to realise the tremendous *non-human* quality of life—it is wonderful. It is not the emotions, nor the personal feelings and attachments, that matter. These are all only expressive. . . . Behind in all are the tremendous

unknown forces of life, coming unseen and unperceived as out of the
desert to the Egyptians. . . .

(21 ix 1914)

These were the forces which the 'Study' particularly celebrated, and
started to fashion into coherence; but where the 'Study' has to spend
pages discovering its sense of the Male and Female principles, *The
Rainbow* was to create them, quite straightforwardly, in its first five
pages. The 'Study' obviously allowed Lawrence unusual space and
freedom to work out his sense of these 'tremendous forces', but *The
Rainbow* builds where the 'Study' only, for the most part, ponders and
experiments. Significantly, that September letter to Campbell goes on
to question the whole problem of ideas in a vacuum—which is exactly
where the 'Study' was putting them.

> But letters are no good. Why should we drift away, if we have a bit of
> hope in common, and a bit of courage. We are all struggling for the
> same liberation, if not for the same ulterior purpose. We must strug-
> gle together, and try to pull all in one direction, even if we're quite in
> the dark and don't see what we're pulling at. Which is preaching
> enough.

(21 ix 1914)

That desire to make ideas count, to participate in a common struggle,
for people to work together 'for the same liberation', was one which
would recur for the remainder of Lawrence's life. Not that it was a
wholly new sense, even in 1914; we know from the recollections of the
Chambers family how the young Lawrence had always had a yearning
for his friends to form groups, for them to work and think and
(perhaps) live together.

But it is significant that when he wrote to Campbell, Lawrence was
(for the first time in almost eight years) not working on a novel. He was
working on ideas; and for the first time since, perhaps, 1908 he was
surrounded by people he liked and trusted and found compatible. His
sense of a novel as his main outlet, his main mode of contact with his
own country and with those like him, which had inevitably been the
case while he was living in Germany and Italy, could be—for the
moment—less important. The Murrys, Campbells, Koteliansky, the
Cannans, Gertler, the Hampstead circle—these allowed Lawrence to
feel part of a group, an incipient community. And as Lawrence wrote, it
was not just letters which would keep them together—and in the
autumn of 1914, it was not novels either. It could be 'hope in common',
'the same liberation', 'one direction'. And this itself was fostered by a
common bond with his friends which at any other time would have
been lacking; a hatred of the War, and a determination not to be drawn

into it. The War did not, Lawrence said, 'alter my beliefs or visions' (21 ix 1914), but it did serve to focus them and redirect them, and to make him feel that beliefs could be shared more directly than through the words of a novel. The War made him realise, in particular, the state of European society that led to it; it made him want to generalise about history from the tendency of his own generation; it made him think much harder about 'the state' and its demands upon its citizens than he had probably done since his Fabian days in Croydon in 1910. The outbreak of War made him want to consider man's needs as a social being; how far he was himself, and how far he could, or should, be compelled by the state.

It was in the 'Study' that he began to sort all this out. 'It will be about anything but Thomas Hardy, I am afraid—queer stuff—but not bad' (05 ix 1914). Hardy in fact offered Lawrence the perfect link between his own two main interests; he saw Hardy's characters submitting themselves to the judgement of their society, in spite of their ability suddenly to break away and behave as the people they really were. For Lawrence, that was their tragedy—that they gave up the quest for the unknown which they were, for the sake of conforming to the judgement of the known which they also recognised.

> The vast, unexplored morality of life itself, what we call the immorality of nature, surrounds us in its eternal incomprehensibility, and in its midst goes on the little human morality play, with its queer frame of morality and its mechanised movement; seriously, portentously, till some one of the protagonists chances to look out of the charmed circle, weary of the stage, to look into the wilderness raging round. Then he is lost, his little drama falls to pieces, or becomes mere repetition, but the stupendous theatre outside goes on enacting its own incomprehensible drama, untouched.
>
> *(Phx 419)*

The character in a 'little human morality play' corresponds closely to that character conceived 'in a certain moral scheme'—and 'the certain moral scheme is what I object to' (05 vi 1914)—which Lawrence had been redefining his novels against in 1913 and 1914. He wanted his novel characters to 'look into the wilderness raging round', to be 'their own true beauty' (24 xi 1913); and the War's outbreak confirmed precisely his sense of the pressures of society, of 'mechanised movement' and the 'charmed circle' which prevented people being the 'pioneers' they should be: 'pioneers venturing out with the code of the walled city upon them', who 'die in the bonds of that code, free and yet unfree, preaching the walled city and looking to the waste' (*Phx* 419). Such would be the fate of those people who, like Skrebensky, were bricks 'in the whole great social fabric' (*R* 328), and who all the same

responded to that outer freedom, that fearfulness of the waste. This is
what Lawrence saw in Hardy which seemed so appropriate to him in
the first autumn of the War. And the Anton Skrebensky he would
create early in 1915 was to be a character exactly like those he describes
in Hardy, 'preaching the walled city and looking to the waste'.

But a major difference was that *The Rainbow*, as rewritten, would
have to deal with those ideas in altogether another form from the
discursive prose of the 'Study'. Lawrence remarked about the 'Study'
in November 1914 that it was 'supposed to be on Thomas Hardy, but
in reality [is] a sort of Confessions of my Heart' (18 xi 1914); he would
not be able to say that, or anything like it, about *The Rainbow*. Recent
criticism of Lawrence has, very properly, taken the 'Study' very seriously as a combination of warehouse and chopping-block for Lawrence's ideas in the months before writing *The Rainbow*. While acknow-
ledging the sense such critics have made of the relation between the
'Study' and *The Rainbow*, I still wish to place the stress differently;
because the 'Study' does not have the problems of a created novel,
because it is a self-indulgent (though creative) piece of work, because it
establishes no tone, because its method and style are widely variable,
because if its first few pages read like a modern *Rasselas*, the rest of it
goes deeper into incomprehensibility than any of Lawrence's later
'philosophical' writings; because, above all, it is a springboard for ideas
which (as it sees) need to be worked out in novels and in living, but
which it rewrites in Hardy's novels rather than writing for itself. It
ends, as it has to, with a chapter stressing the difference between
metaphysic and fiction, and finally returns to the necessity for art:

> There shall be the art which knows the struggle between the two
> conflicting laws, and knows the final reconciliation, where both are
> equal, two in one, complete. This is the supreme art, which yet
> remains to be done. Some men have attempted it, and left us the
> results of efforts. But it remains to be fully done.
>
> (*Phx* 515–16)

As Mark Kinkead-Weekes says, *The Rainbow* 'is an attempt at a supreme fiction'[27] to correspond to that demand for a 'supreme art'. But I
disagree with Kinkead-Weekes when he suggests that the 'Study'
'enabled' Lawrence to write *The Rainbow*; I prefer to stress the novel's
fundamental difference from the 'Study'. It is not enough simply to say,
as he does, that a novel cannot be a treatise, that ideas 'have to be
embodied in human relationships'.[28] Lawrence learned from the
'Study' his problem with a public voice, but that did not enable him to
write *The Rainbow*: it only sharpened the problem of doing so. Almost
all the choices he makes in *The Rainbow* about how to make his characters real, how to embody their condition, are not learned from the

'Study' at all. *The Rainbow* returns to the problem of inventing a new language for experience, and that language is not the language of the 'Study'. In the 'Study', ideas fall into neat shapes and patterns; Male can be played off against Female, Law against Love. Even their reconciliation in some 'supreme art' sounds like a pattern. I would suggest that the problem of the 'Study' is both a problem of isolation, of ideas in a void; and of language, in that what can be absolute in the 'Study' is simply impossible for a novel. (What, fortunately, Hardy does for the 'Study' is recall Lawrence to the problems of lives where such a language would be absurd; and even when he is rewriting Hardy most obviously, Lawrence can still make more actual sense of him than when he is moving around the coloured blocks labelled Male and Female.) Lawrence's two-fold sense that he needed people 'struggling for the same liberation', and that he needed a novel, both left the 'Study' behind. The liberation he would work out during 1915; the novel he started as soon as he ended the 'Study', around the end of November 1914. 'The body of it is so new' (05 xii 1914), he told Pinker; that 'body' included both its structure and its language.

The Rainbow is one of the great, complicated novels of the language; the experiences with which Lawrence is concerned need a special language, and accordingly he invents it. It is one of the great ironies of people's reaction to him that his language has so often been assumed to be careless, repetitive and banal—as when Joyce started *Lady Chatterley's Lover* and reacted against 'the first 2 pages of the usual sloppy English'[29]—when, in the case of *The Rainbow* at least, it is innovative, experimental and deliberate.

But is is also true that, in so far as Lawrence is a linguistic experimenter, his experiments sometimes fail—or only half succeed. He has continually to remake his own terms, so that words like 'unknown' or 'self' or 'darkness' are continually redefined by their context. This is natural; all language which strives to reach an extraordinary pitch of meaning has to redefine itself as it does so; there is no ready-made vocabulary to be used; words have to acquire peculiar pressures of sense which only their use, their context, their redefinition of context and their context's redefinition of *them* can achieve. All this is true and yet it is still not the last word on Lawrence's prose in *The Rainbow*; we have always to consider failure and half-success as well as success when we discuss it.

And 'prose', too, is really a misnomer. We have the problem of a style and a language which continually draw attention to themselves, and yet which are indivisible from the larger purpose of the book; we have to be able to say what the novel is about before we start to discuss its language or style. And that phrase 'what the novel is about' is itself a subtle perversion of truth; what the novel is *about*, to give that word 'about' its full force, is what it intends to do to us as well as what it succeeds in doing. *The Rainbow* is the kind of novel where we sometimes feel the pressure of intention without absolutely knowing what is intended. [The novel has aims, purposes, which are rarely stated and never consistent,] and which yet live on from page to page because Lawrence was, above all novelists of his time, a propagandist for his ideas, for what he felt people could make of themselves and their lives. We know that *The Rainbow* is a hugely ambitious novel, trying for a sense of life which is truer than had ever been created before, even when we are feeling we do not understand it. We are conscious of attempts as well as of successes, when we read it; that is part of the space it manages to create for itself; our efforts to reach its meaning are a considerable part of our experience of it.

To make this clearer, I suggest a comparison between a heightened—but comprehensible—passage from *Sons and Lovers*, and the start of the relationship between Tom and Lydia in *The Rainbow*. The earlier novel offers, apparently, something rather similar to the 'elemental embrace' of the latter: Paul and Clara 'had met, and included in their meeting the thrust of the manifold grass-stems, the cry of the peewit, the wheel of the stars' (*SL* 430). It would seem impossible for them to do better than this. We are given sentences like 'It was all so much bigger than themselves that he was hushed', and 'they were only grains in the tremendous heave that lifted every grass-blade its little height, and every tree, and living thing' (*SL* 430–1). These scenes in *Sons and Lovers*, coming into the novel (I suspect) in its last rewriting in the autumn of 1912, had begun to embody experiences which were life-giving for a relationship; and yet, as I pointed out above, had to be directed by a very firm authorial hand into failure and incompleteness.

But even if this stage in the relationships of Paul and Clara is left slightly incoherent, there is still a marked difference between what they are allowed to experience, and what Tom and Lydia realise. Clara and Paul are one with the cycles and forces of nature; the rhythm of their sexual experience corresponds to that of the world which is wheeling round them. Again, although Clara's strangeness to Paul is emphasised, it is the strangeness of a wild animal: 'What was she? A strong, strange, wild life, that breathed with his in the darkness through this hour' (*SL* 430). If the characteristic word for Clara is 'wild', the corresponding word for Lydia in *The Rainbow* is 'unknown'. Clara is something essentially ordinary, however wild and strange and exciting she is; Lydia takes Tom to another world of experience altogether. Lawrence's commentary on Tom and Lydia ignores the usual psychological explanations of behaviour; he insists on a language which is religious, on experiences which see beyond personality and self into 'the world that was beyond reality' (*R* 29). Fulfilment is not even a matter of being at one with the wheeling universe, but of allowing the impersonal self to

be 'small and submissive to the greater ordering' (*R* 40). Lawrence's
vocabulary for the relationship becomes full of words like 'beyond': the
world 'beyond reality', 'beyond all this, there was herself and himself
which should meet' (*R* 39). That sense of the beyond, of the unknown,
is the realm of experience on which Lawrence is concentrating; for the
first time in his career he is concerned to express a sense of people's
lives which is not mainly dependent on their past. The awareness
which he describes between Tom and Lydia exists almost in spite of
their past lives; 'They were such strangers, they must for ever be such
strangers . . . such intimacy of embrace, and such utter foreignness of
contact!' (*R* 49). But that strangeness itself necessitates a meeting on
impersonal ground. Both Tom and Lydia get beyond the 'him' and
'her' which they know. Not always, and not continually; things go
wrong, jealousies and angers develop, alienations occur. But they are
rooted in a new awareness of each other.

I suggested above that *The Rainbow* can briefly create things which
the 'Study' can take pages to illustrate. An example is the very start of
the novel. The first few pages have been widely described as 'a dream of
pastoral community',[30] 'an impassioned prose poem',[31] an 'evocation of
the Brangwen farm' (*Delavenay* i 450). They are not really any of these
things. It is vital to notice that the first chapter is divided into two
(something very rare in a Lawrence novel), with Part I comprising
these famous introductory pages, and Part II starting 'About 1840, a
canal was constructed . . . ' (*R*11). The second part has a date, facts, a
family history, members of a family; it contrasts with the timelessness,
the explicitly stated 'poem' of Part I, with its ballad-like, unindividual-
ised characters of Mrs Hardy, Mrs Brangwen, Tom Brangwen, Lord
William. Details—such as the way the 'women' apparently have their
own homes ('Her house faced out from the farm-buildings and
fields')—should alert us to the very special tone and method of the first
part. In it, Lawrence is charting aspiration and impulse, not rural life.
The 'women' of Part I are not just sexually female; we have every
reason to suppose that the Tom Brangwen we eventually get to know in
Part II is a 'Brangwen woman'—wanting 'another form of life than
this', 'looking out . . . towards the activity of man in the world at large'
(*R* 9). We can compare with them Tom's fascination with the foreigner
at Matlock, his satisfaction that Lydia is foreign, the way he always
wants something more. The Brangwen women of Part I indicate the
direction of Tom's, Anna's and Ursula's aspirations; the Brangwen
men set our minds towards Lydia and Will and (in a rather different
way) Anton Skrebensky. Part I offers a version of the 'Study's philosophy of Male and Female, but—like a ballad (and even the chapter title
has something of the ballad quality—'How Tom Brangwen married a
Polish Lady')—what Lawrence achieves is both true and impersonal.
He also creates the start of a more traditional kind of novel: 'About

1840. . . .' But that novel, too, exists in the spell of that other knowledge, the timeless account of impulse and aspiration and fulfilment, always modified and always re-enacted by each succeeding generation. The pattern is set in motion, and reshapes itself as we watch.

We are aware, from the start of Part II, that for Tom Brangwen sex and marriage are going to be tremendously important. 'His innate desire [was] to find in a woman the embodiment of all his inarticulate, powerful religious impulses' (*R* 20). We find him asking 'where was life, in that which he knew or all outside him?' (*R* 25). On the one hand he lives a perfectly ordinary life, working on the farm. On the other, we find him insistent that there must be something more, something which can meet and answer those 'powerful religious impulses'. He knows he will only become commonplace and brutal if he lives simply for the moment—for the flirtation, the drink, the companionship of men at the Red Lion. Yet he knows of nothing which could make his life different, though he feels it must somehow come through a woman.

He ends up frustrated at the glimpses of other modes of life he has, occasionally, experienced—as with the foreigner and the girl at Matlock. But nothing materialises; and simple resistance 'to the action of the commonplace unreality which wanted to absorb him' is no longer enough (*R* 26). He turns to drink; that is something which can break down the ordinariness of his life and allow him to escape it by achieving 'this kindled state of oneness with all the world, which is the end of youth's most passionate desire' (*R* 28). He needs that sense of a life beyond himself and his own, though he can only achieve it 'by obliterating his own individuality'. It is at this point that he sees Lydia for the first time. '"That's her," he said involuntarily' (*R* 29). He is at last, in the novel's terms, confronted by life which is not his own, but which he has to acknowledge and respond to. Falling in love, as Lawrence describes it in Tom, is not simply a psychological event; it is an answer to one's deepest needs to have a sense of life beyond the everyday—to have a knowledge of the eternal.

> She had passed by. He felt as if he were walking again in a far world, not Cossethay, a far world, the fragile reality. He went on, quiet, suspended, rarified. He could not bear to think or to speak, nor make any sound or sign, nor change his fixed motion. He could scarcely bear to think of her face. He moved within the knowledge of her, in the world that was beyond reality.
>
> (*R* 29)

If we compare that with the description of Birkin in 'The Wedding Ring' (see above, p. 53), we can see how specifically religious the language of *The Rainbow* has become: 'knowledge of her', 'as if a new creation were fulfilled' (*R* 32), and the final realisation: 'And then it came upon him that he would marry her and she would be his life' (*R* 40). If we try to replace it with what would seem the appropriate language of psychology, we run up against a brick wall. Tom feels that Lydia 'would bring him completeness and perfection' (*R* 41); 'it made him know perfection' (*R* 82), 'his eyes opened on a new universe' (*R* 59). We would normally imagine someone demanding that his wife bring him 'completeness and perfection' would need more the physician than the divine; it sounds thoroughly neurotic.

In *The Rainbow*, it is the language Lawrence wishes to use. He wishes us to realise Tom's life, and to realise our own lives, in terms of what is beyond them and only barely understood. It is an extraordinary ambition, and absolutely fundamental to the way his writing and thinking developed after *Sons and Lovers*. It can smash great holes in the psychological realism of his work—so that, for instance, we can hardly imagine what keeps Ursula and Skrebensky together in their last relationship; we see them so frequently in their relation with what lies beyond them. It can seriously interfere with the book's truth to social history. But in the case of Tom and Lydia and the first section of the novel, I think it is a triumphant success. They are a strikingly odd couple, at moments very close, perfectly mutual, but always returning to a kind of distance which unsubmissively acknowledges and accepts the other; and that is what, for Tom, brings him 'in contact with the unknown, the unaccountable and incalculable' (*R* 59).

At no point is this sense more finely created than in the scene of Lydia in childbirth. Little Anna will not stop crying; her passion is both childlike, and real beyond the confines of childlike terrors. It is a genuine response to the incomprehensible thing which is happening. What Tom finally does, to answer it, is far more than kind or ingenious. He takes her out into the rain, to the barn where the cattle are being fed, and establishes in her a sense of otherness—cattle, rain, lamplight—as he works at feeding the animals. The little girl, totally immersed in her grief and loneliness, is shocked and stimulated into the birth of another awareness. It is no use telling her that she cannot see her mother tonight, that she must be independent; but Tom brings her (and us with her) to such an awareness of impersonal life going its own way, that it counters her self-absorption. He sits with her,

> listening to the snuffing and breathing of cows feeding in the sheds communicating with this small barn. The lantern shed a soft, steady light from one wall. All outside was still in the rain. He looked down at the silky folds of the paisley shawl. It reminded him of his mother. She used to go to church in it. He was back again in the old irresponsibility and security, a boy at home.
>
> (*R* 79)

It is not just the past he feels when he looks at the shawl, any more than
it is when he says to the wondering Lydia: 'We've been here above *two*
hundred years' (*R* 37). He is aware of the strangeness of such con-
tinuities in the life of one person; the fact that he is Tom Brangwen, and
yet never *simply* Tom Brangwen. It is in such ways that he knows he
does not 'belong to himself' (*R* 40); he has no such fixed self to belong
to, he knows he is a meeting-point of change and continuity as well as a
self. His life goes far beyond its personal limits.

Anna grows quiet, exactly as we do as readers; we are stilled by the
description of the barn, of Tom's feelings, of the child growing into
quietness and sleep; finally by Tom's own sense, as he goes upstairs to
see his wife, of being—for all his pain—released, at peace.

> He went downstairs, and to the door, outside, lifted his face to the
> rain, and felt the darkness striking unseen and steadily upon him.
>   The swift, unseen threshing of the night upon him silenced him
> and he was overcome. He turned away indoors, humbly. There was
> the infinite world, eternal, unchanging, as well as the world of life.
>
> (*R* 81)

That is a realisation which we, as readers, can also come to. The last
sentence, with its force as a summing-up, significantly appears to have
been written into the proofs of the novel in the late summer of 1915; like
that other memorable phrase 'he knew he did not belong to himself',
which was also written into the proofs, it represents the kind of conclusion about Tom's experience which Lawrence had been working
towards for the previous three years.

But the language in which he creates the substance of Tom's religious awareness is, for the most part, also an ordinarily descriptive language. Those cows in the barn are real cows, the rain outside real rain;
they are not symbols, they are not portents. Yet a sentence like 'All
outside was still in the rain', with the totality of 'All outside', suggests
through the ambiguity of 'still' that steady continuity of which the
individuals are, for the time being, made aware. Life 'outside' is pulsa-
ting, changing, continuous; inside, individuals are listening, 'together',
'at home' in the expressive phrase of the paragraph's last sentence.
They are living, momentarily, in the knowledge of both worlds.

That is the success of the first section of the novel. It is not a pre-
industrial paradise, but at least its characters have a chance of realising
continuity in their lives as well as change. Lydia, in particular,
responds to that; after all she has been through, she wants simply to
live with Tom at the Marsh Farm. The second chapter's title is appropriately flat and expressive: 'They Live at the Marsh'. We can see in that
the sense of something settled, 'inside', 'together', 'at home'. But we are
also made aware of the kind of human limitation implicit in such

knowledge; we are told that 'To this she had reduced her husband' (*R* 104). Tom has vivid moments of wanting something more than the 'long, marital embrace' (*R* 129), and resenting 'how fixed everything was, how the other form of life was beyond him' (*R* 91). But he can, eventually, cope with that feeling—or at least, we live with the contradiction of it; because it is only a half-truth, it ignores what his marriage is.

Lawrence keeps his most completely biblical language to describe the marriage of Tom and Lydia after two years; the passage ends the third chapter, and the focus is beginning to turn from them to Anna.

> They had passed through the doorway into the further space, where movement was so big, that it contained bonds and constraints and labours, and still was complete liberty. She was the doorway to him, he to her. At last they had thrown open the doors, each to the other, and had stood in the doorways facing each other, whilst the light flooded out from behind on to each of their faces, it was the transfiguration, the glorification, the admission.
>
> (*R* 95–6)

This is the kind of language which makes *The Rainbow* so distasteful to some people; they ask what reason Lawrence has for using such inflated words as 'transfiguration', 'glorification', and 'admission'; they ask what a phrase like 'she was the doorway to him' actually means. These are not irrelevant questions; they have to be asked, and somewhere in our answer (if we are honest) must be an admission that the language is abstract, and that although he has used the word 'transfiguration' at least once before (*R* 39), Lawrence is not here adding very much to our understanding of the word. Any discussion of this passage must consider the extent of its success, and not simply its success. And our sense of what Lawrence is trying to do—of the kind of gestures he is making—is surely a large part of our response to this passage. We understand his kind of interest when we hear that language; we do not register the precision of his thought. The language suggests that Tom and Lydia's fulfilment is a very different thing from their sensual satisfaction, and that what they are for each other's fulfilment is mutual and private. 'To the rest of the world there seemed no change' (*R* 96); but Lawrence used the word 'transfiguration' for their sense of each other; they make all things new, they are not simply their old selves Tom Brangwen and Lydia Lensky. They are more, for each other, than such selves could ever be.

And yet—has this language the triumphant realistic and suggestive success of the description of Tom in the barn with little Anna? It is, of course, a description of Tom and Lydia towards the end of the first part of the novel. It has the weight and function of a summary, not the

excitement of a discovery. I suggest, all the same, that the language
excludes us. It is a language of miracle and mystery, and to appreciate
it fully we need to be ecstatically involved. It is a repetitive, ritual
language—'the transfiguration, the glorification, the admission'—so
that if the ritual can be established in our minds, and the ecstasy of
realisation is accomplished too, then (doubtless) the passage is lumin-
ous with meaning. But I am left, in the end, knowing that this is one of
the passages where the novel's significance lies for me not in its expres-
siveness, but in its attempts to express. Lawrence obviously felt,
increasingly, in the course of 1915, that there must be a way to involve
us in that 'infinite world, unchanging, as well as the world of life'
which he redefined yet again as he revised the novel. But his problem as
a novelist tends to be that of a writer who knows the answers before he
asks the questions; 'transfiguration' is a word which is detached from
the experience of living, and which tends to belong to ecstatic appreciation of it instead. It is a word perhaps impossible to use successfully in
the dynamic relations of a novel; it tends to detach its significance from
those relations.

There are, however, passages more puzzling still than this one, and
which raise even more directly the problem of what Lawrence felt a
novel should be doing when he wrote *The Rainbow*. A strikingly odd
example is the end of Chapter 10 (the first 'Widening Circle' chapter).
The chapter ends with a description of Christmas at the Brangwens,
and how the children 'lived the year of Christianity' (*R* 280). But that is
succeeded by a final page and a half about Resurrection; it is worth
asking what this is for, and to whom it refers. It seems to start as a
dramatic extension of the childrens' reaction, with a narrator asking
the questions for them. They have been feeling the onset of Easter:

> But why the memory of the wounds and the dead? Surely Christ rose
> with healed hands and feet, strong and sound and glad? Surely the
> passage of the cross and the tomb was forgotten? But no—always
> the memory of the wounds, always the smell of grave-clothes? A
> small thing was Resurrection, compared with the Cross and the
> death, in this cycle.
>
> So the children lived the year of Christianity . . .
>
> (*R* 280)

The passage, for all its rhetoric, is still concentrating on the children's
reaction. But it moves steadily further away from them into a consider-
ation of 'the passion of the human heart' (*R* 281), and ends:

> Can I not, then, walk this earth in gladness, being risen from sor-
> row? Can I not eat with my brother happily, and with joy kiss my
> beloved, after my resurrection, celebrate my marriage in the flesh

with feastings, go about my business eagerly, in the joy of my fellows? Is heaven impatient for me, and bitter against this earth, that I should hurry off, or that I should linger pale and untouched? Is the flesh which was crucified become as poison to the crowds in the street, or is it as a strong gladness and hope to them, as the first flower blossoming out of the earth's humus?

(*R* 281-2)

The version in the January–March 1915 MS, and the typed revised version of April–May, was even more extensive; it was only cut down to its present length in proof. I imagine that most readers of the novel find this sudden change and development almost impossible to understand; Kermode is surely exceptional in singling it out as unobtrusive.[32] We lose the children, we lose Ursula; what began as a dramatic extension of experience has taken wing and flown away. Even more than the passage about 'transfiguration', this is prose which we have to take on its own terms, and either be carried away by it, or feel excluded by it.

Lawrence's interest in Resurrection is not explained in the novel; but it can be found at several points in the 'Study', and particularly in a letter to Gordon Campbell of December 1914: 'In the mediaeval period, Christianity did *not* insist on the Cross: but on the Resurrection: churches were built to the glorious hope of resurrection. Now we think we are very great, whilst we enumerate the smarts of the crucifixion' (19 xii 1914). Lawrence is distinguishing between the ways in which the various symbols of Christianity are seen at different periods; he finds the modern period obsessed with 'the sad plight' of man, and detaching the crucifixion from the only context which really gives it meaning—one which includes the resurrection: 'Christianity should teach us now, that after our Crucifixion, and the darkness of the tomb, we shall rise again in the flesh . ' . ' (19 xii 1914). He goes on to insist that

It is very dangerous to use these old terms lest they sound like cant. But if only one can grasp and know again as a new truth, true for one's own history, the great vision, the great, satisfying conceptions of the world's greatest periods, it is enough. Because so it is made new.

(19 xii 1914)

The passage in *The Rainbow*, like the passage in the chapter 'Italians in Exile' in *Twilight in Italy* (revised in early autumn 1915) certainly belongs to the same way of understanding the modern period: observing that our modern sensibility insists on pain rather than joy, on Law rather than Love, on Spirit rather than Flesh, on 'consummation in the spirit' rather than on 'consummation in the flesh' (*Phx* 468–9). In the

'Study', and in his letter to Campbell, Lawrence makes a good case for both this way of describing change, and for this kind of language. In *The Rainbow* he does neither, and in particular he ignores his own caveat that 'it is very dangerous to use these old terms'. The sense of joy given in *The Rainbow* is peculiarly Biblical and mannered: 'eat with my brother happily, and with joy kiss my beloved, after my resurrection, celebrate my marriage in the flesh with feastings' (*R* 282). Not many readers will find this a language appropriate for the 'consummation in the flesh' denied by the modern era.

But there is apparently another reason why Lawrence should have chosen to use this language in the novel. The end of Chapter 10 of *The Rainbow* was not written in the middle of December, despite its similarity with the letter to Campbell. Lawrence probably reached the end of Chapter 10 around the end of January 1914; and it can hardly be a coincidence that in at least three letters he wrote about then, he used the language of resurrection. He told Cynthia Asquith that, 'being risen from the dead, I know we shall all come through, rise again and walk healed and whole and new, in a big inheritance, here on earth. It sounds preachy, but I don't quite know how to say it' (31 i 1915). And he had written to E. M. Forster how he hoped that man could 'come to his new issuing, his wings, his resurrection, his whole flesh shining like a mote in the sunshine' (28 i 1915). This fascination with resurrection in no way explains the passage in *The Rainbow*, but it does correspond to the novel's sense of the words racing away with the narrator. I would suggest that Lawrence's own feelings—'now I don't feel so dead' (31 i 1915)—made the expression of the ideas in his novel rather easier, and so more extreme, less part of the novel's content. We have, for once, an example of the novel's language drawing on resources alien to the book, and made to serve an aim peculiar to its author.

This was something almost inevitable for an author like Lawrence, whose idea of a novel was not of an artistic entity, but an occasion for continual exploration and re-creation. The classic case of this, however, is I think to be found at the end of the novel. There has been a good deal of discussion of this ending, ranging from Leavis's insistence that the optimism at the end is 'a note wholly unprepared and unsupported',[33] to Stephen Miko's belief that 'this is Ursula's vision too, and as such it has both a dramatic and a thematic relevance to what has gone before'.[34] As at the end of Chapter 10, we need to ask 'who is the dramatic protagonist at the end?' Is the vision of the new society, of the 'creation of the living God' (*R* 495), Ursula's own? Does she speak with the voice of the novel?

The last chapter starts with Ursula feeling that she should give up her attempts to gain 'that fantastic freedom, that illusory, conceited fulfilment which she had imagined she could not have with Skrebensky' (*R* 484–5). She decides to be like her mother: 'Her mother was simple and radically true. She had taken the life that was given. She had not, in her arrogant conceit, insisted on creating life to fit herself'. Feeling like this brings Ursula 'a bondaged sort of peace' (*R* 485), and she writes to Skrebensky, proposing marriage: 'you were[35] natural and decent all through, whilst I was so false.' (*R* 485) Immediately after this she goes out, 'feeling the seething rising to madness within her' (*R* 486), and walks until she is 'very wet and a long way from home, far enveloped in the rain and the waving landscape' (*R* 487). I suggest that we hear an echo of Tom Brangwen in the barn, 'at home', with the rain 'sputtering on to her shawl, and the light of the lantern swinging, flashing on a wet pavement' (*R* 78); movement outside, stillness inside, at the centre. Only, this time, Ursula is forcing herself back 'home'; 'She must beat her way back through all this fluctuation, back to stability and security' (*R* 487). She is demonstrating how she has just made a life-choice which actually contradicts her real sense of life as 'very splendid, free and chaotic' (*R* 486).

'Suddenly she knew there was something else.' The sentence strikes us before we know what the 'something' can be. There is 'something else' beside the 'stability and security' she is working her way back to; there is 'something else' she has been repressing in herself. 'Some horses were looming in the rain, not near yet. But they were going to be near' (*R* 487). The question of whether she actually meets flesh-and-blood horses, or whether the whole experience is visionary, is irrelevant. Whether the horses are real or not, her experience at this juncture makes them matter internally, emotionally, psychologically, psychically. It is she who makes the significance of the encounter, out of the way in which it serves to challenge her decision. Her experience with the horses is a terrifying encounter with 'something' utterly destructive of the 'ordered world of man' (*R* 489) which she has tried to set her heart on.

What she recovers after that experience is not, however, the full security which she imagined she had at the start of the chapter. She is no longer threatened with destruction by that 'looming power', but she is spent, utterly, after her escape:

> . . . she lay as if unconscious upon the bed of the stream, like a stone, unconscious, unchanging, unchangeable, whilst everything rolled by in transience, leaving her there, a stone at rest on the bed of the stream, unalterable and passive, sunk to the bottom of all change.
> (*R* 490)

Her alliance has been broken with the temporal, would-be-domestic everyday self which wishes to escape into marriage with Skrebensky. She has also escaped the self which revealed such dominant power over

Skrebensky. She is now, instead, at the furthest possible remove from change, her state corresponding to the 'eternal stillness that lies under all movement' which Lawrence celebrated in his November 1913 letter to Henry Savage. But she needs to grow back into some individuality again; a person cannot simply *be* that stillness, though it must underlie them. She has just enough dumb purpose left to get back home, and into bed. But the delirium that possesses her beats round and round the question of her links with her past, with Skrebensky, with her family. She feels trapped by the temporal self she has been, by the unreality of her alliance with the temporal:

> 'I have no father nor mother nor lover, I have no allocated place in the world of things, I do not belong to Beldover nor to Nottingham nor to England nor to this world, they none of them exist, I am trammeled and entangled in them, but they are all unreal. I must break out of it, like a nut from its shell which is an unreality.'
>
> (*R* 493)

It is at this point that we perhaps first start to lose touch with the Ursula whose struggles have involved us; she herself feels she has to break out of the shell which encloses her, and experience the world as it demonstrates 'a new knowledge of Eternity in the flux of Time' (yet another of those phrases which entered the novel only at its proof stage; the TS had only been modified to read 'to create a new world').[36] The last pages of the novel become a vision of that world.

> Nay, when she looked ahead, into the undiscovered land before her, what was there she could recognise but a fresh glow of light and inscrutable trees going up from the earth like smoke. It was the unknown, the unexplored, the undiscovered upon whose shore she had landed, alone, after crossing the void, the darkness which washed the New World and the Old.
>
> (*R* 494)

Like all visions, this experience is not personal, not individual experience belonging to a person created; it has to be our experience too, if it is to make sense. The danger to a novel's dynamics when such material becomes its substance is, again, apparent; the appeal is so very much to us as readers, directly, and not through something created. When Ursula comes to think of Skrebensky, he no longer exists as a person either. 'He was something of the past, finite. He was that which is known. She felt a poignant affection for him, as for that which is past. But, when she looked with her face forward, he was not' (*R* 494). The earlier part of the novel created its visionary experience through our sense of lives led and feelings lived. This later part is much more propagandist for its experience.

There are reasons for this, too, which lie outside the actual novel. The experiences of two sisters, contrasted, were the origin of the substance of this novel; each won through to the man who really answered her. This had been the state of the novel right through to the first 'Rainbow' of the spring of 1914. When Lawrence began to rewrite the book in November 1914, it was still with a sense of the whole novel of two sisters and their eventual marriages; we know that at the end of December, it was still planned as a book 'about marriage in three generations',[37] and Lawrence wrote 300 pages of it (roughly up to the end of Chapter 6) before deciding to change it radically and keep the second half of his material for another novel entirely. 'I am going to split the book into two volumes: it was so unwieldy' (07 i 1915), he told Pinker. Mark Kinkead-Weekes is surely right to suggest that the reason for this was the introduction of so much new material at the start of the book, in the lives of Tom and Lydia in particular.[38] But this change in the book's structure meant that the logical and original ending—Ursula's marriage to Birkin, Gudrun's to Gerald Crich—vanished. The book would have to end, instead, at some indeterminate point before those marriages; and Lawrence chose to end it with the end of Ursula's affair with Skrebensky. In the course of the three years it took to write, the book had taken on other interests entirely from its original conception of 'the relationship between man and woman'; it had come to be a religious novel of the search for self, and self-fulfilment, through love and marriage. Each generation's search and fulfilment is that of its marriage—except for the last, where Ursula does not reach the relationship which enables her to come to her fulfilment or her sense of self. She is isolated where the whole point of the earlier generations in the book had been that they should, in one way or another, be together. Lawrence confronted a void at the end of his novel; not just in the lack of Ursula's marriage partner, but in the realisation of his own deepest concerns; without that partner, there could be no created end to the third generation's search for fulfilment.

I suggest that this accounts for the very special tone of the ending, and of some of the passages written in the latter part of the book (and of those rewritten during revision). The ending inevitably hangs its rainbow out over a void, and Ursula's experience becomes more picaresque as she goes through a series of significant experiences of the modern world; and in the absence of a revelation of the character's own needs, another element altogether starts to enter the novel. As at the end of Chapter 10, something which belonged to Lawrence's problems with making sense not only of his book, but of his society, made a forced entry into it.

In the spring of 1915, Lawrence confronted not only a novel that needed to be finished; he was in the position of any man who has

become aware of a gap between the life he can call his own, and the life
he shares as a member of society. The more modern the history
recounted by *The Rainbow*, the more it brought to a head the problem of
being an individual in a society, inescapably in and of that society. The
War, more than anything else he had ever experienced, brought home
that problem for Lawrence; it made him realise it as both man and
artist. As a man, he could say that he was separate—at a cost; he had
lived abroad for two years, anyway, and he could have a life with a few
others, in some real or longed-for colony or *rananim* (as he had learned
to call it in 1914); he made plans with the Murrys for an island
rananim, and later (with Lady Ottoline Morrell) planned a community
of an exclusive kind at Garsington Manor. But, as an artist, those
solutions were open to him no more that they had been to a man like
William Morris, in the latter half of the nineteenth century, who also
felt that gap between himself and his society, between his ideals and his
social realities, between what he could do as a writer and what he could
imagine; 'an essential question for Morris was whether writing was a
way of both doing *and* dreaming'.[39]

Lawrence's association with Bertrand Russell provoked his final and
strongest realisation of that dilemma. As a result of their meeting on 6
February, and the ensuing correspondence, Lawrence's language about
his own role in society underwent a significant change. The idea of a
colony vanished, for the moment, to be replaced by the idea of Revolution. Russell made Lawrence feel that society could change, and that
they could change it; and Lawrence wrote to Russell within a week of
meeting him:

> There must be a revolution in the state. It shall begin by the
> nationalising of all industries and means of communication, and of
> the land—in one fell blow. . . . Which practically solves the whole
> economic question for the present.
>   . . . There comes a point when the shell, the form of life, is a prison
> to the life. Then the life must either concentrate on breaking the
> shell, or it must turn round, turn in upon itself, and try infinite
> variations of a known reaction upon itself. . . . Now either we have to
> break the shell, the form, the whole frame, or we have got to turn to
> this inward activity of setting the house in order and drawing up a
> list before we die.
>   But we shall smash the frame. The land, the industries, the means
> of communication and the public amusements shall all be national-
> ised. Every man shall have his wage till the day of his death, whether
> he work or not, so long as he works when he is fit. Every woman
> shall have her wage till the day of her death, whether she work or
> not, so long as she works when she is fit—keeps her house or rears
> her children.

Then, and then only, shall we be able to *begin* living. Then we shall be able to *begin* to work. Then we can examine marriage and love and all. Till then, we are fast within the hard, unliving, impervious shell.

(12 ii 1915)

But we have to make a distinction between the way in which Lawrence used the word Revolution, and the force which Russell gave it. Lawrence himself wrote to Gordon Campbell, explaining what he meant, that 'It is not politics—it is religion' (24 ii 1915). And Russell—a man who believed in political solutions—found that when he and Lawrence planned to give a course of lectures together, 'When he talks politics he seems to me so wild that I could not formally work with him'.[40] The real problem between them was that Lawrence always knew that 'It is not a political revolution I want, but a shifting of the racial system of values from the old morality & personal salvation through a Mediator to the larger morality and salvation through the knowledge that ones neighbour *is* oneself' (24 ii 1915). What finally angered Russell beyond bearing in the summer of 1915 was Lawrence's insistence on revolution in this sense; not only did it not matter to Lawrence *how* the social revolution happened—'we hadn't thought it out, and there wasn't any need to think it out'[41]—Lawrence's schemes always appeared ludicrously impractical to Russell. 'He kept reiterating that London doesn't really exist, and that he could easily make people see it doesn't, and then they would pull it down'.[42] Lawrence wanted the birth of a new spirit, a new desire for truth, a new realisation of self. And although Russell was impressed by Lawrence's passionate belief in change, fundamentally he wanted a new system of democratic control in England. Lawrence didn't believe in democracy and insisted on religion:

Believe me, in the end, we will unite in our knowledge of God. Believe me, this England, we very English people, will at length join together and say, 'We will not do these things, because in our knowledge of God we know them wrong'. . . . This isn't ranting, it is pure reasoning from the knowledge of God and the truth. It is not our wickedness that kills us, but our unbelief.

(14 v 1915)

The need for change he called (briefly) revolution sprang from a desire for a wholly new society, with new goals: 'The highest aim of the government is the highest good of the *soul*, of the individual, the fulfilment in the Infinite, in the Absolute' (15 vii 1915). What kind of policy (and Russell continually stressed their need to be practical) could achieve *that*? In Lawrence we see not only what Russell saw—'he has not learnt the lesson of individual impotence'[43]—but one of the classic twentieth-century dilemmas; a belief that the very forms of society ('the hard, unliving impervious shell') are both rigid beyond your capacity to change them, and have (none the less) to be changed; but nothing less than a total revolution of individual and social attitude can make any difference to people's predicament—or your own.

In the spring of 1915 Lawrence was in this dilemma; feeling that he knew, in himself, what was wrong with his society, and yet being unable to transfer that knowledge (or even the desire for it) to other people, except in wish-fulfilment. Russell, a long time later, remembered Lawrence going

> into long tirades about how one must proclaim 'the Truth' to the multitude, and he seemed to have no doubt that the multitude would listen. I asked him what method he was going to adopt. Would he put his political philosophy into a book? No: in our corrupt society the written word is always a lie. Would he go into Hyde Park and proclaim 'the Truth' from a soap box? No: that would be far too dangerous (odd streaks of prudence emerged in him from time to time). Well, I said, what would you do? At this point he would change the subject.[44]

Russell would not have listened to Lawrence in 1915 if that had been all Lawrence could offer him; but the general point is, all the same, a real one. Russell's political philosophy and 'Principles of Social Reconstruction' could at least be written down in the form of lectures, given to an audience early in 1916, and published as a book afterwards.[45] What could Lawrence do, full of a sense of insight into the deepest predicament of his age, and also believing

> that one is not only a little individual living a little individual life, but that one is in oneself the whole of mankind, and ones fate is the fate of the whole of mankind, and ones charge is the charge of the whole of mankind. Not *me*—the little, vain personal D. H. Lawrence—but that unnameable me which is not vain nor personal, but strong, and glad, and ultimately sure, but so blind, so groping, so tongue-tied, so staggering . . . there is something I *must* say to mankind—& I can't say it by myself—I feel so dumb and struggling.
>
> (24 ii 1915)

The answer to his problem might be assumed to be 'write novels and stories'—that always had been his way of expressing his sense of the needs of his age. But the point still holds which Russell's probably garbled recollection of 1915 preserves: 'in our corrupt society the written word is always a lie.' Lawrence made a number of remarks of that kind in the spring and summer of 1915, all of them contemporary with his actual completion of *The Rainbow*. They express his predicament acutely.

To begin with, it is significant that he did not tell Russell about *The Rainbow* in the letters he wrote him while finishing the book. In fact he did quite the opposite; he remarked that 'I am ashamed to write any real writing of passionate love to my fellow men. Only satire is decent now. The rest is a lie' (12 ii 1915). One would not guess from that that he was currently engaged on the last four chapters of the novel, which (perhaps) contain satire, but which also contain 'passionate love to my fellow men'. But in the world of *Realpolitik* in which he sensed Russell lived, perhaps he felt *The Rainbow* could have no place. To put it another way, the novel had taken its own shape, and had its own logic in its sense of 'eternity'; a revolution in the state was not a possibility it could naturally accomodate. Once again, Lawrence was in in a position where the novel he was finishing had been overtaken in its version of self and society by its author's own experiences; the speculations which increasingly filled the mind of its author would have to be accommodated in another kind of writing altogether. As soon as the novel MS was finished, Lawrence was able to start doing what he had been planning throughout the second half of February—'begin a book about Life—more rainbows, but in different skies—which I want to publish in pamphlet form week by week—my initiation of the great and happy revolution' (02 iii 1915). This was the writing he told Russell about—the writing designed to 'start a campaign for this freer life' (26 ii 1915). Completing *The Rainbow* made him 'very excited' but the philosophy made him feel 'very profound. . . . It is my revolutionary utterance' (02 iii 1915).

And a novel was not, for Lawrence, a 'revolutionary utterance'. He talked with Murry on 22 February, and Murry put their conversation in his diary.

> In the evening we talked—about the Revolution. Lawrence said it was no more use writing novels; we had first to change the conditions, without which either people would not hear, or our novels be only a tale. . . . [He] said: 'What novels we could write, if we wrote of the whole good we knew, instead of the good that may be in this world!' We loosely planned a scheme for publishing weekly pamphlets in which the Revolution should be expounded by us individually.[46]

The novel could be (and in Lawrence's mind certainly was) other things than a 'revolutionary utterance', and in the long run it might count for more. But at the very moment of finishing it he wanted something more immediate in which to express his sense of what people needed and what he could do for them. He had written to Russell rather poignantly about man's ultimate desire 'to work for humanity':

> That is every man's ultimate desire and need. Now you see the vicious circle. Shall I go to my Prometheus and tell him beautiful tales of the free, whilst the vulture gnaws his liver? I am ashamed. I turn my face aside from my Prometheus, ashamed of my vain, irrelevant, impudent words. I cannot help Prometheus. And this knowledge rots the love of activity.
>
> (12 ii 1915)

That, of course, completes the circle of the dilemma; because he could (as Russell so cruelly pointed out) find no way into an immediate relationship with the people he wanted to communicate with. He was, in the end, forced back on being a novelist; what he could do, in his society, for his society, had to be in his publishable writing, and in his novels. All the summer of 1915 he struggled to find a way of approaching his audience directly: 'art after all is indirect and ultimate' (14 ix 1915) he told William Hopkin. 'One must start direct with the open public' (16 viii 1915) he wrote to Cynthia Asquith.

It seems certain that he adapted *The Rainbow* to make it approximate more fully to that ideal of directness, though he could not do much more to it than modify it. Two days after his conversation with Murry, he wrote to Campbell that 'art which is lyrical can now no longer satisfy us: each work of art that is true, now, must give expression to the great collective experience, not to the individual . . . I can see nothing to begin on, but a social revolution. For I write my novels, & I write my book of philosophy, & I must also see the social revolution set going' (24 ii 1915). So far as it could be, the novel was being co-opted into that 'social revolution'; Murry recalled Lawrence saying that 'Art . . . is a social activity' at just the same time.[47] Lawrence was writing the last chapters of *The Rainbow*; in Ursula's vision we get something very similar to the ideas of social change expressed in the letter of 12 February to Russell, with its prevailing metaphor of the 'hard, unliving, impervious shell'.

> And again, to her feverish brain, came the vivid reality of acorns in February[48] lying on the floor of a wood with their shells burst and discarded and the kernel issued naked to put itself forth.
>   . . . .this was all husk and shell lying by, all husk and shell, she could see nothing else, she was enclosed still, but loosely enclosed. There was a space between her and the shell. It was burst, there was a rift in it.
>
> (*R* 493)

And, of course, the people in the book's last paragraph 'would issue to a new germination'; the vision of a new society breaking out of the old is drawn directly from that metaphor, and out of the same hopes; and perhaps, too, out of the same impotence in realising such hopes. The last pages are trying both to end a novel deprived of its original end, and to be a triumphant public utterance. Lawrence modified them a good deal in revision; when he finished the last paragraph in March, Ursula 'knew . . . that the new growth should take place, the vast forest of mankind should spring up urgent and young out of the brittle, marshy foulness of the old corruption';[49] the ending we now know must have been introduced at the proof stage, in August. 'She saw in the rainbow the earth's new architecture, the old, brittle corruption of houses and factories swept away, the world built up in a living fabric of Truth, fitting to the over-arching heaven' (*R* 496). When we find Lawrence himself writing to Cynthia Asquith in August that 'We are a nation which must be built up according to a living idea, a great architecture of living people, which shall express the greatest truth of which we are capable' (16 viii 1915), then we realise how little it is Ursula who speaks to us out of the novel at that moment. The fabric of the novel is being stretched by a vision which grows out of the particular needs of the author.

This happens most dramatically at the end; but similar things happen throughout the last section. The life of Winifred Inger—Ursula's teacher—is only lightly touched in by the novel; but it is striking the way her sexual perversity is seen as typical of her situation in society, exactly as homosexuality is seen in the 12 February letter. 'Sodomy only means that a man knows he is chained to the rock, so he will try to get the finest possible sensation out of himself' (12 ii 1915). Winifred is not only lesbian, but the novel enacts a symbolic marriage between her and Ursula's uncle Tom, who 'had come to a stability of nullification' (*R* 344). Both Ursula and the novel treat Winifred and Tom as archetypes of the modern world; people past desire and feeling, simply aware of the sensations of their lives, cynical about the 'pure ugliness' of Wiggiston (where Tom is colliery-owner); neither they nor the place are created—they are produced as evidence, and their lives made symbolic. Ursula is briefly fascinated by them—then frees herself. 'No more would she subscribe to the great colliery, to the great machine which has taken us all captives' (*R* 350). The polemic is strikingly obvious, down to the 'us all' of that sentence; the allocation of Tom and Winifred to a symbolic Wiggiston is a kind of shorthand for a real analysis of society; their marriage is a way of demonstrating 'the repeating of a known reaction upon myself' (12 ii 1915) which 'is sensationalism'. When the demonstration is over, they have nothing further to offer the book, and are dismissed to imperfect felicity. And Chapter 13 starts the novel again with an Ursula who might as well not have lived through the Wiggiston episode at all; but the point, of course, is not that *she* should, but that *we* should.

A different kind of problem, where the novel's determined involvement with society is perhaps more interesting, is the last relationship between Will and Anna, at the end of Chapter 8. This was written into the TS of the book in April or May 1915; there was no equivalent for it in the MS written in January. Lawrence makes the new relation between Will and his society stem directly from his new relation with Anna: 'He had at length, from his profound sensual activity, developed a real purposive self' (*R* 283). The January MS contains only a brief note to the effect that Will and Anna were 'resolved into satisfaction' by their new relationship—'cleared, resolved, freed'—and that Will's woodwork class makes him feel that 'at last he was doing something in the world, for the world'.[50] Knowing what Lawrence was to make of modern industrial society in the Wiggiston passage, it may surprise us that he should talk so simply about Will turning 'with interest to public life' (*R* 238), but in July we find him telling Russell about 'the *most fundamental* passion in man, for Wholeness of Movement, Unanimity of Purpose, Oneness in Construction' (15 vii 1915). And he noted on the TS of Russell's lecture plans that 'It isn't *the others* we are interested in, it is *the Whole*, the Whole of us. We want to make a Whole Movement, Unanimous'.[51] And indeed, when he revised the novel's proofs at the end of July and start of August, he introduced a new sentence to sum up Will's new situation: 'He wanted to be unanimous with the whole of purposive mankind' (*R* 238).

What Will goes through in these last pages of the chapter is, as Colin Clarke says, done rather quickly and simply—the whole description of the public activity after his new passion with Anna is done in less than a page and a half; but it certainly is not, as Clarke suggests, 'reassuring, not to say cosy'.[52] The significant thing is that Lawrence should have wanted to put it in at all—that he should have wanted to move from a profound description of sensual behaviour to a description of the consequent relationship with society at large. It bears out my suggestion that, after February 1915, Lawrence tended to write much more directly about his characters' involvement with society; and that the later in 1915 that he actually worked on the novel, the more likely he was to make such an involvement explicit. The passage about Will and Anna stresses their 'heavy, fundamental gratification' (*R* 238), and then goes on to describe Will engaged in what Lawrence referred to as 'the *most fundamental* passion in man'. The pun is appropriate; Will's life makes sense in Lawrence's terms because his sexual self and his social self are united. My only hesitation is that the rather explicit language about purposes in the passage reveals its first-draft quality; so that, in April, he summed up the matter: 'The house by the yew trees was in connection with the great public movement at last. It gained a new vigour thereby.'[53] It sounds unreal because it is so tenuous a link. In proof revision, Lawrence changed 'public movement' to 'human endeavour', but it does not add very much to the sentence. Does a woodwork class for village boys really bring such results? Lawrence is overstressing his point because he so very much wants to make it.

The Rainbow demonstrates nothing so simple as an author using the events and feelings of his everyday life as material for his books, though we know that Lawrence certainly did that from his very earliest work. *The Rainbow* shows us Lawrence trying to divert an almost completed novel into a new channel—one more passionately concerned with society as he saw it in 1915. That channel, too, even though experimental and partial, ran in a direction which accorded better with his own sense of himself as a writer. He wrote to Russell in February: 'If I know that humanity is chained to a rock, I cannot set forth to find it new lands to enter upon. If I do pretend to set forth, I am a cheating, false merchant, seeking my *own* ends' (12 ii 1915). The 'new lands' of Tom Brangwen's awareness of 'the infinite world, unchanging' are less important in the second half of the book; a primarily religious vision is subtly modified to include a vision of a new society. The authorial influence is at its strongest when Lawrence makes his characters responsible for observations which he feels *he* needs to make, in response to his new sense of what a novel should be. A final example of that is the section immediately before Skrebensky's final return, when Ursula is considering the nature of society. She thinks of it, we are told, as 'the area under an arc-lamp, wherein the moths and children played in the security of blinding light' (*R* 437). Yet she is also aware of 'the glimmer of dark movement just out of range', 'the eyes of the wild beast gleaming from the darkness'. And indeed we recognise the existence of both such awarenesses in her, too. But the passage goes on to ignore the dramatisation of a character, and to introduce a new voice—an authorial one.

> Yea, and no man dared even to throw a firebrand into the darkness. For if he did he was jeered to death by the others, who cried 'Fool, anti-social knave, why would you disturb us with bogeys? There *is* no darkness. . . . Fool and knave, how dare you belittle us with the darkness?'

> (*R* 438)

To make the point absolutely clear, Lawrence replaced the MS reading 'base knave'[54] with 'anti-social knave' in his revision of the TS; and to make the passage more strident still, he replaced 'introduce the darkness'[55] with 'belittle us with the darkness' in proof revision. He makes the point superficial by vulgarising it, and he quite forgets poor Ursula, standing by this passage and having, in theory, to bear the responsibility for it. When *The Rainbow* annoys us, it is not so often because of its complexity as because of its sudden and apparently inexplicable facility; what we had thought was only possible through careful creation is, instead, sketched briefly and left to stand. A passage such as that just quoted has the pressure of a man's belief behind it, but not the authority of his creating hand. Even a passage as intensively revised as the last page of the book was, interestingly enough, amended yet again by Lawrence in the copy he gave to his sister at the end of September 1915; the ringing phrases about the earth's new architecture and the living fabric of Truth were replaced by this: '[She knew that the] fight was to the good. It was not to annihilation but at last to newness. She knew in the rainbow that the fight was to the good' (*Delavenay* i 479). That suggests how temporary a resting place for his ideas the rhetoric of the ending actually provided. The printed ending stressed the book's relationship with the society which, he hoped, would be its audience; the emendation returns the book, a little, to the consciousness of Ursula. It is as if he were still discovering that he had other ways of making the book relate to society than by making it a triumphant and prophetic vision of change.

A study of *The Rainbow* charts the change in Lawrence's belief in the novel form as a crusading and liberating expression of sexual fulfilment (as the first 'Sisters' had been), through to his still developing demonstration of the kind of change he felt his society most needed. Between these two poles, it succeeds in being a great novel; it creates the moral, religious and social needs of men and women as the nineteenth century gave way to the twentieth. Lawrence himself felt that after 'nearly three years of hard work' he had 'at last got it pretty much to its real being' (23 iv 1915); we can see how that 'being' itself changed over the years, for good and bad. But even while he was ending it, he was aware of the novel he would have to write next; at the bottom of both the MS and the TS, where composers have sometimes written 'Glory to God', Lawrence wrote 'End of Volume I'. He was already looking beyond it, forward to *Women in Love*.

5 *Women in Love*

What did Lawrence want his novels to be, after *The Rainbow*?
Lawrence, after expounding *The Rainbow*, said that he felt that he
would write one more novel, and no more. He was sad, because he
was a forerunner, like John the Baptist before the Christ, whose
place it was to give up and surrender.... 'So I suppose my
achievement begins and ends with preaching the revolution of the
conditions of life—why not?'[1]

Murry made that diary note in February 1915, and *The Rainbow* had
begun to incorporate something of that 'revolution of the conditions of
life' as Lawrence finished it during February and revised it from March
till August. Its final social optimism is what Lawrence himself wished
to communicate to the people of England in the summer of 1915. But
by mid-October he had lost that optimism about the future of society;
his magazine *The Signature* had failed to capture an audience, public
meetings in a room above Fisher Street brought no success, and he
found the unchanging pointlessness of the war a final demonstration of
the end of man's purposive belief in society (and in himself). Cynthia
Asquith noted in her diary: 'the war he sees as the pure *suicide* of
humanity—a war without *any* constructive ideal in it, just pure sense-
less destruction'.[2] He decided to emigrate to America, but on the
November day when the Lawrences' passports arrived, he also heard
that Methuen had surrendered to the police all unsold and unbound
copies of *The Rainbow*, had recalled all unsold copies from the book-
shops, and would be facing charges of publishing an obscene book. The
news must have come with depressing aptness; just as he was deciding
not to work for England any more, his novel was charged with being
unfit to be read by English people.

But the idea of going to America, which had emerged as a spontaneous reaction to the hoplessness of the war, gave way to a revised idea
of community—of *rananim*. In November 1915 Lawrence began to meet
a number of people 'who have the germ of the new life in them' (20 xii
1915), and whose enthusiasm for the idea and hostility to the war made
him feel that a community abroad was a real possibility. Robert
Nichols, Dorothy Warren, Philip Heseltine, Dikran Koumidjian,
Suhrawardy, Aldous Huxley—all declared themselves potential set-
tlers; and instead of the community being a kind of England-in-spite-

of-itself (as planned in the spring) it became unmistakeably an escape from the England which actually existed, and from the war. It was to celebrate a new life, a life lived apart from English society, the English past and the actual moment of history; it would be a self-sufficient community of souls achieving spiritual satisfaction in the only way possible to them. It represented (and continued to represent for all Lawrence's life) the appeal of a community which was outside English society as Lawrence had known it; it was to be a community outside history, time and place. Lawrence was obviously much attached to the idea of a complete escape; but without a revolutionary idea of society, such an escape had to exist outside the realm of all the things which attached him to his own time. It was an idealist sort of escape because it rested on the belief that individuals together could achieve what they could not achieve as members of conventional society. There was always an air of unreality about Lawrence's proposed *rananims*, both now and for the next ten years; they were really a response to the particular effects of the War, and for Lawrence they were a way out of the contradictory feelings which the War imposed on him. In the age of the mass, authoritarian state, he wanted to assert the integrity of the free individual; but he also wished to create and live the life of a community. Caught between freedom which was illusory and involvement which was unbearably painful, he invented *rananim* as a means of bridging the gap between society and individual fulfilment; as such, *rananim* summed up the basic contradiction in Lawrence's response to his society and to himself as an individual: it offered relief from both.

By mid-November, the Lawrences had passports, a destination, and a colonising group. But they did not go. For one thing, the very idealism of *rananim* was something that, in the end, Lawrence always shied away from. For another, to leave the country one needed military exemption, and some of the group almost certainly would not have got it. Lawrence himself queued up at Battersea town hall to be attested for exemption, but left the queue before his turn came. 'I must say', he wrote immediately afterwards, 'I feel again a certain amount of slow, subterranean hope. . . . It is only the immediate present which frightens me and bullies me. In the long run I have the victory; for all those men in the queue, for those spectral, hazy, sunny towers hovering beyond the river, for the world that is to be' (12 xii 1915). The men in the queue—the men for whom Lawrence has the victory—'were very decent'. He obviously wanted to offer them more than a spiritual *rananim*: he felt more deeply attached to them. He abandoned the queue and with it the immediate prospect of America, and went to live in Cornwall.

His months in London had seen the end of his belief in 'revolution' and in 'doing anything' publicly—the end of his hope to change his society by other means than by his writing. Cornwall was, from the start, seen as more than a refuge; it was to be a creative centre, after all. Lawrence wrote to Katherine Mansfield: 'We must begin afresh—we must begin to create a life all together—unanimous. Then we shall be happy. We must be happy. But we shall only be happy if we are creating a life together' (30 xii 1915). Lawrence never answered the question of what actually could be created, in such a way; in the end, his only creation of 'a life together' would be in the pages of his novels. *Women in Love* would be his finest rejection of society, his most complex statement of attitude to the prevailing ideology, his own most intense ideological statement: his realisation of the contradictions of his own position as man and writer. He wrote it in Cornwall, and it became more important than any community he had ever planned.

Community in the sense of being 'unanimous' itself receded in importance very quickly. Throughout the autumn of 1915 Lawrence had been insisting to his friends on the importance of unanimity, and he had expressed his strongest hostility to the merely personal. 'I am sick and tired of personality in every way,' he had written to Katherine Mansfield (12 xii 1915). But in Cornwall he gave up the corresponding insistence on unanimity of purpose as something which could transcend the merely individual; it was as if he were gradually stripping himself of those beliefs which had so far sustained his belief in community itself. Koteliansky must have written to him in the first week of January complaining that there was no real harmony between the proposed group of colonists; and in a remarkable reply Lawrence declared himself 'willing to give up people altogether'. 'There is my intimate art, and my thoughts, as you say. Very good, so be it . . . I am not going to urge & constrain any more: there are no people here in this world, to be urged' (06 i 1916). And he told Katherine Mansfield that he was not going to 'strive with anything any more—go like a thistle-down, anywhere, having nothing to do with the world, no connection' (07 i 1916). That was clearly a reaction from his feelings the previous September, when the Fisher Street meetings were being planned, about working for change and not caring if people were hard to convince; but even if Lawrence felt temporarily relieved of the *care* for humanity which had dominated him the previous year, we can still see a contradiction between the insistent casualness of such a remark, and how he actually behaved during 1916. He wanted a kind of freedom from society and care, a kind of new, free individuality; but he also hated individuality, and remained a writer deeply concerned with the existing) relation between the individual and his society. On the one hand, 'I feel very estranged' (24 ii 1916): on the other, 'Yet still one can be an open door, or at least an unlatched door, for the new era to come in by. That is all' (09 i 1916). He declared himself uncaring, yet the idea of the new, of change, dominated him. He wrote to Ottoline Morrell at the start of February:

> The only thing now to be done is either to go down with the ship, sink with the ship, or, as much as one can, *leave* the ship, and like a castaway live a life apart. As for me, I do not belong to the ship; I will not, if I can help it, sink with it. I will not live any more in this time. I know what it is. I reject it. As far as I possibly can, I will stand outside this time, I will live my life, and, if possible, be happy, though the whole world slides in horror down into the bottomless pit.
>
> (07 ii 1916)

We must realise that this was not a final, impassive declaration. It represents something that, for the rest of Lawrence's life and his career as a writer, remained possible for him. His description of feeling 'as if my heart had once more broken' (*Phx II* 326) while looking down on the modern world from Monte Cassino in 1920 suggests the pain of such a separation. But most of all it could affect his writing deeply; his novels were henceforward written in a way that could always stand back from the world of men and the world of his own past experience. Lawrence was never blithe about the possibility of separation that opened up for him in 1916; standing 'outside this time' was never simple, or desirable, or even possible for very long. But the artist who sometimes did stand outside his own and his culture's present and past starts here: the wanderer, the biting satirist, the exponent of new religions of body and spirit starts here.

It was also typical of him that within four days of such a letter, he should be collaborating with Philip Heseltine on plans for the private publication of important books—notably *The Rainbow*: 'I myself believe that there is something to be done by private publishing' (11 ii 1916). In such contradictions, we can understand Lawrence. He could no more give up the hope of changing people, of advancing society, than he could finally escape from that fundamental belief in progress and advance which had been one of his inheritances from his mother, and from the nineteenth century. And he could not escape from either the desire, or the job, of writing novels to express that belief. He might feel unutterably alienated, but he could still express that desire to affect people, to alter the course of their lives.

> I feel quite anti-social, against this social whole as it exists. I wish one could be a pirate or a highwayman in these days. But my way of shooting them with noiseless bullets that explode in their souls, these social people of today, perhaps it is more satisfying. But I feel like an

outlaw. All my work is a shot at their very innermost strength, these banded people of today. Let them cease to be.

(15 ii 1916)

His new philosophical work 'Goats and Compasses', the revised *Twilight in Italy*, *The Rainbow* as written in 1915—all were works subversive of conventional ideology, shots at the conventional 'innermost strength' because so totally opposed to conventional belief. 'I want to blow the wings off these fallen angels. I want to bust 'em up. I feel that everything I do is a shot at these fallen angels of mankind' (15 ii 1916). 'No more adhering to society. I am out of the camp, like a brigand. And every book will be a raid on them' (17 ii 1916). It was probably the successful completion of the first half of 'Goats and Compasses' which gave Lawrence the confidence to say that he was, finally, 'out of the camp'. But 'any man of real individuality tries to know and to understand what is happening, even in himself, as he goes along' (*Phx II* 276), he wrote in his 'Foreword' to *Women in Love*; what he felt he had understood in the spring of 1916 was his own social role, for ever outside the conventional ideology of society—and yet strangely attached to that society, still. He had moved on from one social role, of self-made educator of feelings, the idealist exponent of advance, to another: that of critic and mystic. Bertrand Russell was the kind of writer he himself refused to be; Lawrence wrote to him that 'One must be an outlaw these days, not a teacher or preacher. One must retire out of the herd and then fire bombs into it' (19 ii 1916). Lawrence's antogonism to society does not often sound as absolute as this, and we need to understand it as the corresponding swing of the pendulum to that which had carried him into such fervent social hope in 1915. And the important thing even about those 'bombs' was that they would make people realise things, and not simply destroy them. But never again would this particular pendulum swing so far back the other way. One of his major concerns for the rest of his writing life would be what place he had, as a writer; what relationship with society, what contact, what responsibility.

The Lawrences moved into their new home at Higher Tregerthen, near Zennor, in March; 'a tiny settlement, all to ourselves' (11 iii 1916). It may have been 'to ourselves', but as soon as they were all settled, Lawrence began to write again. The mood in which he did so is summed up in a letter to Ottoline Morrell:

One must forget, only forget, turn one's eyes from the world: that is all. One must live quite apart, forgetting, having another world, a world as yet uncreated. Everything lies in *being*, although the whole world is one colossal madness, falsity, a stupendous assertion of not-being.

(07 iv 1916)

That 'other' world might in theory be brought about by a colony, a *rananim*; but it could also be something created by the novel which Lawrence was about to write. A novel could take its stand against the prevailing ideologies of both rigid class structures and democratic opinion; it could assert a new world, an uncreated world of the spirit. That same month, Lawrence wrote to Catherine Carswell that she was 'so intrinsically detached, so essentially separated and isolated, as to be a real writer or artist or recorder' (16 iv 1916); that suggests how important such a stand-point seemed to him as an artist in 1916. *Women in Love* shows both its author's attempt to adopt such a stand-point, and his ultimate failure to do so.

But, interestingly, the novel he first thought of writing was not the continuation of *The Rainbow* at all. The recent prosecution and destruction of the first part of that novel may have made the writing of its second part too tender a matter; at all events, Lawrence's mind went back three years, to that amazingly creative spring of 1913, and the half-finished novel he had come to call 'The Insurrection of Miss Houghton'. He had stopped work on that novel because it seemed too outrageous to be published. That would not stand in his way in 1916. He wrote to Germany for the MS; he waited almost exactly a month for it. But in the middle of the war, it is hardly surprising that it never came. Sometime in the last ten days of April he began *Women in Love*, 'the second half of *The Rainbow*' (01 v 1916).

He had begun to wish to deny belonging to a culture, a country or a society, altogether: 'I hate the whole concern of the nation. Bloody false fools, I don't care what they do, so long as I can avoid them, the mass of my countrymen: or any other countrymen' (18 iv 1916). And yet only a week later he was engaged on the novel, and insisting that there was no inconsistency in his attitude:

> I am doing another novel—that really occupies me. The world crackles and busts, but that is another matter, external, in chaos. One has a certain order inviolable in one's soul. There one sits, as in a crow's nest, out of it all. And even if one is conscripted, still I can sit in my crow's nest of a soul and grin. Life mustn't be taken seriously any more, at least, the outer, social life. The social being I am has become a spectator at a knockabout dangerous farce. The individual particular me remains self-contained and grins.
>
> (26 iv 1916)

But this novel, at least, does more than grin at the society of its production, just as its range and activity shows more than a 'particular me' involved in it. Lawrence could write, 'I feel I cannot *touch* humanity, even in thought, it is abhorrent to me.' And yet he was writing a novel: 'a work of art is an act of faith, as Michael Angelo says, and one goes on writing, to the unseen witnesses' (01 v 1916). Faith meant faith in others sharing his stand-point, aware of their contradictions as he was aware of his, aware of both the pain of alienation and the danger of individuality. A novel is an act of faith in its capacity to communicate with its readers, and to be for them what it can be for its author.

But never had Lawrence been so certain that what he was writing would meet with little or no response in its potential readers. 'Already it is beyond all hope of ever being published, because of the things it says,' (01 v 1916) he was saying within a week of starting it. 'It is a terrible and horrible and wonderful novel. You will hate it and nobody will publish it,' (25 x 1916) he told Pinker after it was finished; 'It is enough for me that it is written, in this universe of revolving worlds' (03 x 1916). He was right about its prospects; no-one would publish it for four years, and most people found it incomprehensible. Cynthia Asquith saw the TS in 1918, and we can consider her a potentially sympathetic ordinary reader; she wrote in her diary:

> It is interesting—painfully so, and full of extraordinary bits of stark writing, but what is it all about and *why*? It seems a *mis*application of such a wealth of strenuous analysing and writing. Surely he is delirious—a man whose temperature is 103?—or do I know nothing about human beings? It is all so *fantastic* to me and 'unpleasant'—morbid to a degree. I don't know *what* to think about it.[3]

Sixty years on, it is easy to forget just how difficult its first readers found *Women in Love*. Today's critics go through the book like lions through a paper hoop; critical guides exist in which the crooked is made straight and the rough places plain. But as late as 1930, as whole-hearted an admirer of Lawrence's genius as F. R. Leavis could complain that 'To get through it calls for great determination and a keen diagnostic interest . . . never again does he come near to offering, as here, a parallel to the turgid, cyclonic disasters of Blake's prophetic books'.[4] In 1945 George Orwell felt confident that 'with few exceptions Lawrence's full-length novels are, it is generally admitted, difficult to get through'.[5] Above all, *Women in Love* made its first readers feel that it was a mad book. *The Observer* headed its review 'A Mad World' and commented: 'page after page reads like the ravings of some unfortunate being subjected to the third degree'.[6] Rebecca West, for many the voice of the *avant-garde*, wrote that 'many of us are cleverer than Mr D. H. Lawrence and nearly all of us save an incarcerated few are much saner'.[7] *John Bull*—admittedly a special case—remarked that 'most of his characters are obviously mad'.[8] The *London Mercury* felt that 'one would have to sweep the world before getting together such a collection of abnormalities';[9] even John Middleton Murry, who was staying with the Lawrences when the book was first written, and who shared in discussions which found their way into it, remarked in his review that it was 'five hundred pages of passionate vehemence, wave after wave of turgid, exasperated writing impelled towards some distant and invisible end; the persistent underground beating of some dark and inaccessible sea'.[10]

What did its readers find so hard? Fundamentally, like Cynthia Asquith they asked 'what is it all about and *why*?' Those are still the right questions. *Women in Love* is a book whose relationship with the world of its production is particularly complex—as its author's own remarks about it might suggest; on the one hand, 'most people won't even be able to read it' (03 x 1916), on the other he felt he had 'knocked the first loop-hole in the prison where we are all shut up' (11 x 1916).In exactly the same way, in the book, Birkin both rejects society utterly—he would like 'everybody in the world destroyed' (*WL* 141)—yet replies to Ursula, when she asks him 'why do you bother about humanity?', 'because I can't get away from it' (*WL* 144). And, as she sees, he wants to be a 'Salvator Mundi' (*WL* 144). The novel, too, is committed and remains committed to the society of its production, both by being written as a publishable novel submitted to publishers in the normal way when finished, and by continually dwelling on the social worlds of twentieth-century England.

And yet, as a novel, it insists continually that people of heightened consciousness both should and do live in a different world. At one point Gerald asks Birkin 'where's your special world?' Birkin answers: 'Make it. Instead of chopping yourself down to fit the world, chop the world down to fit yourself. As a matter of fact, two exceptional people make another world. You and I, we make another, separate world' (*WL* 230). Birkin believes this, and the novel offers it as something we too can believe. The novel is designed to 'knock a hole in the wall', just as Birkin feels that 'to know, to give utterance, was to break a way through the walls of the prison' (*WL* 209); the novel's Foreword offers the book as a 'passionate struggle into conscious being' (*Phx II* 276). Yet to understand that 'conscious being' in yourself, or in the created characters, is to insist on another world from twentieth-century English society. The more we understand *Women in Love*, the more it serves to alienate us from the society in which we are reading it and understanding it. *Women in Love*, like all novels, is in a continually shifting relationship with the society of its production; it dramatises that society, it may even reflect it, but it also creates its own world; in this case, an insistently other world. Because although *Women in Love* seems to deal at great length with the society of its day, it works a vital transmutation upon the society it presents. To take a single example; the novel starts with two women sitting in a room discussing marriage. As has been pointed out, this is a starting-point reminiscent of a number of nineteenth-century novels. We seem to be in a world stressing moral

choice and the opportunities of women in society. David Cavitch writes
of the two sisters: 'like vain or superior ladies in fiction of more than a
century earlier they are afraid that all married men are bores and that
married life will not sustain the sense of heightened significance, the
romantic vividness, that they require in life'.[11] But 'romantic vividness'
certainly is not what these ironical young women desire. And four times
in these first few pages we are told that one or the other of them is
frightened. Cavitch says that they are frightened of the bad marriages
they might make—men and romance being so incompatible. But the
novel's stress goes far deeper than this: 'in their hearts they were frightened' (*WL* 8). In the world of the Regency novel which Cavitch
evokes, fear is an emotion which young ladies would experience about
spinsterhood, not about marriage. Gudrun and Ursula's talk is light,
flippant and clever; it is also obvious that they feel more than they
admit. Three times, in fact, Gudrun tries to end the conversation;
emphatically she does not want to pursue the ideas her sister offers her,
about children, about being reckless, about their father. Both of them
jump at the chance of going to see the wedding, as an escape from the
crevasses which keep opening beneath the conversation.
 We are told something of the origin of Ursula's fears first:

> As she went upstairs, Ursula was aware of the house, of her home
> round about her. And she loathed it, the sordid, too-familiar place!
> She was afraid at the depth of her feeling against the home, the
> milieu, the whole atmosphere and condition of this obsolete life. Her
> feeling frightened her.
>
> (*WL* 11)

She is conscious of the gap between her cheerful ironies and her fundamental feeling. The contrast is violent. Both sisters cope so well with
conventionalities (or the lack of them), so elegantly and superciliously;
but neither can face 'this obsolete life'. The novel has indeed offered us
a scene reminiscent of the social intercourse of a Regency novel; it also
suggests, immediately, that social life as Gudrun and Ursula
experience it is both frightening and obsolete.
 The sisters walk through Beldover—'a dark, uncreated, hostile
world' (*WL* 13). Gudrun's reaction is that 'It's like being mad, Ursula'
(*WL* 2). Critics commonly distinguish Gudrun's reaction—which they
see as bad—from Ursula's; the crucial thing is that, like the narrator,
both sisters respond to the scene not as it is but in terms of the feelings
which it provokes in them. Beldover is less described, than rendered in
terms of heightened consciousness—terms which presumably made
Cynthia Asquith write 'delirious' and *'fantastic'* about the book's
descriptions. It is not a mining village but a kind of hell through which

Gudrun is led, as she asks what *her* world can be, if this is 'the world'. As in the first scene, what she says is different from what she actually experiences. She is actually shocked, bewildered and frightened, but she says: 'It is like a country in an underworld. . . . Ursula, it's marvellous, it's really marvellous—it's really wonderful, another world. The people are all ghouls, and everything is ghostly' (*WL* 12). Words like 'wonderful' and 'ghouls' sound forced; but only in that way can she create her sense of 'another world' and enjoy her fear. Later in the chapter, as the sisters watch the wedding party go into the church, she sees each person as 'a complete figure, like a character in a book, or a subject in a picture, or a marionette in a theatre, a finished creation' (*WL* 15); and we again see her almost consciously insisting on her world, on her right to *make* a world. We cannot simply say that Gudrun's view of Beldover is biased, or foolishly unaware of the social reality of the place; the narrator himself uses words like 'amorphous', 'aborigine', 'brittle', 'magic', 'obsolete', to create *his* vision of the world, and those too are words describing the heightened consciousness of someone who finds this world an alien world, a species of hell. A phrase like 'It's like being mad' would come as naturally from the narrator as from Gudrun. He shows us an ordinary cabbage stump, or a street, and we register it as an artefact of hell. 'I think we've all gone mad,' says Ursula in 'Water-Party'. 'Pity we aren't madder,' replies Birkin—and, again, the narrator would agree with him (*WL* 188).

So when Gudrun sees Gerald, and thinks of him as 'a young, good-humoured, smiling wolf', as someone who 'did not belong to the same creation as the people about him' (*WL* 15), I suggest that we find Gudrun's language one of discovery and revelation ('Am I *really* singled out for him in some way, is there really some pale gold, arctic light that envelopes only us two?')—not something we could judge inadequate (*WL* 16). It is the language of someone discovering the mystery of another human being; the language of someone fated to a certain kind of experience: it has nothing to do with the way that people should (or do) behave in society. The novel's dream-like quality comes from the way it turns the normal world into a species of hallucination—a vivid, unreal panorama. Beldover, 'as if seen through a veil of crape', its chimney smoke rising 'in steady columns, magic within the dark air' (*WL* 12), is a compelling vision of the real world turned unreal.

This is true, too, of an incidental aspect of the book to which the early reviewers and critics often drew attention, but which modern criticism largely ignores—the continual detailed description of clothes. Even chapters apparently cast in the mould of conventional realism instruct us to focus our attention on the unreality of the perceived world, and on the violence of our relationship with it. There is a vivid contrast between the brilliant clothes of the two girls, the blackened place, and the hostile inhabitants. In 'Coal-Dust' two labourers watch the girls:

> They saw the two girls appear, small, brilliant figures in the near distance, in the strong light of the late afternoon. Both wore light, gay summer dresses, Ursula had an orange-coloured knitted coat, Gudrun a pale yellow, Ursula wore canary yellow stockings, Gudrun bright rose, the figures of the two women seemed to glitter in progress over the wide bay of the railway crossing, white and orange and yellow and rose glittering in motion across a hot world silted with coal-dust.
>
> (*WL* 126–7)

The repetitive second sentence helps create the phantasmal appearance of the girls; they are glamorous in the full sense of enchanting. Rebecca West, in 1921, noted the 'sheer meaningless craziness' of the 'extraordinary descriptions of women's clothes',[12] Murry said much the same thing,[13] the *Saturday Westminster Gazette* reviewer (who had fun with the whole novel) thought that '"Enter a purple gown, green stockings, and amber necklace" would do for a stage direction if *Women in Love* could ever be dramatised'.[14] It is right to notice the clothes; they are clearly meant to be noticed. They individualise the characters against the world. The labourers watching Gudrun and Ursula are, strictly, in another world—and that everyday world is both temporal (with its momentary pang of lust) and unreal. Gudrun's clothes are, appropriately, the most often described, just as her keeping of herself to herself (very different from Birkin's conception of singleness) always isolates her and keeps her disturbingly separate. She leaves the Pompadour café with Birkin's letter, and just where we might have expected a sentence or two about her feelings, we get this:

> She was fashionably dressed in blackish-green and silver, her hat was brilliant green, like the sheen on an insect, but the brim was soft dark green, a falling edge with fine silver, her coat was dark green, lustrous with a high collar of grey fur, and great fur cuffs, the edge of her dress showed silver and black velvet, her stockings and shoes were silver grey. She moved with slow, fashionable indifference to the door.
>
> (*WL* 434)

We learn, half a page later, that she is 'frozen with overwrought feelings' and violently angry with Birkin: 'Why does he give himself away to such *canaille*?' (*WL* 435). Giving herself away is precisely what Gudrun will not do; the description offers a curious mixture of Gudrun exposed (even the taxi which collects her has lights 'like two eyes') and Gudrun concealed. Halliday's reading of the letter aloud obviously touches her deeply, by what it says as much as by how he reads it: 'I want to go,' (*WL* 434) is her instant reaction. She conceals herself by leaving, and crushes the letter in her hand as she goes; but she is also making a public gesture. So she presents herself only as a 'form'; glossy, fashionable, the greens and silvers and blacks like a shell over her feelings. The 'sheen on an insect' confirms this sense; she is deeply concealed against the moment of public exposure. The description of her clothes is Lawrence's way of suggesting her true tension at such a moment, the terror of her isolate self, always buried yet always fearing exposure, always in danger of giving itself away.

The first part of the novel is constantly aligning the experience of the individual consciousness against the moeurs of established society, and suggesting that such opposition is the norm of contemporary life. Gudrun and Ursula both go to a wedding, but, like the people taking part in it, seem hardly aware of the social reality of the ceremony. The wedding breakfast in Chapter 2 turns into a discussion of race and nationality, hinging on the individual's 'pleasant liberty of conduct' (*WL* 32). Chapter 3, 'Class-Room', lacks all sense of the social reality of teaching children in a school; education is discussed entirely in terms of the arousing of an individual's consciousness. In Chapter 4, 'Diver', we do get a momentary sense of what is possible for a man, but not for a woman, in society; but that chapter too finds its centre in a discussion of the independence of the proud individual, set like a swan against the geese of society. In Chapter 5 we find Birkin's assertion that 'first person singular is enough for me' (*WL* 61)—and so on. We have been in a number of carefully distinguished social worlds, but their vividness is given the quality of a dream rather than of a reality; the individual's consciousness makes them dream-like.

This is particularly odd since in this novel, more than in any of his others, Lawrence creates a wide spectrum of society and shows us what Gudrun feels to be 'the whole pulse of social England' (*WL* 470). But the novel is not so simplistic as to set the claims of the individual consciousness against the threat of the social world, and say simply that the individual's only hope is to depart from the mass and cleanse himself (as *St Mawr* was to say in 1925).[15] *Women in Love* is a greater novel than *St Mawr* because it creates situations in which individuals would like to be free, and where freedom is not so easily attained; where a tension between liberation and constraint (social, sexual, economic, cultural) is continually reinforced. We can see such a tension in Gudrun in the Pompadour, where it makes her brittle to the point of fragility. Birkin, throughout the novel, would like to be free, independent and self-satisfying: 'The old way of love seemed a dreadful bondage, a sort of conscription . . . he wanted to be single in himself, the woman single in herself' (*WL* 223). Rolling in primroses, he prefers the 'new-found world of his madness' (*WL* 120) to the 'regular sanity' (as well he might). 'Why form any serious connections at all? Why not be casual, drifting along, taking all for what it was worth? And yet, still, he was damned and doomed to the old effort at serious living' (*WL* 340). He is as separate as a man can be, from the social world; his job keeps him unlocated and he feels he can give it up at any moment—'tomorrow perhaps' (*WL* 147). Yet it is his doom, his fate, to be attached to the world. When he defines for Ursula what he means by 'the last thing one wants', he says 'I don't know—freedom together' (*WL* 147), itself a paradox and a limitation of himself. Love haunts him, yet seems a 'conscription'—a word which in 1916 could only suggest the recently (and for England uniquely) introduced military conscription: the state's ultimate binding of the individual. He expresses his commit-ment to Ursula by giving her rings; yet also insists that he bought them only because 'I wanted them' (*WL* 341). He insists that people do not matter, yet it is commitment to have dinner with Hermione and say goodbye to her which provokes the quarrel in 'Excurse'. The novel shows Birkin moving in and out of phase with the social world; the same man who rolls naked among the primroses also 'looked a failure in his attempt to be a properly dressed man' (*WL* 88) in Halliday's London flat. Proud singleness can only be suggested in 'freedom together', and the idea of going away with Ursula instantly suggests his need of still further people.

> 'To be free,' he said. 'To be free, in a free place, with a few other people!'
> 'Yes,' she said wistfully. Those 'few other people' depressed her.
> 'It isn't really a locality, though,' he said. 'It's a perfected relation betwen you and me, and others—the perfect relation—so that we are free together.'
>
> (*WL* 356)

Lawrence in fact gives Birkin notably more sense of commitment to others than he ascribed to himself; just before starting the novel, he remarked that 'It isn't scenery one lives by, but the freedom of moving about alone' (25 iii 1916)—and the 'few other people' never material-ised for him.

It might be argued that the paradoxes of the novel are simply con-fusions, reflecting contradictions in its author. If *Women in Love* were another sort of novel, then they might well be. But *Women in Love* is a very carefully constructed experimental novel, designed to elicit para-dox rather than fall helplessly into it. Its very structure is a refusal of simple narrative progression; its clear-cut, often unlinked chapters fol-low not the sequence of a particular narrative but the progress of

particular concerns—like individuality, freedom, love and consciousness. Birkin's confusions are the necessary links in a chain of thoughts,
as are Ursula's insistencies. The novel is constructed to elicit from its
characters the complexities attendant upon their advanced lives; it
interweaves theory and experience, idea and counter-idea, knowing
and being. 'All vital truth contains the memory of all that for which it is
not true,' (19 xii 1914) Lawrence once wrote; the same could be said of
a novel like *Women in Love*. A simple narrative necessarily suggests the
progress of thoughts to a conclusion; the characters of *Women in Love*
(and we ourselves) only reach realisations, are not aware of truths.
When we find Birkin both as obstinate and as unclear at the end of the
novel about what he wanted from Gerald, as he had been at the beginning, we don't need to blame a confusion in Lawrence's own heterosex-
ual and homosexual impulses (as, for instance, Scott Sanders does);[16]
we need to realise that Gerald is a focus for Birkin of his need for more
than a single intimacy, his need for 'other people', his desire for
'another kind of love'; it is something the novel has dramatised, not
something it has reached a conclusion about or is offering as a truth.

The novel as a whole, in fact, is asking what kind of freedom—or
individuality—is possible for a man like Birkin; his attachment to
Gerald has the force of a necessary, if unwanted, bond. The Pompadour crowd are distinguished by their deliberate freedoms; when
Gerald asks about them 'All loose?' Birkin replies 'In one way. Most
bound, in another' (*WL* 66). Gerald himself tells the Pussum that he is
'afraid of being bound hand and foot' (*WL* 73) before she gives herself
to him; but she is loose with Gerald only to ensnare Halliday. The
young men in Halliday's flat flaunt their freedom from convention by
being deliberately nude; but they are people trapped in their own
'repetition of repetitions' (*WL* 216). What Birkin offers Ursula is never
as free as his own discovery, in Chapter 8, of 'the new-found world of
his madness': 'he would be free in his new state'. 'As for the certain
grief he felt at the same time, in his soul, that was only the remains of
an old ethic, that bade a human being adhere to humanity' (*WL* 120).
But he has just been knocked over the head by Hermione, and his
experience offers a temporary relief from caring rather than a final
break; never again does Lawrence allow him to be so free of the 'old
ethic'. Indeed, both Birkin and the narrator insist on the 'connection
with life and hope' which human beings need (*WL* 286). But Birkin's
primary insistence is on his doctrine of 'free, proud singleness' (*WL*
287); that kind of individualism is his primary recourse against the
society which he hates. 'He said the individual was *more* than love, or
than any relationship' (*WL* 299).

At least, this is what Birkin would like to think. It is an assertion
made in a context which modifies it; Birkin is, in fact, neither free nor
proud nor single. Right at the end he breaks down over the death of

mechanised industry. Yet the vision of total change is utterly untrue to history; and it is certainly untrue that most miners had to work 'much harder' after mechanisation. Lawrence goes on: 'And yet they accepted the new conditions. They even got a further satisfaction out of them' (*WL* 259). What he means by 'satisfaction' is reduction, self-immolation in the machine; he is talking about souls, not about working selves. Lawrence's own later description of the modernised industry at Moorgreen pit as he saw it in 1925 is surely far more realistic:

> The pit is foreign to me anyhow, so many new big buildings round it, electric plant and all the rest. It's a wonder even the shafts are the same. But they must be: the shafts where we used to watch the cage-loads of colliers coming up suddenly, with a start . . . while the screens still rattled, and the pony on the sky-line still pulled along the tub of 'dirt', to tip over the edge of the pit-bank.
>
> It is different now: all is much more impersonal and mechanical and abstract.
>
> (*Phx* 823)

That is the reaction of a man naturally puzzled and alienated by an enlarged industry, nostalgic for the past. But what he had described in 'The Industrial Magnate' is the counterpart of his analysis of emotions in the novel; 'sensation' in sexual relations is re-created in industrial terms. Gudrun, both repelled and fascinated by Gerald as he spurs his horse at the railway crossing, is satisfied in the same way as the miners are satisfied by Gerald's demonstration of power, and Lawrence is surely very acute about such a response. That does not meant that the miners of England behaved as 'The Industrial Magnate' says they did; the novel is, once again, creating in its own terms the consciousness of the age.

The chapter is, in fact, more concerned with myth than with history. When Lawrence describes the difference between Gerald and his father, he is not directing our attention to a change in the general outlook of industrial management between 1880 and 1914; he is describing his sense of a fundamental change in Christian society in post-Renaissance Europe. The Crich family is a mythic analogue, not an historical reality. Lawrence is primarily concerned with spiritual change, and presents the miners as the willing participants in that change: 'Gerald was their high priest, he represented the religion they really felt. . . . They were exalted by belonging to this great and super-human system which was beyond feeling or reason, something really godlike' (*WL* 259–60). Lawrence is defining his novel's interest in society—the destruction of man as a social being. Gerald and his colliers are seen committing themselves to 'the great social productive machine': 'This was a sort of freedom, the sort they really wanted. It was the first great step in undoing, the first great phase of chaos, the substitution of the mechanical principle for the organic' (*WL* 260). Such freedom is like that of the London Bohemian circle; freedom without any belief in 'the ultimate unison between people—a bond' which, Birkin insists, is the only thing which holds the world together (*WL* 169). 'The Industrial Magnate' chapter creates a picture of a world from which the individual must free himself, and one to which he is almost fatally attached; it is the world of modern consciousness.

That was the extent to which Lawrence was prepared to take his novel. Of all the novelists writing in 1916, he was in a unique position to describe the actual conditions of industry as the working man experienced them. Yet he not only ignored or transmuted his knowledge of the actual conditions, he ignored events like the South Wales miners' strike of July 1915—which was a stand taken against a nation at war, against the power of a centralised government, and against the power of the local coal-owners. The novel's strike is considered metaphysically, not economically. He ignored the wartime plan for nationalising the coal industry—something his own political programme of February 1915 had looked forward to, as a necessary step in the revolutionising of society. The worlds he is concerned with in 'The Industrial Magnate' are created worlds, not realistic ones. *as he ignored*

The final location of the novel is the Tyrol; but this, too, is hardly a realistically created setting. The Tyrol is constantly described as an 'other' world; it is the most extreme 'other' world of the novel, and affects all the characters deeply. Even while journeying to it, Ursula is conscious of leaving behind 'the old world' (*WL* 438); she means England, which, like the Continent glimpsed from the train, is only 'the superficial unreal world of fact'. She and Birkin are making a 'final transit out of life'; they lose all sense of 'the old world', being concentrated not 'on the world, only on the unknown paradise' (*WL* 437). Ursula feels herself 'projected' out of the world she knows—the world of her own past—which starts to feel like an obstacle to her newly developing, alienated self. Her past self starts to feel like 'a little creature of history, not really herself' (*WL* 440).

At the guest-house, the process is carried still further. 'She wanted to have no past' (*WL* 460); and after her initial fears of this 'different world', she develops an unnatural self-confidence—something really rootless. The Alps are 'the navel of the world' (*WL* 450) and give the people an 'other-world look' (*WL* 453); they intoxicate Ursula with 'a conceit of emotion and power' (*WL* 457), releasing inhibition and stimulating consciousness. For Gudrun the place is 'her place', cutting her off finally from responsibility to Gerald (or anyone), and from any possibility of creative relationship. She reaches her own final isolation here. Gerald responds to the freedom with a release of energy, skiing as a man 'projected in pure flight, mindless, soulless, whirling along one perfect line of force' (*WL* 474). Only Birkin cannot bear it—or could not, without Ursula; this world, more real than real, frightens him. Its dream of freedom is so powerful, glimpsed in the house itself, set 'in the midst of the last deserted valleys of heaven . . . deserted in the waste of snow, like a dream' (*WL* 449).

England and the past vanish for all the characters—but particularly for Ursula. The place seems to offer the freedom which the real world denies, to be indeed the 'nowhere' which Birkin wanted, to be a release from the 'other world' of home: 'That old shadow-world, the actuality of the past—ah, let it go!' (*WL* 460). Once Ursula had insisted on 'the world that's given—because there isn't any other' (*WL* 355). Now she too has too a vision of 'a new world of reality':

> What had she to do with parents and antecedents? . . . she was herself, pure and silvery, she belonged only to the oneness with Birkin, a oneness that struck deeper notes, sounding into the heart of the universe, the heart of reality, where she had never existed before.
> (*WL* 460)

Ursula certainly does not want to spend the rest of her life in the Tyrol. Her vision of a separate, individual self, at one with Birkin, is rather different from his original idea of life with those 'few other people'. And yet, once and for all, she seems to have released herself from the 'old world' which Birkin, too, wants to be free of; she can now match him, and together they can just 'wander off'—or, as the novel presents them, live in their own world.

Gudrun, too has a final vision in the Tyrol:

> If she could but come there, alone, and pass into the infolded navel of eternal snow and of uprising, immortal peaks of snow and rock, she would be a oneness with all, she would be herself the eternal, infinite silence, the sleeping, timeless, frozen centre of the All.
> (*WL* 461)

It is a vision both hallucinatory and repulsive; but she is not actually going to put her boots on and start climbing. The vision, like so much of the novel, mediates between a real, actually apprehended world, and the world of a fulfilling imagination. The novel is an attempt to convince us that such experiences of the world are, for us, indeed our truest experience of it; we truly 'make the world we do not find'.

And each character in the novel makes such a world of his or her own. More obviously than the other characters, Gerald has such a world, back in England; but he gives it up without a pang and apparently receives neither telegrams nor anger from Shortlands. The Tyrol offers him an utterly satisfying physical world, but all he can do (as ever) is 'see this thing through' (*WL* 362). 'There must be a conclusion, there must be finality' (*WL* 519); his kind of unsatisfied physical and psychic longing finds its conclusion in self-abnegation and a desire to kill Gudrun—and so have her 'finally and for ever'. His longings revolve inwardly and tempt him, as Gudrun too is tempted, into a 'oneness with all', a final relief and sleep; but as he actually *does* set off upwards after half-strangling her, we know that his only destiny is to become that 'sleeping, timeless, frozen centre of the All' which was the culmination of Gudrun's vision. He wants to 'come to the end—he had had enough', but all he can do is simply keep going–and we should remember the mocking irony from Chapter 4 of 'he's got *go*, anyhow' (*WL* 53). But where does the 'go' go to? Finally, into nothingness; 'he slipped and fell down, and as he fell something broke in his soul, and immediately he went to sleep' (*WL* 533). Such an ending is a marvellous combination of realism, vision and parable; the world Lawrence makes for Gerald is a perfect interpenetration of the worlds of fact and spirit; his physical death is a spiritual tragedy.

Gudrun's 'world' is harder to define; yet she, too, struggles to achieve one. As an artist, she remains unattached to place; Beldover, London, Sussex, Shortlands are all simply resting places for her. She flirts with the idea of marriage to Gerald, with 'what he represented in the world' (*WL* 469); but her genuine knowledge of the 'whole pulse of social England' makes her recoil in irony from the idea. All she can believe in—and always ironically—are the 'perfect moments' of her life. She rejects the whole of conventional society, in withering irony. That makes her sound like Birkin, but unlike him she has no vision of ideal relationship, or of a way of life. She is, we could say, entirely unspiritual, and there is a price to be paid for that. She can construct fantasy worlds with Loerke, and as an artist she can insist that 'my art stands in another world' (*WL* 484); but that has to be enough for her. The novel leaves her wondering '*wohin?*'—'she *never* wanted it answered' (*WL* 528)—unattached, unbelieving, terrified, playful as and when she needs to be, perfectly cynical; surviving. She finds a solution to the problem of living in this world posed by the novel; her individuality hardens into obstinate personality. But she survives, as it is her fate to.

Ursula begins the novel with a place to which she belongs (unlike Gudrun), a job, a past she has grown up from; only her future is empty. She ends the novel with no past and no desire for anything in the present which 'this world' can give her. Her future is, simply, to live with Birkin, to 'come down from the slopes of heaven to this place, with Birkin' (*WL* 460). Reality is a matter of belonging 'only to the oneness with Birkin'; from that point onwards, she can wander the world with no trace of regret. When, indeed, Gudrun offers Ursula her own arguments about accepting the world as it is—'the only thing to do with the world, is to see it through' (an argument terrifyingly true for Gerald)—for 'you can't suddenly fly off on to a new planet', Ursula replies 'One has a sort of other self, that belongs to a new planet, not to this. You've got to hop off' (*WL* 493). It is an answer Birkin would be proud of. And that is where the novel leaves her.

Birkin, of course, is the most consistent believer in new worlds in the whole novel. Early on, he plays with the idea of 'a world empty of people, just uninterrupted grass, and a hare sitting up' (*WL* 142)—though we should note how his unworldly words are followed shortly afterwards by the careful 'carpeting' of his rooms. But the world he wants most often is the 'world of proud indifference' (*WL* 282) with Ursula, where he is 'a strange creature from another world', where they can 'wander away from the world's somewheres, into our own nowhere' (*WL* 355). I have already suggested both the extent to which they want to do that, and the degree to which the vision is unrealised. Birkin's faith in 'the mystery' and in living with Ursula in a world of their own—and in ceasing to care, as he ceases to care about everything in the world except Gerald and Ursula—remains central in the novel, a provocative centre which is true to the presentation of the world as the novel creates it.

With his novel finished—'another world'—Lawrence hardly felt like publishing it: 'It seems such a desecration of oneself to give it to the extant world' (20 xi 1916). Such remarks apparently confirm his sense of the artist's necessary detachment; in the novel it is Loerke who feels that the work of art 'has no relation to anything outside that work of art' (*WL* 483), and we are told by Gudrun that Loerke '*is* an artist, he is a free individual' (*WL* 522) because he has 'an uncanny singleness, a quality of being by himself, not in contact with anybody else, that marked out an artist to her' (*WL* 474). Lawrence obviously knew what it was to feel that. And yet, if *Women in Love* survives as a significant novel, it must be because it succeeds in having a relation with the world outside it; as Ursula puts it, 'The world of art is only the truth about the real world' (*WL* 485). And Lawrence also knew what it was to feel 'a gnawing craving in oneself, to move and live as a real representative of the whole race' (23 xii 1916). The artist perhaps has to feel that. Critics write about Lawrence's misanthropy as if it must have damaged him profoundly as a novelist: 'you cannot make fiction out of hatred for humanity'.[21] There is no evidence that Lawrence ever tried to; it is also true that while writing and revising *Women in Love*, he felt utterly alienated from the world of England. The kinds of purposes he had felt in 1915, culminating in the vision of a new world which took over the end of *The Rainbow*, were things which would never get into his novels again. The Foreword he wrote for *Women in Love* in 1919 sets out to make it sound a wholly personal work, in fact: 'This novel pretends only to be a record of the writer's own desires, aspirations, struggles;

in a word, a record of the profoundest experiences in the self'
(*Phx II* 275–6). Most readers probably feel that there are moments
when it reads primarily as a reflection of the 'deep, passional soul'
(*Phx II* 276) of its author; and yet *Women in Love* also demonstrates an
author having the confidence that the soul he confronts in himself is
also 'a real representative of the human race'. And through his creation
of the novel's characters we see him living out the contradictions of his
own position as an artist.

In its stress on the individual, *Women in Love* stands as one man's
response to his own deliberate social isolation, as the record of his own
'struggles'. But it is also representative of a hatred of the ideology of his
society; it creates individuals in worlds of their own, making the happi-
ness they cannot find, standing against the social world which has
reduced human society to the ugliness of Beldover, the repetitiveness of
the Pompadour, the insentient mental fibre of Breadalby and the human
tragedy of Shortlands. *Women in Love* makes no sort of compromise with
the problems it obviously causes for its readers; it transmutes social
reality into the play of heightened consciousness, and says that *that* is
our true world. It insists on vision, on impracticality, on the deathliness
of social bondage and liberated personality alike; but it is a novel which
also creates worlds of other people and other attachments. It represents
an idea of what Lawrence in 1916 thought both art and individual
consciousness should be; but it also creates imaginative worlds full of
life, not only of individuality. Eschatological critics make much of the
titles Lawrence considered using for it, in the later summer of 1916:
Dies Irae, The Latter Days. It was not, however, a weaker sense of England's doom that made him revert to the earlier title *Women in Love*.
Such a title suggests the free play of irony, the colloquial inquiringness,
which underlies the book. It isn't *Men in Love*—though it might have
been: but are they in love? What are the women in love with—themselves? *Does* Gudrun love Gerald? Does Ursula not love Birkin 'too
much' (as he insists)? In such ways, the title opens up the world of the
book quite undogmatically; and in such realism is the strength which
keeps it alive as a novel. It is the strangest of Lawrence's books; it
shows the real world falling into phantasmagoria; but like the African
sculpture so often discussed, it is a high pitch of art, it is a desperate
creation of the almost unbearable.

6 *The Lost Girl*

The first thing to say about *The Lost Girl* is that Lawrence wrote all of it in 1920. This needs saying because almost every discussion of the novel in the past twenty years has assumed that it was started in 1913; those making this assumption have included Cavitch, Daleski, Delavenay, Hough, Kermode, Leavis, Miko, Moore, Moynahan, Niven, Pritchard, Sanders, Sagar, Schorer, Roberts and Tedlock—as comprehensive a list of Lawrence scholars as one could find. This is not the place to discuss the actual relationship between *The Lost Girl* and its predecessors—some scenes from the 'Paul Morel' of 1911, an unfinished novel-fragment 'Elsa Culverwell' of 1912–13,[1] the lost 'Insurrection of Miss Houghton' of 1913 and the lost beginning to a novel which Lawrence wrote in Capri in 1920. *The Lost Girl* certainly took over the situation of the real-life provincial family and household used in the first three of those; it is equally certain that in the case of the first two, though the family and household are identical to those described in the first part of *The Lost Girl*, the actual treatment, the tone, everything but the bare outline of Lawrence's borrowing from the real-life Cullen family of Eastwood, are quite different. Everything in Lawrence's letters describing the full-scale novel version of the family and daughter which he wrote in 1913, 'The Insurrection of Miss Houghton', sounds utterly unlike the novel he wrote in 1920; critics who have tried to believe in the identity of the two works have been puzzled and disappointed when unable to see *The Lost Girl* as 'really a stratum deeper than I think anybody has ever gone, in a novel' (11 iii 1913)—Lawrence's description of 'The Insurrection' while writing it. It is much better to give up trying to guess what the vanished 'Insurrection' was like, and to concentrate on two other questions; why should Lawrence have gone back to pre-war material at all, in 1920; and what does that tell us about the novel he then wrote?

Between 1917 and 1921, Lawrence tried to write novels while knowing that the two he thought his finest could have no effect on his contemporaries; *The Rainbow* was banned in England and only obtainable under the counter in America, and *Women in Love* stayed unpublished until the end of 1920. The war may have ended in 1918, but publishers were slow to change their mind about Lawrence; it is worth remembering that the only book he published in 1919 was the tiny volume of poems called *Bay*, and the only work of fiction he got into print was the short story 'Tickets Please'. His feeling of impotence as a novelist was not helped by the discovery in the winter of 1919 that his agent Pinker had never even sent the TS of *Women in Love* to his American publisher Huebsch (who had handled his previous five books). In that winter Lawrence still had the MS of *Aaron's Rod* on his hands, but with the publication of *Women in Love* and the republication of *The Rainbow* at last being considered, he seems to have felt a need to offer his publishers and his public something less difficult—and something not liable to legal action, either. *Aaron's Rod* was both awkward and unfinished; Lawrence wanted to use the suggestion of a popular novel to allay his publishers' qualms about taking on *Women in Love*. He wrote to Huebsch at the start of December 1919 that 'When "Women in Love" is really published, I shall have another novel ready—not before—a more possibly popular one' (03 xii 1919). Secker heard about the project for a popular novel in exactly the same way. He was considering taking on *Women in Love*—'Do that, and you have my eternal allegiance'—as well as *The Rainbow:*

> If you do this, "The Rainbow" as a Vol. I of "Women in Love", then I must make a sort of permanent agreement with you. I am waiting for MS. of a novel three parts done, "Mixed Marriage," which I left in Germany before the war. This would make a perfect selling novel when I've finished it.
>
> (27 xii 1919)

'Mixed Marriage', as Lawrence was now calling 'The Insurrection', was obviously being offered as bait—to the extent of having its true nature concealed. It had actually been given up in 1913 because it had become unpublishable—'it was *too* improper' (05 iv 1913)—and was abandoned in favour of a novel which would sell. Now, in 1919, Lawrence was offering it as 'a perfect selling novel'. He can hardly have forgotten why he abandoned it; but clearly he planned to rewrite it. At least it was a substantial corpus of a novel, with unrealised potential, and Lawrence wished to attract, to convince and to mollify his publishers.

Post from Germany into a strike-torn Italy that winter was, however, terribly uncertain, and Lawrence waited in Capri until the second week of February before the MS arrived. What happened then, however, indicates his problems with the 1913 material, and how much he had to alter it. He worked on it for about a fortnight, remarking that he was writing 'a new novel' (13 ii 1920); but after moving to Taormina in Sicily at the end of the month, he 'scrapped all the novel I did in Capri—have begun again—got about 30,000 words, I believe, done since I'm here' (22 iii 1920). The 1913 material obviously needed to be rewritten entirely, and could neither be simply completed, nor (at the first attempt) recast. A remark to the American publisher Seltzer suggests why: 'I am doing Mixed Marriage—it should be more popular—one withdraws awhile from battle' (09 iii 1920). His main concern was to make the novel 'quite *unexceptionable*, as far as the Censor is concerned' (16 i 1920), as he had told Secker; and if that meant withdrawal from battle—well and good.

The Lost Girl was written very fast, and finished in just over eight weeks. During the first half of its composition, Lawrence continually told his correspondents how 'it does so amuse me' (09 iv 1920); and that, too, was its recommendation for Secker. 'It is I think an amusing book, and I don't think it is at all improper: quite fit for Mudies. I wish it could be serialised. Do you think there is any possibility?' (29 iv 1920). The novel which 'should be more popular' than *The Rainbow* or *Women in Love* was, in Lawrence's mind, turning into one which might make him a good deal of money; not only was Secker offering it to the libraries, Lawrence had actually asked him if he wanted to do it at all 'or shall I go to a commercial firm?' (09 iv 1920). Secker was decidedly a specialist publisher of literature. And all summer Lawrence tried to get the book serialised; he clearly made serial publication a priority over book publication, since although the novel was corrected by mid-June, Secker did not see the corrected version until late in August because the corrected TCC was, Lawrence insisted, *'for serialising purposes'* (24 vi 1920), and he wanted a magazine editor to have it. The TS he sent to America never even got to a publisher, but made a round of magazine editors—though all of them rejected it. Seltzer did not see the book until Secker sent him a set of proofs of the English edition in October. *The Lost Girl* was the first—and the last—novel Lawrence ever tried to get serialised. He failed because it was simply not designed as a serial—Carl Hovey of the *Metropolitan* commented that 'it is too attenuated and too descriptive to chop up into instalments'.[2] The idea of serialising it only occurred to Lawrence right at the end of the period of composition; it seems simply to have added another dimension to his hopes for the book's commercial success.

We should, however, remember another 'pot-boiler'—the first 'Sisters'—which developed into 'an earnest and painful work' (05 v 1913), before dismissing *The Lost Girl* as a commercial enterprise. In fact, it suffers from more complications than those simply resulting from a man like Lawrence trying to write for money. *The Lost Girl*'s relationship with England is most peculiar. On the one hand, as Lawrence told Catherine Carswell, it was meant to be 'comic—but not satiric' (31 iii 1920); and James Houghton's sales, Alvina's experiences with men before Ciccio, Mr May's work as manager—all are comic but not satirical, though Woodhouse is certainly small-minded. And yet, as the same letter from Lawrence contined, 'At the moment I feel I never want to see England again'; and when Alvina finally sails away from England, there is a description both stronger and stranger than satire:

> England, beyond the water, rising with ash-grey, corpse-grey cliffs, and streaks of snow on the downs above. England, like a long, ash-grey coffin slowly submerging. She watched it, fascinated and terrified. It seemed to repudiate the sunshine, to remain un-illuminated, long and ash-grey and dead, with streaks of snow like cerements. That was England! Her thoughts flew to Woodhouse, the grey centre of it all. Home!
>
> (*LG* 347)

She feels that her vision is 'like looking at something else', and it strikes oddly against the prevailing tone of the first two-thirds of the book. It is visionary in the way that Alvina's experiences in Italy will also be, and it repudiates England with an astonishing violence. H. L. Mencken thought that 'the story goes to pieces immediately the old gal leaves home';[3] it is more true to say that the novel takes a new direction altogether, and ceases to be comic; as if it had suddenly realised its subject for the first time, and could sweep away England as an unreal vision.

As if to confirm this, the novel bridges the gap between Alvina's life in Woodhouse, and her departure for Italy with Ciccio,[4] with some confusion. Alvina is, certainly, determined not to be taken in either by Ciccio or by the Natcha-Kee-Tawara troupe; there are similarities with the reaction of another English virgin from the Midlands, Yvette in *The Virgin and the Gypsy*, to the sensual male who attracts her. But Yvette cannot avoid the literal and symbolic flood of passion which envelops her in spite of her caution. Alvina simply walks away from Ciccio at the start of Chapter 9, and literally closes her door on him. He gets her back by appealing to her non-verbally; he sits and sings and plays his mandoline, looking at her with 'a deep, deep sun-warmth', 'somehow sweet to her' (*LG* 253–4). It is a fleeting but vital encounter, and confirms her passion for him; they go back to Woodhouse, and sleep together in the great mahogany bed of the Houghtons, which leaves her 'absurdly happy' (*LG* 280). But for no good reason, the relationship crumbles. Nothing is said, nothing happens, but Alvina leaves the troupe and takes a job in Lancaster as a nurse. She and Ciccio only get together again by chance, when he sees her in the street, and goes to her house; again he sings and plays, again she responds; but this time she goes to London with him, and they get married.

These events have a strange inconsequence. They have a superficial truth: Alvina's reserve, her class and her Englishness conspire to resist Ciccio and everything he stands for. And Lawrence is deliberately making their encounters nŏn-verbal, mysterious, instinctive. But we have no sense of Alvina knowing what it is that dissatisfies her, or how she responds to Ciccio. Ciccio simply looks at her, she recognises the look, and they can go away and get married and go to Italy. She goes through no realisation, conscious or unconscious, of her feelings or of his. She simply gets off the hook temporarily, in Lancaster; and then, just as mysteriously, she gets on it again. Her resistance to Ciccio does not even take the form of thinking about him; she just goes away and does something else.

This problem stems largely from having a heroine whose inner life is never the centre of our interest; who, compared with a Birkin or a Kate Leslie, in effect has no inner life—the way the book is written effectively prevents it. The tone of the first third of the book is ironic, slightly superficial in an attractive way, witty and successfully comic. Alvina's first sense of a darker side to her nature comes in her sudden friendship with Alexander Graham; he baffles her, but overwhelms her; those around her decide what is best, and she loses him. It happens swiftly, comically, with its own kind of truth—but the inner life of Alvina is not part of that truth. The same is true of her encounters with Albert and Arthur Witham. They enter and leave her life making hardly a ripple on its surface; she quickly knows that she cannot devote herself to either of them. Again, the encounters are rendered deftly, neatly and ironically—typified by the sustained metaphor of Albert Witham as a fish the far side of an aquarium wall. 'His impression was of uncanny flatness, something like a lemon sole' (*LG* 82). Could she have children by him?

> Why not his curious, pale, half cold-blooded children, like little fishes of her own? Why not? Everything was possible: and even desirable, once one could see the strangeness of it. Once she could plunge through the wall of the aquarium! Once she could kiss him!
>
> (*LG* 105)

But she cannot. She sees him in Chapel, 'staring away from everything in the world, at heaven knows what—just as fishes stare—then his dishumanness came over her again like an arrest' (*LG* 106). Such passages are comic rather in the popular style of *Mr Noon*, a style Lawrence employed in 1920 and which I discuss in Chapter 7; whether we like the style or not, it is certainly not a style in which much can happen outside the range of the narrator's dominant, flippant rhetoric. The novel is limited to certain kinds of interest in human nature precisely because the rhetoric is itself so rich. Our sense that Albert Witham is impossible for Alvina depends entirely on the narrator's skill and wit, not on any understanding we have of either Witham or of Alvina. The latter does not learn anything from the experience because she is simply sharing the narrator's stand-point. The same is true of James Houghton, one of the novel's real successes. Although Alvina is apparently the sympathetic centre of the book, it is not her business either to understand her father or to communicate her understanding to us. They might just as well be living in separate worlds. James Houghton is a triumph of the narrator's art, with the foam and froth of his 'creative adventure' in women's clothing underpinned by the indestructible shirts made by Mrs Pinnegar; Alvina is a centre used by the narrator rather than a created life. She is, indeed, distant enough for the narrator to engage in a kind of promotional exercise on her behalf which would be inconceivable for any of the other major characters in his novels (with the significant exception of Gilbert Noon).

> Now so far, the story of Alvina is commonplace enough. . . But we protest that Alvina is not ordinary. Ordinary people, ordinary fates. But extraordinary people, extraordinary fates. Or else no fate at all. The all-to-one-pattern modern system is too much for most extraordinary individuals. It just kills them off or throws them disused aside.
>
> (*LG* 107)

Such interventions by the narrator are not a sign of a failure of the novelist; they are natural and even necessary in the kind of narrator-dominated fiction Lawrence is writing in *The Lost Girl*; explicitly comic, the style allows for a good deal of narrative whip and sting, a lot of palpable hits, a lot of witty asides.

The one real exception to this narrative style in the first part of the book is Alvina's mysterious vision of the underworld in Chapter 4, which comes between the deaths of her mother and Miss Frost. She visits the mine Throttle-Ha'penny, and on returning to the surface sees Woodhouse 'like a vision', a world 'bubbling iridescent-golden on the surface of the underworld' (*LG* 64–5). An underworld of miners 'in their enslaved magic' suggests the forces of darkness which, if liberated, 'would cause the superimposed day-order to fall' (*LG* 65). She is clearly having a vision of psychic power as well as of a particular place; she feels that 'what was wanted was a Dark Master from the underworld'. Like Gudrun's vision of Beldover in *Women in Love*, it is a vision of the sources of power and magic, of marvellous and subversive forces in the self and in society. In the novel, it bubbles up for a moment, then vanishes; when Alvina meets Ciccio we have no sense of her as a woman who has had such visions. It is a passage utterly characteristic of Lawrence, but not of the Lawrence of *The Lost Girl*; it is significant that a passage as haunting as this should be so strange in the actual world of the novel.

The forces with which the novel really is concerned come into focus
with the advent of the Natcha-Kee-Tawara troupe; but along with
them comes a typical character in *The Lost Girl*—Mr May, a splendid
comic character of almost entirely incidental importance to the book,
whose one apparent intervention in the action is ludicrously incredible.
He is supposed to instigate a system of private detectives to follow
Alvina when she joins the troupe, because of the danger of her falling
into the White Slave traffic. The episode is both clumsy and absurd,
but because Mr May is so essentially unimportant a character he can
be used for it. Like Molly Bloom, the narrator obviously feels 'well as
well him as another'.[5] The Natchas, however, are the first sustained
indication of the book's aspiring to another kind of interest than the
incisively comic. They are spread rather thickly over the central
section, but it is not their presence so much as their language which
makes difficulties for us. They present something of the same problem
as Mellors' dialect in *Lady Chatterley's Lover*; how seriously should we take
the pseudo-Red-Indian in which they talk? Madame, to be sure, uses the
language as a cover for her feelings. But, for instance, in the ceremony of
admitting Alvina to the tribe, it is first used with a kind of double-edged
irony—so that her new name changes from Vaali to Viale, and thus to
L'Allée and Allaye. Alvina is being set up as mistress for Ciccio, and all the
talk of 'Stoop, stoop Allaye, beneath the wings of Pacohuila' (*LG* 242) is
only a jocular and slightly sinister way of admitting it, and disguising it at
the same time. 'The ragged chant of strong male voices' is 'resonant and
gay with mockery' (*LG* 240); like Mellors' dialect it is also an isolating and
destructive mockery. But then, it also sounds as if the tribe does, after
all, believe in its pseudo-Red-Indian: 'WE ARE THE
HIRONDELLES' (*LG* 241) they chant, with no trace of mockery. It is
a male language for the tribe, with Madame (as mother) speaking it to
keep them together; it is also, like the whole affair of the troupe,
palpably something the narrator enjoys relaying. It takes wing from the
Red Indian language and style which Lawrence had found in the
Fenimore Cooper books he enjoyed so much (the actor in the bear's
skin being taken directly from *The Last of the Mohicans*); but he actually
uses them exactly as Dickens uses Sleary's Horse-Riding in *Hard
Times*—to suggest art, gesture, instinct, melodrama and passion,
combined in an unsentimentalised and slightly raffish outfit, and
meaning more than the slightly childish outward appearance would
suggest. The members of the troupe are, significantly,
European—French, German, Italian, Swiss—and their natural
language is gesture. As in *Hard Times* we have the contrast between the
'solid permanent fact' of Woodhouse and the troupe's liberation of
feeling. We see Ciccio, 'on his bay horse with a green seat, flickering
hither and thither in the rear, his feathers swaying, his horse sweating,

his face ghastlily smiling in its war-paint' (*LG* 174); the troupe is more than histrionic, it expresses the deeper feelings which Woodhouse hates (and hates the Natchas for expressing). It shows cruelty as well as love, malice as well as yearning, sensuality and sexuality. Lawrence perhaps over-uses the Natchas because they allow him to make so many of the points which could not be made by the ironic narrator; they are continually symbolic. The novel tends to mark time during the central section while they symbolise the same kind of things for over a hundred pages. But, as usual, the narrator directs their exits and their entrances just so long as he feels they will serve his purpose. And the novelist determined to produce a 'popular' novel perhaps finds it natural to draw from writers as successful as Dickens and Cooper.

But the creation of a relationship between Alvina and Ciccio, which is part of the dramatic function of the troupe in Woodhouse, also exhibits a major weakness; the book presents a relationship between two symbolic representatives rather than between two human natures. It needs to demonstrate a relationship which it has neither developed nor explored. It shows us Alvina after she and Ciccio have made love, going back to her washing-up:

> Her inside burned with love for him: so elusive, so beautiful, in his silent passing out of her sight. She wiped her dishes happily. Why was she so absurdly happy, she asked herself? And why did she still fight so hard against the sense of his dark, unseizable beauty? Unseizable, forever unseizable! That made her almost his slave. She fought against her own desire to fall at his feet. Ridiculous to be so happy.
>
> (*LG* 280)

Katherine Mansfield's criticisms of the novel were written out of a total lack of sympathy with it: but she was outraged as an artist by this scene. 'Take the scene where the hero throws her in the kitchen, possesses her, and she returns singing to the washing up. It's a *disgrace*' (*Nehls* ii 52). 'His hero and heroine are non-human,' she remarked; immediately after this scene Alvina forgets all about her desire to 'fall at his feet', answers an advertisement, and within twenty pages is working as a nurse in Lancaster. We are not invited to understand why she behaves as she does. We can, indeed, discuss her recoil from an over-reaction to Ciccio; we can decide that her enslavement is a stage she has to get over; but the important thing is that the novel does not talk like that. It splits them up, then reunites them when she hears him singing; they behave as creatures of the novel, not as characters in it.

This is particularly disturbing because at such a point Lawrence is entering on just that territory which he had made peculiarly his own, in the novel: the perception and presentation of what it is that makes a relationship possible or impossible. It is something we are aware of continually in *The Rainbow* and in *Women in Love*, but we can see it clearly too in as odd a novel as *Aaron's Rod*, in the relationships of Aaron with Lottie and with the Marchesa. Lawrence explores the bare fringes of this territory in *The Lost Girl* when he offers a character like Albert Witham; but his mind is too firmly made up about Ciccio and Alvina to allow him any room for exploration. There is no possibility of 'the flow of our sympathetic consciousness' (*LCL* 104) in us towards the characters or their modes of feeling during the first two-thirds of the book. Instead, we are on a conducted tour.

If, in fact, we consider *The Lost Girl* simply in terms of the things which we know interested Lawrence in the early twenties, it is striking how thinly it copes with them. The idea of male friendship is there, but never gets much further than exclamations like those of Geoffrey to Ciccio at the Gare de Lyon: 'I shall never see thee again, brother, my brother!' (*LG* 349). The Natchas are a kind of illuminated exhibition of things which Lawrence feels are important; but they are also repetitive and sometimes boring. The idea of male dominance which haunted Lawrence in the twenties is there, too, but only in the form of a dominant man who finds no real resistance in his woman. The idea of both men and women going beyond marriage into a fuller relationship with the world beyond them, and with each other, is not important in this novel. Lawrence's sense of the situation of the individual set against a mass society, which had been made explicit for him by the War, again barely enters this book, although it is the only one of his novels in which the main action extends into the period of War. The problem of the individual isolated in a community which is also naturally his own—like Gudrun, or Birkin, or Aaron—is hardly important in the case even of Alvina. And although the novel would appear to answer the charge made by many critics that Lawrence habitually damages his novels by making them preach and prophesy—and, indeed, in 1930 F. R. Leavis, conscious of just that charge, suggested that *The Lost Girl* was Lawrence's 'best *novel*'[6]—yet its narrative of events largely untouched by 'thought-adventure' suggests the very weakness of a Lawrence novel which does not create that habit in its characters, in order to provoke it in its readers. *The Lost Girl* is curiously undynamic in its relation with us; its narrative method tells us what should interest us, and displays wit and irony of an attractive kind as it makes its demonstrations. But for most of the first two thirds of the book it falls into the trap of its own easiness, and has a weaker effect than we might have imagined. Carl Hovey noticed this in 1920, when he was trying to view the book as a potential serial; he told Robert Mountsier that it was 'by way of being wonderful in details' but, oddly enough, 'it does not carry a great effect as a whole'.[7] Its easiness is obviously partly a result of being made deliberately popular: we should remember Lawrence's own sense that 'one withdraws awhile from battle'—*The Lost Girl* is not a book that sets out to challenge its readers much.

However, bringing Alvina and Ciccio together is more effective than we might have expected. I have already suggested the strangeness of the novel's attitude towards England, as Ciccio and Alvina leave it. What is striking in that passage, and thereafter, is that Alvina is allowed to see and to experience with the acuteness of the narrator himself. The same is true of the journey across Europe; the narrator vanishes, the experience becomes that of Alvina at first hand. And, fortified by Lawrence's characteristic genius in reporting travel, the journey takes on symbolic proportions of its own: 'for the first time she realised what it was to escape from the smallish perfection of England, into the grander imperfection of a great continent' (*LG* 351). Her growing tiredness, set against the increasing magic of what she sees, culminates in the final uphill struggle to Califano itself, and the ultimate contrast between the squalor of the house with the mountains outside, 'glimmering and marvellous in the evanescent night' (*LG* 369). Her journey from one world to another ends in cold terror, that first night; horror at the cold, at Ciccio, at being 'lost—lost utterly' possesses her.

> Then deliberately she got out of bed, and went across to him. He was horrible and frightening, but he was warm. She felt his power and his warmth invade her and extinguish her. The mad and desperate passion that was in him sent her completely unconscious again, completely unconscious.
>
> (*LG* 370)

It is an almost identical situation and experience to that of Dollie Urquart in Lawrence's later story 'The Princess', when—in terror of the cold and the wildness of *her* place among the mountains—she turns to Romero for warmth. The huge difference is that, unlike the Princess, Alvina does not keep herself to herself, even in extremity. She recognises that giving herself to him like this has the force of a marriage bond. The episode is a fitting end to a chapter which contains the first deeply interesting experiences Alvina has had in *The Lost Girl*; it is the other-worldliness of her whole experience, not just Ciccio's passion, which makes her for the first time 'unconscious'. The symbolic chapter has this inevitable ending.

In such an experience, the first words of the next chapter inform us, 'There is no mistake about it, Alvina was a lost girl' (*LG* 370). 'She's not morally lost, poor darling' (12 v 1920), Lawrence reassured Catherine Carswell, though obviously he liked the *risqué* title. Alvina is lost to her previous experience, but in a way that, paradoxically, is more important than being found or known. She is both exhilarated by the beauty and magic, and drained by a place as hostile as it is beautiful. It seems to destroy her past, it denies her future, it attacks the self she has always been. She experiences the things which, together, her upbringing and England have protected her from; passion, the loss of significant language, a violent and non-Christian past. It is a 'strange valley of shadow' which she is now 'threading' (*LG* 379); the image is appropriately that of a dangerous pilgrimage. She is 'beyond herself'; as well as being realistically dirty and alien, Califano is also the place of an obscure spiritual testing, in which Alvina lapses away from the self she has always been. She would lose herself finally if she stayed there—'she could never endure it for a life-time' (*LG* 378)—but she submits to place and experience as if instinctively recognising its importance. She submits as she submits to Ciccio, with a 'sort of acquiescent passion' (*LG* 378). Ciccio almost vanishes from her everyday consciousness; he is a figure seen ploughing in the distance, or walking through a room engaged in some unknown task. And then, suddenly, he is kissing her—and that, too, is 'a strange valley of shadow'. In Califano Alvina grows aware of her own capacity to respond unconsciously and instinctively.

In such ways, the last three chapters of *The Lost Girl* are exploratory in a way that the rest of the novel has not been. As so often in Lawrence's novels, the very end of the book reaches out to say things—perhaps obscurely—which are the fruit of the whole book's experience, but which have, strictly, little place in it. In the last chapter, again, Ciccio suddenly changes; he talks to the men of Pescocalascio about politics, about religion, and fiercely excludes Alvina from his male world. There had been no evidence of his having any interests beyond bicycling and mandoline playing, in Woodhouse. But in Pescocalascio he suddenly foreshadows men like Aaron and Lilly; the novel is just starting to reach out for ideas about a man's world, and masculine dominance, which are to become so important in *Aaron's Rod* and *Kangaroo*. The last three chapters of the novel are striking because they start to behave as characteristic Lawrence novels do—provocatively, in a dynamic relationship with their characters and their audience. Most of the book had dealt with matters which its wit had encouraged us to think of as thoroughly comprehensible. But as Alvina goes into her new, mysterious experiences at the end, Lawrence goes so far as to refer to her 'mediumistic soul' (*LG* 372). She goes like a clairvoyant into those experiences. It is an altogether unsupported assertion about Alvina's character, but obviously Lawrence was starting to feel that she could be a medium for his own revelations.

Another potential development in the book is its attitude to the War. For once, Lawrence is dealing with people whose lives are directly affected by war; the men face conscription, the wives and children face loneliness at home. That war of troops and army conscription never happens in *Women in Love* (though other sorts of conscription do); neither Lilly nor Aaron has to go through the war, Somers is rejected. Only Mellors, in the novels, is actually called-up; and he is grateful for a chance to get away from his wife Bertha. Ciccio, however, actually faces conscription, and Alvina will be left behind expecting a baby. There is a strange new note in his anger with the 'them' who are responsible:

> 'I'll come back, Allaye,' he said quietly. 'Be damned to them all.'
> She heard unspeakable pain in his voice.
> 'To whom?' she said, sitting up.
> He did not answer, but put his arms round her.
> 'I'll come back, and we'll go to America,' he said.
>
> (*LG* 400)

Ciccio is starting to be aware of that outside world of compulsion which up to this point both he and the novel have avoided—though it is the world of Lawrence's protagonists from Ursula onwards. Here, it is unprepared for, and it ends with the ending of the novel half a page later. The war—which could have been vital for a narrative starting in 1913, 'the last calm year of plenty' (*LG* 11)—has not, after all, been the focus of the individual's relationship with his world. At the end it is only a belated *deus ex machina*.

For a novel written in hopes of commercial success, *The Lost Girl* did not do very well—at least in England. It was not serialised in either England or America, and its first printing in England of 4000 copies took four years to sell out. It was awarded the James Tait Black prize for fiction (which brought in £100), but it must have been ironical for Lawrence that *The Lost Girl* should be awarded such a prize in the year of *Women in Love*'s publication. It only just obtained the backing of the library market which Secker's print order of 4000 had been designed to supply; and it obtained no more orders from the libraries after their initial purchase. Lawrence's attitude to the finished work may be judged by his uncomplaining compliance with Secker's urgent request for him to rewrite a page which the libraries objected to (and which would have jeopardised the whole of their order). Two years later he resisted all attempts by Seltzer to make him change a few passages in *Aaron's Rod*, and the changes he made to *Women in Love* because of threats by Philip Heseltine were done very angrily and carelessly. But he rewrote the page of *The Lost Girl* without a murmur; his diary records the event dispassionately, and his only comment to Secker was 'Put not your trust in the British public' (10 xi 1920). Again, he was prepared to tolerate Secker's apprehension about the title *The Lost Girl*; Secker preferred the alternative *Bitter Cherry*, and Lawrence was prepared to accept that, so long as the title *Women in Love* (which also worried Secker) remained unchanged. The suggestion Lawrence made about *The Lost Girl* as a title indicates his attitude to the book: 'More selling, I'm sure' (31 v 1920). But, as he confessed to Koteliansky when the book finally appeared, 'I am not wildly interested in it' (03 xii 1920). Immediately on finishing it, indeed, he had told Mackenzie that he was not sure of the direction it had taken. Mackenzie's Sylvia Scarlett had, he thought, been wrong in looking for something permanent in relationship—at least his Alvina had a 'questing soul'—but, all the same, 'I believe neither of us has found a way out of the labyrinth. How we hang on to the marriage clue! Doubt if it's really a way out' (10 v 1920). *The Lost Girl* does tend to treat marriage as if it were 'a way out'—until those final chapters.

The Lost Girl is a paradoxical novel in that its strengths of description, wit and irony, and local comedy, are its least forward looking or exploratory feature; while its exploratory parts are arbitrary and abbreviated. It is clear that Lawrence knew this; when he reread the novel in typescript, he observed that 'It's different from all my other work: not immediate, not intimate—except the last bit: all set across a distance. It just came like that' (11 vi 1920). The distance it was 'set across', of course, was the gap which was opening between Lawrence and the England he had recently left—not simply the geographical gap, but the gap between the community of which he wrote, and which he remembered so well as to re-create it in extraordinary detail in *The Lost Girl*—and the deliberate isolation from it which he was imposing on himself. *The Lost Girl* looks back to, and lovingly re-creates, a pre-war England; but it is also a novel straddled across a sense of England which had changed vitally in Lawrence, during the last seven years. To bridge the gap which he himself had opened between that England, and the England in which he now no longer had any belief, Lawrence developed a kind of jocular, popular, narrative style: as if to assert that, if he chose to, he could indeed appeal to a public. The style itself, though, is a voice which grows lonelier the longer we listen to it. *The Lost Girl* does not simply represent Lawrence's attempt to write a commercially successful novel; it reveals the tenuousness of his links with the very community he knew best in the world, at the same time as it shows his amazing recall of it. The novel only takes wing when it escapes the 'coffin' of England, and is able to develop ideas that have no roots in the life which up to then it has shown. It is the revealing final paradox of *The Lost Girl* that, in it, Lawrence should write best of things which, on the one hand, he had left behind totally—and of things which, on the other hand, he could not show he believed in.

7 Aaron's Rod

The form *Aaron's Rod* takes is that of a journey or progression: in time, in place, above all in ideas. Geographically, it moves from a small mining community in the English Midlands, via London, to Novara, Milan and Florence; its final action takes place, however, in the recesses of a soul. It moves from a conventional scene of settled married life to the brief amours of a smart metropolitan set; to upper-class living in gentility and wealth, and thence to the cosmopolitan life of an American Marchesa; but it ends with two men alone. It moves very deliberately from the old world of England just recovering itself after the war, through a bright metropolitan world attached to the old as if the war had never been, to a rootless world of expatriate living, finally through a world which is literally exploded to a 'nowhere' of mystic relationship. Aaron, the man who makes all these journeys, starts as a checkweighman and secretary of his local Union branch; but he finally accepts the role of follower in a relationship which seems to have no existence in society at all. All these progressions give *Aaron's Rod* its structure; it is a novel concerned to move its hero (and us) through a sequence of ideas and significant experiences which get increasingly remote from conventional domesticity; and which finally sets us down outside our community, our culture, our expectations and our society, altogether.

It has, of course, had a bad press. At best, it has been seen as picaresque; usually it has been criticised as quite formless. Daleski writes of the 'flabby flesh of its structure',[1] Alcorn sees it as 'one of Lawrence's most uneven and ill-organised books'.[2] 'When we consider the technical brilliance and originality of *The Rainbow* and of *Women in Love*, we can only conclude that Lawrence is no no longer concerned with form in the novel'.[3] Eliseo Vivas writes of its 'technical clumsiness';[4] Keith Sagar, in 1966, was damning: 'The novelist to a large extent shares the doubts and vacillations of his characters. The vision of disintegration has overwhelmed the integrity of the artist, which cannot create firm values out of the chaos he contemplates.'[5] The odd thing for a novel apparently so confused and despairing is that Lawrence obviously believed in it as serious, and as saying something he particularly wanted to say: 'It is the last of my serious English novels—the end of The Rainbow, Women in Love line. It had to be written—and had to come to such an end' (08 x 1921). He obviously thought it progressed to some point, even if that point were the end of a road.

118

What has made critics more confident in their judgement of the novel as clumsy or disorganised has been their knowledge of the way it was written. They look at the sustained creative effort which gave rise to *The Rainbow* and *Women in Love*, and are a little shocked to find that it took Lawrence over three years to write *Aaron's Rod*—and that he wrote it spasmodically. What would be natural in another writer is, in Lawrence's case, taken as damning evidence of his unconcern. But the history of *Aaron's Rod* is, anyway, complicated by the circumstances of its start.

Lawrence began it sometime between October 1917 and February 1918, but probably not before moving to Berkshire in January. The important thing about this date, however, is that *Women in Love* had for over a year utterly failed to find a publisher in either America or in England; and, of course, *The Rainbow* too counted almost as an unpublished novel. Lawrence had no publisher interested in his work; to start another novel in that situation is, therefore, the astonishing thing, not the fact that it went spasmodically. 'I am doing . . . another daft novel. It goes slowly—very slowly and fitfully. But I don't care' (21 ii 1918). There was very little point in caring; it was 'another daft novel' because that was how publishers, and even friends, had seen *Women in Love*. All novels were daft at *that* moment in time. Surprisingly, he was still 'slowly working' at it in September 1918, 'though I feel it's not much use. No publisher will risk my last, and none will risk this, I expect. I can't do anything in the world today—am just choked.—I don't know how on earth we shall get through another winter—how we shall ever find a future' (1 Kix 1918). He does not seem to have done any work on it during 1919—which was, for Lawrence, a year in which he painstakingly tried to make enough money to leave England; a third unpublishable novel would not have helped him. It is significant that when he found publishers interested in his work again (Secker, Seltzer and, as it turned out, Huebsch, were all considering *Women in Love* by the end of 1919), he did not go back to *Aaron's Rod* but, as I pointed out, made himself agreeable by offering the old 'Insurrection' as 'a perfect selling novel' (27 xii 1919). *Aaron's Rod*, however little of it had so far been written, clearly could not be manipulated into being popular.

Lawrence did, however, either actually start work on it again, or at least plan to, within two months of finishing *The Lost Girl* in the summer of 1920. He told Secker in mid-July that 'I have got it ⅓ done, and it is very amusing. But it stands still just now, awaiting events. Once it starts again it will steam ahead' (18 vii 1920). He moved it on a little further during September 1920: 'I did more than half of *Aaron's Rod*, but can't end it: the flowering end missing, I suppose—so I began a comedy which I hope will end' (29 xi 1920). The 'comedy' was the novel *Mr Noon*—which turned out to be, in the end, 'rather impossible only

funny' (12 vi 1921). With its first part set entirely in the England of
Lawrence's own adolescence, it clearly did not stand in need of 'events'
to supply it. It was designed to be in three parts: up to 1913, up to 1914,
and ending in 1919. And yet it was not, apparently, as important to
Lawrence as *Aaron's Rod* was; 'funny, but a hair-raiser' (04 iv 1921), it
attracted him simply because it *was* outrageous. He wrote it with great
glee—with a continual acid and insinuating commentary on small-town
bourgeois morals and traditional habits of marriage. It was obviously
easier to write than *Aaron's Rod*. I suspect that if *Aaron's Rod* had really
been as spasmodic and picaresque as critics have suggested, Lawrence
could have found plenty of material and humour for it, just as he found
them for the scandalous other novel. The way *Aaron's Rod* alternated
with *Mr Noon*, indeed, suggests that the comic-outrageous style of the
latter literally could not mix with the satiric-serious style of the former.
Mr Noon was started in May 1920; *Aaron's Rod* was worked on during
July and September, *Mr Noon* in December and January, *Aaron's Rod* in
May 1921. And however easily he wrote it, Lawrence never did finish
Mr Noon, and made no real efforts to have it published. *Aaron's Rod* he
ended by being determined to make it end; and he insisted on its
publication too.

He finished it, indeed, in a little over a month; and he insisted to both
his American and his English publishers how serious it was—though
he was sure they would not like it. 'I will have the book published. It is
my last word in one certain direction' (10 xi 1921). We can further
distinguish it from *The Lost Girl*, and from the uneasy rag-bag it has so
often been thought to be, by noting Lawrence's obstinacy in making
changes in it for Seltzer—a publisher he was particularly grateful to
and whom he had no wish to offend. Seltzer had asked for changes: but

> the essential scenes of Aaron and the Marchesa it is impossible to me
> to alter. With all the good-will towards you and the general public
> that I am capable of, I can no more alter those chapters than if they
> were cast-iron. You can lift out whole chunks if you like. You can
> smash them if you like. But you can no more alter them than you can
> alter cast iron.
>
> (14 i 1922)

Lawrence was not acting on a point of principle; he had tried on at least
two occasions to make the changes Seltzer was asking for. But the book
was itself, and not to be changed.

And he knew it would not be popular. Neither his American nor his
English agents liked it. 'Everybody hated *Aaron's Rod*—even Frieda'
(15 xi 1921), he told Donald Carswell. But 'it is what I mean, for the
moment' (30 vii 1921) he told Seltzer; it was what he *meant* that he
knew would not be liked. To begin with, the novel chronicles the life of
a man who abandons his wife and two small children, without a word,

and walks off into the night. True, he makes sure they have some money—he has a legacy they can live off. But when that is exhausted, 'she must look out for herself' (*AR* 176). 'I call that almost criminal selfishness,' says the man he is talking to. 'I can't help it,' replies Aaron. That is an insistence which the novel makes as well as Aaron; he has to do what he does.

It is a striking way to start a novel: especially as the whole first chapter goes by, in vivid detail, without us knowing that this domestic scene is Aaron's last night at home. And yet the chapter has an uncanny ability to separate Aaron from his surroundings. It proceeds as a sequence of sense impressions as well as a narrative of events. We know that Aaron is putting a Christmas-tree in its pot, is carrying it in, is talking to his wife; but we are aware of an inner stillness, of the sound and touch of the Christmas-tree branches, the feel of the cold air to a man with no coat on; the sound of water dropping into a bowl, the 'curious soft explosion' of the blue ball breaking, the stream of cold air from the ventilator, the rush of sound from the flute. The sequence cuts off Aaron's inner life from the normal domestic scene around him; we feel what it is really like to be him in this situation, and his wife's remarks about the Union—or the quarrelling of his children—or Millicent's kind of attention-seeking—are simply a surrounding noise. His life goes on in the middle of them, anyway. His dourness, though, is comic, like his perverse refusal to buy Christmas-tree candles except when sure the shop has none; both are defences against this thoroughly ordinary life. 'The war was over, and everything just the same. The acute familiarity of this house, which he had built for his marriage twelve years ago, the changeless pleasantness of it all seemed unthinkable. It prevented his thinking' (*AR* 19). This is the world which Lawrence decides Aaron should simply walk away from. The novel is as perverse and as obstinate as Aaron himself. It gives no more explanation for his behaviour than the feelings I have just indicated. Aaron and his wife bicker, but they get on as well as most couples. The children are irritating, but small children *are* 'tiresome and amusing in turns' (*AR* 122). His Union is arguing pointlessly; but that is the nature of such things. Aaron's stillness, his separateness, suggest another world, however: a world of his own.

In a way, *Aaron's Rod* is taking up an idea which had been lying dormant in Lawrence's work for eight years. Aaron does what Mr Morel in *Sons and Lovers* threatened to do to his family: walk out on his security and on theirs. Just a year after completing *Aaron's Rod*, Lawrence told the Brewsters how 'he had not done justice to his father in *Sons and Lovers* and felt like rewriting it', and how he now saw in his father an 'unquenchable fire and relish for living' (*Nehls* ii 126). In *Sons and Lovers*, the father has not the spirit to carry out his threat to leave: 'he had not even the courage to carry his bundle beyond the yard-end'

(*SL* 59). But, even in the earlier novel, we know something of his reasons for wanting to leave: 'He was shut out from all family affairs. No-one told him anything . . . as soon as the father came in, everything stopped. He was like the scotch in the smooth, happy machinery of the home' (*SL* 81). By contrast, Aaron fits very well into the family and the home. He actually puts the children's Christmas-tree in its pot before he has his dinner—we should compare Mr Morel eating his dinner before going upstairs to see his wife and the baby born that day. But Aaron shows us what it is to suffer from 'the smooth happy machinery of the home', not just to operate it. 'When you've had enough,' he says, 'you go away and you don't care what you do' (*AR* 152). Mr Morel may have had more than enough, but it is Aaron who leaves. The whole viewpoint of the novel has changed, from the position of moral superiority which the earlier book adopts towards Mr Morel, to the idea of a man doing what he really wants in the later book. By making Aaron a hero rather than a moral example, and by offering no more conventional explanation for his going, and by making him so consciously uncaring, Lawrence—and the novel—are making a statement about the real nature of the individual's life in his society. So far as society is concerned, Aaron is thoroughly reprehensible—doing what Lawrence described to the Brewsters as 'misbehaving and putting ten fingers to his nose at everything' (08 v 1921).[6] He is bad-tempered, comic and perverse; but he trusts the strength of his feelings.

And *Aaron's Rod* is the kind of novel which demands that we, too, should trust them. On three occasions in the novel, people ask Aaron directly why he abandoned his family: Josephine Ford, Sir William Franks, and finally Aaron himself. Interestingly, Lilly never asks. Nor does Aaron's wife; what she says is, 'Tell me what you have against me' (*AR* 151). She feels irresistibly that his leaving home must be an attack on her, and that is the only way she sees it. But Aaron clearly did not leave home as a result of his feelings about her—only two chapters from the end he is still feeling that 'I am married to Lottie. And that means I can't be married to another woman' (*AR* 310). He leaves home in response to instincts—about love, about singleness—which both he and the novel only gradually come to realise. He has no answer which could satisfy the curiosity of a Josephine Ford or a Sir William Franks. Josephine, because it is her nature, assumes that the answer must be to do with love, either lost or sought; and Sir William, having tried the obvious solutions—'Not that you loved any other woman?' 'You just left off loving?' 'Mere caprice?'—can only fall back on 'Well, well! Well, well! Life! Life! Young men are a new thing to me!' (*AR* 176–7). 'I went away . . . from it all,' (*AR* 176) is what Aaron says, and that is what the novel rests on too. It is taking a considerable risk in so doing; the England which Aaron has to get away from is only sketched in the masterly first chapters, and in the London scenes. But the novel is as obstinate as Aaron in not providing us with scenes of psychological or eschatological horror for Aaron to run from. It assumes that normal family life, English style, and the normal cultivated world, metropolitan style, are enough, given the attitude women have and which we see particularly in 'More Pillar of Salt'. It is as if Lawrence, believing in the escape first and foremost, chooses to show Aaron making it from a situation of placid conventional responsibility—in order to insist that it is *that* important.

Lottie's attitude is clear in 'More Pillar of Salt'. To start talking to her, in her way, is to accept that marriage is an emotional battle of wills. It is also clear that she wants neither explanation nor quarrel. She wants submission. For his part, Aaron—after his first nostalgia for love and marriage—is incapable of responding to her unspoken appeal. ' "What have you come for?" she cried again, with a voice full of hate. Or perhaps it was fear and doubt and even hope as well. He heard only hate' (*AR* 149–50). Aaron has gone back out of tenderness and half-admitted love; like his house, his marriage appeals to him as a kind of refuge, a place for the return to old feelings, to the old way of life. Like Lot's wife, he looks back. But when he thinks back to the episode later on, he finds

> The illusion of love was gone for ever. Love was a battle in which each party strove for the mastery of the other's soul. So far, man had yielded the mastery to woman. Now he was fighting for it back again. And too late, for the woman would never yield.
>
> (*AR* 155)

The chapter ends with him vowing 'life single, not life double'. 'To be alone . . . surely it is better than anything' (*AR* 155). And in that frame of mind he leaves England and goes to Novara; the 'it all' which he tells Sir William he has left behind is the state of marriage, of relationship, in his society.

I imagine that most readers will protest at this point (if not before). I think the novel is designed to make us protest. After all, what it is effectively saying is absolutely the reverse of the conventional analysis of marriage and the relationship of the sexes in the twentieth century. Marriage in our culture has been traditionally male-oriented; the man has been free to pursue his own life (whatever that involves) and the woman has had to take responsibility for home and children. Aaron himself apparently has such a marriage; when he thinks back over it, he remembers Sunday evenings at home: 'At this hour he himself would be dressed in his best clothes, tying his bow, ready to go out to the public house. And his wife would be resenting his holiday departure, whilst she was left fastened to the children' (*AR* 191). And in the first

124   *D. H. Lawrence and the Idea of the Novel*

chapter, too, it had been Aaron who went to the pub while Lottie stayed in:

> 'There's no knowing what time you'll be home,' she said.
> 'I shan't be late,' he answered.
> 'It's easy to say so,' she retorted, with some contempt.
> He took his stick, and turned towards the door.
> 'Bring the children some candles for their tree, and don't be so selfish,' she said.
> 'All right,' he said, going out.
> 'Don't say *All right* if you never mean to do it,' she cried, with sudden anger, following him to the door.
>
> (*AR* 22)

She is right to be angry: he does not mean to do it. Most readers would sympathise with her anger, and with her attempt to boss him about—after all, he is still going out. But Aaron condemns his wife for her judgement of him, for wanting power over him, for making love a battle-ground. And the novel makes absolutely no attempt to justify Aaron, beyond giving him the kind of soliloquies from which I have already quoted; indeed, it shows him disliking his own obstinacy: 'he hated the hard, inviolable heart that stuck unchanging in his own breast' (*AR* 57). But the novel refuses to be conventionally moral about what he should, or should not, be to his wife and to women in general; it insists that, deeper than middle-class morality, is a self-contained individual self which *must* not be violated. Aaron may be obstinate, unfeeling, even hateful. Very well then—so be it. It may not be just or fair to the woman, but there it is. The man *must* resist.

And *Aaron's Rod* is far more interested in such resistance than it is in analysing the causes of marital tension in early twentieth-century England. Fairness or unfairness to women, to children, to marriage—to Hindu doctors saying unexceptionally liberal things about the British in India, to landladies being warm and friendly—is simply less important. Aaron finds himself disliking 'the whole circumstances' (*AR* 32); the novel strikes out in its own new direction. This, of course, is one of the ways in which *Aaron's Rod* is the end of the line of Lawrence's novels up to 1922. It marks the end of the kind of concern with marriage which had dominated his novel-writing since early in 1913. 'I'll do my life work, sticking up for the love between man and woman' (25 xii 1912), he had written then. Even *Women in Love* had created a strong and even loving relationship between Birkin and Ursula, to stand them in good stead during the end of the old world which the novel continually suggests. *Aaron's Rod* refuses to do that; it finds the tensions of sexual relationships outweighing both love and hope. Lawrence remarked about the novel, while revising it, that 'I like it, because it kicks against the pricks' (30 vii 1921); its first part, at least, is both obstinate and asexual. It has a peculiar confidence in what it is saying, however much we may object to it. Some of the confidence, certainly, is that of deliberate perversity; it shouts, in order to deafen us. Yet it does speak (or shout) with a different kind of voice from novels like *The Rainbow* or *Women in Love*—of that there is no doubt, either; I wish to pursue the nature of that difference.

In the 'Foreword' to *Fantasia of the Unconscious*, Lawrence offered a distinction between his fiction and his essays:

> The novels and poems come unwatched out of one's pen. And then the absolute need which one has for some sort of satisfactory mental attitude towards oneself and things in general makes one try to abstract some definite conclusions from one's experiences as a writer and as a man. The novels and poems are pure passionate experience. These 'pollyanalytics' are inferences made afterwards, from the experience.
>
> (*Fantasia* 15)

He wrote the *Fantasia* at Baden-Baden in the summer of 1921, just after finishing *Aaron's Rod* there; the 'Foreword' was written in the autumn. He began a Venetian novel in September, but it seems not to have got very far; *Aaron's Rod* is undoubtedly the best example of passionate experience immediately preceding the *Fantasia*—especially as Lawrence himself remarked that he only wrote two poems in the whole of the summer (09 x 1921). *Aaron's Rod* hardly came 'unwatched' from Lawrence's pen—it had required a good deal of watching, over the years, to make sure it came at all. But he revised the TS of the novel after finishing the *Fantasia*; and probably revised the TS of the *Fantasia* after that. If the passionate experience of a novel really came first, to be succeeded by a prose development of its ideas, in this case at least the prose exposition could itself have influenced the novel. But is 'passionate experience' really what distinguishes the novel from the *Fantasia*?

There are certainly some obvious links between them. The *Fantasia* shows exactly what Lawrence meant by calling the chapters in which Aaron returns home 'The Pillar of Salt' and 'More Pillar of Salt'; 'never look back. Because if Lot's wife, looking back, was turned to a pillar of salt, these miserable men, for ever looking back to their women for guidance, they are miserable pillars of half-rotten tears' (*Fantasia* 192). Indeed, it sums us all up as Aarons: 'Climb down Pisgah, and go to Jericho. *Allons*, there is no road yet, but we are all Aarons with rods of our own' (*Fantasia* 24). The *Fantasia* insists that 'most fatal, most hateful of all things is bullying' (*Fantasia* 52); Lilly in the novel says 'I think there is only one thing I hate to the verge of madness, and that is *bullying*' (*AR* 328). 'Most men,' says the *Fantasia*, 'are half-born slaves' (*Fantasia* 31); Lilly insists that 'people are not *men* . . . and their destiny is slavery' (*AR* 327). The *Fantasia* asserts: 'Leaders—this is what mankind is craving for' (*Fantasia* 88); Lilly remarks, 'All men say, they want a leader' (*AR* 347). And so on; there is a great number of such parallels; above all, both novel and essay discuss the way men need to resist the ideal love of their wives (and their wives' potential dominance), and need to assert the 'single oneness' (*AR* 343) of the individual, to be 'alone with one's own soul' (*Fantasia* 137).

I think there is no parallel to this identity of essay and novel elsewhere in Lawrence's work. The 'Study of Thomas Hardy' influenced *The Rainbow*, *The Rainbow* influenced 'The Crown', and 'The Crown' influenced *Women in Love*; but beyond one or two small verbal parallels, influence is all we can discuss. *Aaron's Rod* and the *Fantasia* are a different kind of case; we should ask why Lawrence wrote them both, who he wrote them for, and why he should choose to distinguish them in the *Fantasia* 'Foreword'.

The first answer is that they *are* very different; the first and most revealing difference is their manner of approaching their readers. The *Fantasia* is unconcernedly chatty and personal; Lawrence says, about the working man, that 'I would like to save him alive, in his living, spontaneous, original being. I can't help it. It is my passionate instinct' (*Fantasia* 115). On the other hand, he remarks in his 'Foreword', with perfect inconsistency, that 'I really don't want to convince anybody. It is quite in opposition to my whole nature' (*Fantasia* 11). The *Fantasia* is cheerful, sometimes irritatingly facetious; it nudges its reader in the ribs, and then bellows in his ear: 'fight for your life, men' (*Fantasia* 191). It is, indeed, almost entirely oriented to the male reader. Certainly, after a paragraph about men beating their wives out of their damnable self-consciousness (and before several more such paragraphs), it adds: 'Wives, do the same for your husbands' (*Fantasia* 191). But that is purely an afterthought. The *Fantasia* ignores the way in which marriage is a situation *between* two people; it suggests that, if the man regains the proper attitude to it, then the woman—taking a subservient role to her husband, after all—will also have the right attitude. 'Ah, how good it is to come home to your wife when she *believes* in you and submits to your purpose that is beyond her' (*Fantasia* 193). There is nothing about how good it is to be a woman in that situation. The *Fantasia* pushes a point of view just about as far as it will go, offers a certain amount of pseudo-scientific support from ganglia theories—and tries to be cheerful and winning about the matter, too.

But it is Lawrence's first published piece of non-fictional popular writing. His other works of theory or philosophy had either not been intended for publication (like the 'Study') or had not been published (like 'At the Gates'); or, if they had been, like 'Love' and 'Life' in 1918, they had been cool and abstruse. Even the *Fantasia*'s companion piece, *Psychoanalysis and the Unconscious*, written in the winter of 1919–20, had been in a cooler and less popular style. In the early summer of 1920, Lawrence rewrote 'Education of the People' into its present form—it, too, has parallels with *Aaron's Rod*—and that seems to have been his first use of the new style. In his fiction, the popular style is most obvious in *Mr Noon*, which he started in the summer of 1920, though it also gets briefly into *The Lost Girl* (finished in May 1920). It is best characterised by a kind of facetious whimsicality, a continual address direct to the reader, and a good deal of word-play. *Mr Noon* plays on 'spooning': 'Mr Noon was a first-rate spoon—the rhyme is unfortunate, though, in truth, to be a first-rate spoon a man must be something of a poet' (*Phx II* 125). 'Ah, the spoon, the perfect spoon! In its mystic bowl all men are one, and so are all women. . . . If you seek the Infinite and the Nirvana, look not to death nor the after-life, nor yet to pure abstraction; but into the hollow spoon' (*Phx II* 128). The *Fantasia* has nothing quite as gross as this, though the extended soul-in-body-as-damsel-on-bicycle metaphor of Chapter 5, and the love-railway to the New Jerusalem of Chapter 11, are rather wearing. The important thing, however, is not to pick holes but to enquire into reasons.

From 1919 onwards, Lawrence was concerned to establish a reading public of a sufficient size to give him an income enabling him to live and travel as he wanted to. He never made more money than he actually needed—not until 1928, anyway—but he had found it impossible to live by his writing during the War, and his letters about that fact were angry and resentful. From 1919 we can see him looking to America as his potential market and audience; we can also observe him writing carefully, on occasion, for publication. I have pointed out already the origin of *The Lost Girl*. I suggest we can link the advent of what I have called the popular style with this particular approach to an audience. However, from 1919 onwards Lawrence wrote almost nothing while in England; the detailed recreation of English life in *The Lost Girl* and *Mr Noon* is the odder for coming from a man whose dearest wish for the past three years had been to free himself of England, whose book-buying public was largely in North America, and who was to live abroad for all but three and a half months of the remaining eleven years of his life. The combination of the fictional recreation of a world he knew inside out, and the development of a style that rather desperately asserted a connection with his readers which he certainly did not often feel, suggests the kind of contradiction which vitiates *Mr Noon*; and something of the same contradiction gets into most of his works in this immediately post-war period. His attachment to the England he had known, for both his subject and his audience, hardly changed; if anything, it intensified. In 1923 he remarked that his books did not sell in England, only in America. 'But the few Englishmen who do read me, at least understand me' (*Nehls* ii 228). And yet his attachment to England also made him furiously angry; as he wrote in 1921, in *Sea and Sardinia*, 'I must insist that I am a single human being, an individual, not a mere national unit, a mere chip of l'Inghilterra or la Germania. I am not a chip off any nasty old block. I am myself'.[7] And yet, again, a novel is always a product of community, and never simply of an individual. I suggest that the popular style is uneasy precisely because it is, half-jocularly, asserting a link, a common bond, a common awareness, which is actually denied by Lawrence's own genuine feeling of being cut off from England. He would write to Koteliansky shortly before leaving Europe in 1922 that, compared with the days before the War, 'one is eight years older, and a thousand years more disconnected with everything, and more frustrated': he felt 'like you, that I am messing about on the edge of everything' (14 i 1922). The edge was both the southermost tip of Europe, where he was living; and the edge of a community which he both asserted and denied.

Aaron's Rod is the novel rather painfully and slowly written out of this particular realisation; far more, for instance, than *Mr Noon*, it realises this source of trouble. Its English scenes seem to have been written for the most part in England; the trouble it gave during 1920 was in continuing Aaron's progress outside England, for its real theme is how to live as an individual outside the society you know; such a theme grows away from both marriage and society as Lawrence and his English audience knew them.

After Aaron's self-communing in Florence, and his own realisation of this theme, something else happens which indicates what Lawrence is prepared to do with this novel—and which he could not have done with the *Fantasia*. Aaron's meditations have gradually been turning into a kind of tract for the times, and Lawrence makes less and less effort to integrate them into Aaron's actual situation. And then, as if drawing attention to the fact that this excurse beyond the bounds of character and situation can simply be cut off from them, the novel draws a line of dots . . . and returns to a witty and brilliant account of a scene where none of those ideas matters for a second. The novel is a vehicle for the transference of ideas which grow in isolation; but although it may go into the wilderness for the pure contemplation of those ideas, it can also unembarrassedly drop them and apply itself to something else. The *Fantasia* attempts similar casualness; the start of Chapter 4 digresses into a description of the pine woods where it is being written. But it does not make the transition without embarrassment: 'Excuse my digression, gentle reader. At first I left it out, thinking we might not see wood for trees. But it doesn't much matter what we see. It's nice to look round, anywhere' (*Fantasia* 46). And then it plunges into its subject again: 'So there are two planes of being and consciousness. . . .' The novel's obstinacy is more attractive, and its realisation of the isolated character of both Aaron and the ideas is more natural and needs no apology.

Something even more striking had happened three pages earlier in the novel. At that point Aaron's thinking had still been kept in character; he had just realised his freedom outside the idea of himself which he had always had. Now he finds the mask cracked; 'he was at last quiet and free' (*AR* 199). But is not such thinking unnatural for a man whose expressive medium is music, not words? For a moment, the novel hesitates: 'I do but make a translation of the man. He would speak in music. I speak with words' (*AR* 199). But, as if realising that such apologies are no good, it comes clean:

> Don't grumble at me then, gentle reader, and swear at me that this damned fellow wasn't half clever enough to think all these smart things, and realise all these fine-drawn-out subtleties. You are quite right, he wasn't, yet it all resolved in him as I say, and it is for you to prove that it didn't.
>
> (*AR* 199)

The novel not only makes no attempt to cover up the gap which has widened between the created character and the thoughts offered as his experience; it actually attacks the reader for bothering about it. Even the address 'gentle reader', so frequently used in both *Fantasia* and *Mr Noon* for the irony of the old-fashioned mode—gentility is precisely the quality which will be most outraged by such works—is here barely ingratiating. In effect it says that 'gentle reader' novels are not the point; that this is the kind of novel where Aaron's experience is vital and symbolic, so that we had better get on with it, and stop bothering.

The passage has annoyed or saddened most critics. It makes Vivas say that 'the machinery creaks disgracefully'[8]—but what machinery? Sagar doesn't like Lawrence's 'self-conscious apologies to the reader'[9]—but Lawrence is *not* apologising, here. It makes Daleski gloomy about Lawrence's 'weakness'; he 'is no genial Thackeray'.[10] Absolutely right, he is not, and this novel is going its own sweet way regardless of geniality. Like the other so-called 'admission' by the novelist at the end of Chapter 18, the passage is surely a clear warning to the reader about the kind of book this is. Aaron writes a letter to his Novara host: it is an outspoken, rather objectionably self-centred letter. 'Well, here was a letter for a poor old man to receive. But, in the dryness of his withered mind, Aaron got it out of himself. When a man writes a letter to himself, it is a pity to post it to somebody else. Perhaps the same is true of a book' (*AR* 308). Is it really 'a pity' that we are reading this book? There is a lot of irony in the remark. Given the lengthy gestation period of the novel, and the time Lawrence had the TS on his hands during the late summer of 1921— when he made a good many corrections—he could easily have ironed out these problematic passages if he really thought them 'a pity'. But their obstinacy is their strength; the book, they agree, is personal and one-sided. But they offer moments of a far more genuine contact between work and reader than the pleasing, nudging whimsicalities of the *Fantasia*. *Aaron's Rod* is, perversely, better at developing contact with an audience; that is what I meant by suggesting that it was, in part at least, written out of Lawrence's realisation of his predicament as an artist. It is a novel unashamed of its obstinacy, as well as a novel astringently insistent on saying its say; 'they've got to swallow it sooner or later' (24 i 1922), Lawrence wrote to Catherine Carswell about it.

Aaron's Rod has, too, no time for the idea that novels should balance and qualify their insights; it clearly wants us to register Lilly's claim that people should 'submit to a bit of healthy individual authority' (*AR* 119), and it offers him as that authority. It also shows him having his wind knocked out of him by a man who will not submit. But this is not to demonstrate prophecy balanced against realism, outrageous statements about submission qualified by punches thrown to the midriff. If Jim Bricknell punches Lilly, then—momentarily—good for him: as Birkin feels when Hermione biffs him. But Jim Bricknell vanishes with that chapter; not because Lawrence forgets about him, but because he has no more to offer Lilly, or the novel, than his moment of protest and his monomaniacal self-indulgence. The self-indulgence is comic and the protest may be deserved, but Jim has been understood on all sides and can give us nothing more. Lawrence is far more interested in going on with his novel's journeys into ideas than he is in qualifying Lilly's interesting assertiveness by Jim's protest. Lilly, too, is certainly comic as he sits fighting for breath and refusing to let anyone see it— but his ideas are not qualified by Jim's behaviour as they would be in another kind of novel, any more than they are by Tanny's mockery. Such reactions are inevitable; the ideas remain important.

This same 'unembarrassed'[11] quality can be seen in the dialogue with the Socialist Levinson at the end of the book. Lilly had toyed with ideas of leadership in Chapter 9, but he now puts them far more forcefully; and says he agrees with the word 'slavery' cheerfully used by Argyle to describe the optimum condition of the masses:

> 'I mean a real committal of the life-issue of inferior beings to the responsibility of a superior being.'
> 'It'll take a bit of knowing, who are the inferior and which is the superior,' said Levinson sarcastically.
> 'Not a bit. It is written between a man's brows, which he is.'
> 'I'm afraid we shall all read differently.'
> 'So long as we're liars.'

(*AR* 327)

It is typical of the novel that it should make Levinson so sensible and Lilly so extravagant—and should still insist that Lilly is the more interesting and intelligent man. Lilly goes on to agree that military force may be needed to enforce men's voluntary submission. I do not think it is possible to like Lilly; but it is also clear that he is not being made likeable. We may hear the sound of jackboots, but Lilly is pursuing a belief to its natural and bitter end. Two minutes later, however, he smiles a 'peculiar, gay, whimsical smile' and declares he would say 'the blank opposite with just as much fervour' (*AR* 328). It was not a belief after all; he was simply riling the liberal. But his real point is that fundamentally he hates bullying, and he finds Levinson a liberal bully. 'Every man is a sacred and holy individual' (*AR* 328); he believes in leadership, not in bullying. And at this point in the novel, as so often in the twentieth century, a bomb goes off. A bomb is one of those expressions of bullying and uncontrolled individual will which, in this novel, are equated with anarchy. Levinson's kind of liberal socialism means the proper and justifiable throwing of bombs on occasion; but the bomb proves the primacy of the individual self, as we feel the latter struggling clear of the 'awful gulfing whirlpool of horror in the social life' (*AR* 329) the bomb sets in motion.

The novel is, indeed, using a number of different methods to enforce its meaning; it is adventurous in that kind of way. A bomb is a fine way of making vivid the point which Lilly has been arguing; it is the final explosion in a sequence which has rocked the stability of people's lives. And it is striking how, after the blast, we experience the world through Aaron; he always has been a kind of sensitive centre of bodily awareness, and, like him, we feel thrown back on ourselves after the urgencies of the cut-and-thrust argument have been so abruptly ended. Aaron is instantly a man in need; the loss of his flute confirms that. He is very much alone, and he needs more than simply himself to remain human in such a world: 'the loss was for him symbolistic. It chimed with something in his soul: the bomb, the smashed flute, the end' (*AR* 331). At this turning-point, Aaron feels 'driven to bay, and forced to choose' (*AR* 336); does he go on with the world he has known, in one form or other—or does he try something new? The *Fantasia*, too, after a whole book stressing the primacy of the individual soul, suddenly breaks out into a final exhortation in its last chapter: 'if you don't know which direction to take, look round for the man your heart will point out to you. And follow—and never look back' (*Fantasia* 192). But the *Fantasia* does not develop the idea. The novel dwells on it throughout the last two chapters. It takes two forms; the necessary submission of the woman to the man (which has been argued for since the start of the novel), and the submission of the individual to the superior man. And that submission is a mystical submission; we have no idea what it leads to.

The novel uses yet another typical device in coping with the idea. Aaron looks at Lilly, the man he feels is superior, and interrupts him with terse and sardonic objections. 'You'll never get it,' he says (*AR* 346). Lilly asks him if he understands. 'I don't know' (*AR* 346). Lilly asserts the submission of woman to man. 'She never will . . . anything else will happen, but not that' (*AR* 346). And then again, 'You'll never get it' (*AR* 347). Such objections count for a good deal against Lilly's fluent and mystical rhetoric; the chapter is, after all, called 'Words'. Yet we should contrast this chapter with 'Talk'—the chapter of meaningless discussions in London. In the end are Words, and in the end Aaron submits—or is just about to. 'And whom shall I submit to?' (*AR* 347). Lilly's face is 'like a Byzantine eikon' at that moment, a transmutation of the human form into the divine. Aaron's submission is not made simply to another human being; Lilly's eikon-like face is how the soul sees him.

It is all a very long way from that checkweighman putting a Christmas-tree in a tub for his two small daughters. But this is the end of the road, at last. The novel has taken our fondest beliefs about love and home and marriage, and has thrown them out of the window; it ends with the mystical submission of one man to another. It does things novels are not supposed to do; as Lawrence said about it, 'it never turns the other cheek' (30 vii 1921)—it never humbles itself to our judgement. Its ideas about the inferior and superior men are necessarily political, but it washes its hands of politics; anarchists and Socialists are interchangeable in the Italian scenes, and Lilly surely speaks for the novel as a whole when he says that Socialism is not 'every man's problem', because 'to me it is no problem'; 'my alternative . . . is an alternative for no-one but myself, so I'll keep my mouth shut about it' (*AR* 326–7). The point is that he feels bloody-minded, and intends to remain so. For a novel which wishes to move from an argument about the state of marriage to an argument about men, *Aaron's Rod* is notably unfair to its women. In Aaron's dream, in the last chapter, the three collisions of his elbow with the stake are clearly dream versions of his three encounters with women—with Lottie, Josephine Ford, and the Marchesa. But the analogy is terribly crude; are these women only chance encounters, bruising Aaron's elbow as any serpent in Eden might bruise his heel? Each is made vividly alive during her scenes with Aaron; but they have little part to play in the society Lilly imagines, and even Lilly's wife Tanny is conveniently missing from the last chapter. When Aaron leaves the Marchesa at dawn, for instance—and we might compare Gerald Crich leaving Gudrun at dawn—it is simply the end of the affair, because Aaron wants it to be.

But I feel that even such criticisms, serious as they are, do not actually penetrate to the heart of the book, any more than do objections to the novel's noted inconsistencies. I want to come back to the heart of the matter and say why that should be so.

'I am tired of Europe—it is somehow finished for me—finished with Aaron's Rod' (08 x 1921), Lawrence told his American publisher. That was, in fact, wishful thinking; his next novel, *Kangaroo*, would concentrate on Somers' wartime experiences for the whole of a chapter; both *The Plumed Serpent* and *Lady Chatterley's Lover* would find Europe inescapable. But in 1921 *Aaron's Rod* felt as if all its progressions led away from England, away from Europe itself, out into the isolation of the individual soul. The world falls away into nothingness for Aaron as he accepts his mystical charge to submit and follow. It is a remarkable end to the journeyings of Lawrence's other novels up to 1921; Ursula's journeys through the Widening Circles of *The Rainbow*, or the worlds of social England transcended by Gudrun in *Women in Love*. The rich social worlds of those books, the sheer range of human possibility suggested by the existence of a Tom Brangwen *and* a Loerke, a child Ursula *and* a child Winifred Crich—all such things are ignored by *Aaron's Rod*. The novel has become the vehicle for an idea; the essential outline of a journey of dispossession is what is needed to sustain that idea and give it a context. The characters fall away like dead leaves as soon as the novel has finished with them. *Aaron's Rod* says that human community, though fascinating and even sometimes enjoyable, is a lesser thing than the being of the isolated individual, and a lesser thing than mystic purpose. 'It is a queer book,' wrote Lawrence as he finished it: 'it all came quite suddenly here' (27 v 1921). It does have the quality of a sudden and final realisation. Aaron stands in his kitchen, listening to the world around him, feeling utterly cut off from it; and it is so ordinary!

> . . . there came from outside the dissonant voices of boys, pouring out the dregs of carol-singing.
> 'While Shep—ep—ep—ep—herds watched—'
> He held his soapy brush suspended for a minute. They called this singing! His mind flitted back to early carol music. Then again he heard the vocal violence outside.
>
> (*AR* 18)

Nothing at home can breach that isolation; it can only reinforce it. When he goes home for the first time, 'it was like looking at his home through the wrong end of a telescope' (*AR* 51). The sounds and lights of London seem 'all far away . . . unthinkably far away' (*AR* 87). His music is always a stillness, the expression of his isolation. His affair with the Marchesa at first makes him hate her, but soon 'he stood far off . . . his soul stood apart, and could have nothing to do with it' (*AR* 318). Finally, when the Marchesa's husband argues with Lilly that no heart beats alone, that a man's heart always beats 'either with or against the heart of mankind, or the heart of someone, mother, wife,

friend, children' (*AR* 290), then Aaron admits that he, too, once felt
that; but only in the past. 'Is it true for you?' asks Lilly; 'it has been,' he
replies.

That aloneness is what the novel is about, in the end, which is why
both its sexual and social scenes, though so vivid, can be abandoned
without a qualm, just as Aaron leaves his home. Characters can be
inserted, or dropped, without a second's thought; only the fates of Lilly
and Aaron are allowed to be important. Lawrence felt affectionate
towards Norman Douglas, invented Argyle—and in he went. We must
not make too much of anyone in the book. Corinna Wade is a focus for
things which, in *Women in Love*, could have been the hub of a chapter:
'She was charming in her old-fashioned manner too, as if the world
were still safe and stable, like a garden in which delightful culture, and
choice ideas bloomed safe from wind and weather' (*AR* 314). But what
reader even remembers her existence? She floats into the novel,
reminds us of those old days, of the newer world—and vanishes.

The most striking example of this is the novel's attitude to the War.
It has a whole chapter, 'The War Again', full of stories and
reminiscences from Herbertson. Later on, Angus Guest gives his
account of the War. The Marchese and Cunningham are in uniform,
Bricknell moves as if he were. In Novara, Aaron's dinner companions
include a Colonel and a Major, both in khaki. There are soldiers at the
stations and in the streets of Italy; Aaron is robbed by soldiers. Lilly
tells a horror-story of the Russo-Japanese war. And there are, apart
from all these, over thirty direct references to the First World War
itself. Is the novel following some pattern, creating some whole
awareness out of these separate elements? Is the War a turning-point, a
break between the old world beloved of Corinna Wade and the new,
very much post-war world?

It is, I think, impossible to find that pattern in this particular carpet.
The references have the effect of continual, enforced recollection—as if
the subject were too traumatic ever to be forgotten for long. Yet there
seems to be not a single reference to the War as such in the whole of the
last four chapters—just where its symbolic value (if it had any) would
have come to a head. Having been traumatic, the War fades, just as the
world of men is made to fade as Lilly and Aaron walk into the country
in the last chapter. In the end, the novel is no more concerned with
War than it is with society, or with marriage. It is pursuing its theme,
and chronicling a journey out of modern consciousness; the War is
inevitably part of that consciousness, but only part; and it can be left
behind.

Lawrence makes the novel, in fact, a kind of diary of the Europe and
the age he wanted to leave. For the most part it is Aaron who
experiences the places and people, and Lilly the ideas, which the
novelist abandons. As readers, we may well feel left behind too; the

novel is quite capable of ignoring us. There is a kind of hard-edged honesty in such a novel. It does not gambol round us, like *Mr Noon*; by contrast, the *Fantasia* (not being a novel) has to keep an eye on its readers and keep in touch with its audience. *Aaron's Rod* is perverse, mostly very clear, and almost untouched by charm; it is a thoroughly honest novel. It really does exemplify Lawrence's remark to Mabel Luhan, in November 1921, that 'I want to live my life, and say my say, and the public can die its own death in its own way, just as it likes' (05 xi 1921). The novel pursues its idea and chronicles its version of Europe; and leaves well alone.

And yet—it cannot. We do not let it; it will not let us. By being so very single-minded, *Aaron's Rod* forcibly reminds us of all the things it ignores and perverts and glosses over. I said it was a kind of diary of the Europe Lawrence wished to leave; for all the vividness of many of its scenes, it must strike readers who are not Lawrence as less a diary than a slightly bad-tempered collection of ideas and travel-jottings. For all its single-mindedness, it works on us as a novel by virtue of the things Lawrence would probably have valued least in it; its evocations of the Franks' establishment in Novara, the home life of Aaron and Lottie. These fragments of a world which the novel abandons are the most important things in it; they alone create its sense of how people live together, of human society and human needs. Birkin, in *Women in Love*, wonders at one point whether he can give up caring, and just live life 'like a picaresque novel'. But he cannot; 'he was still damned and doomed to the old effort at serious living' (*WL* 340). Aaron, by contrast—and with the full support of the novel—*does* drift on 'in a series of accidents' (*WL* 340); and while working on the novel and finding it recalcitrant, Lawrence himself wondered whether he could 'sort of pimp him picaresque' (26 ix 1920). But the very quality of the picaresque in this book suggests how much more there is to life, even to English life, than the determined individuality of two conceited men. For a novel which isolates its main characters and frees them from a post-war Europe, *Aaron's Rod* is astonishingly rich *in* Europe. As Lawrence wrote in *Apocalypse* (thinking not of society, but of religion), 'I *can* deny my connections, break them, and become a fragment. Then I am wretched';[12] more than any other of his novels, *Aaron's Rod* tries to break those connections with England, with Europe, with the novel, with community, with family, with marriage. I think it fails to break them; but not for want of trying. The novelist who wrote in November 1921 that 'I am tired of here, I can't *belong* any more' (16 xi 1921) knew what it meant to try to break them; knew, too, what wretchedness was like.

8 *Kangaroo*

Kangaroo was Lawrence's first novel written outside Europe; given the attitude to community, to England and Europe, to women and to its readers shown by *Aaron's Rod*, it is natural to wonder what relationship with the past, with Europe, with its audience, with the very idea of what a novel should be, could possibly be shown by its successor. But such questions have not in general been asked of *Kangaroo*—it has not been taken so seriously. Criticism has preferred to think of it as disorganised, self-indulgent and arbitrary; it suffers from 'a carelessness of "form" which goes almost beyond *Aaron's Rod*',[1] 'it isn't really a novel but a special kind of production',[2] it 'flounders on, with its built-in apologies to the reader . . . Lawrence is no longer interested in this novel. If you lose faith in men, then you lose it in your own readers, and inevitably, in your own art.'[3] The fact that the first draft of *Kangaroo* was mostly written in six weeks is in itself enough for many critics—'a remarkable work . . . considering it was written in only about six weeks';[4] it is assumed that its oddities are the result of carelessness, and its descriptive power that of purely incidental genius.

No five hundred page MS is easy to write; and the MS of *Kangaroo*[5] has a good deal of interlinear correction and revision. Lawrence worked equally hard on the TS; worked on it as something he was determined to get into its proper shape. He wrote to Seltzer that he had 'gone through Kangaroo—many changes—it is now as I wish it . . . I have made a new last chapter. Now it is as I want it, and it is good' (16 x 1922). He was to revise the ending yet again, in January. How could he, over a period of months, work on such a MS and TS if he had lost faith in men, in readers, and in his art? Neither financial nor commercial reasons compelled him to write it; rather the opposite, in fact. By 1922 Martin Secker was sure that Lawrence's short stories and short novels would always do better than his novels; only *Lady Chatterley's Lover* would make Lawrence very much money in the whole of his novel-writing career, and that only for particular reasons. Secker was clear in his preference for the shorter fiction; we find him writing to Lawrence's agent Curtis Brown, just after the publication of *Kangaroo*, that

> I am confirmed in my opinion that it would not prove so popular as
> 'The Ladybird' . . . I shall be publishing the short stories 'England,
> My England' in January and under that title, and think it will be

more popular than *Kangaroo*. To show my belief in it, the initial printing order will be 4000.[6]

The printing order for *Kangaroo* had only been for 3000 copies. I suggest that if Lawrence worked on a novel like *Kangaroo*, we cannot think of him as really writing only 'a supreme travel book, with commentary that is at times earnest philosophic point-putting and at other times journalistic chitchat';[7] he was writing a novel because a novel interested him, because he had some belief in what he could do in a novel that he could not do in an essay or a short story.

And there is another point that has generally been overlooked by criticism. None of Lawrence's well-known essays on the novel date from the years of *Sons and Lovers*, *The Rainbow* and *Women in Love*; apart from bits of the 'Study of Thomas Hardy', and the early versions of the essays on American literature, the essays on the novel all date from the years 1923–5—just those years when, in majority critical opinion, Lawrence had forgotten what a novel really was, and was producing turgid flounderings. 'Surgery for the Novel—or a Bomb' dates from February 1923—less than a month after Lawrence wrote the last words of his final revision of *Kangaroo*. 'Why the Novel Matters', 'The Novel and the Feelings', 'Art and Morality', 'Morality and the Novel', and 'The Novel' all appear to have been written in the early summer of 1925, between the completion and the revision of *The Plumed Serpent*. Whatever we think of the novels which Lawrence wrote in these years, it is striking how his belief and interest in the form did not change; and if one of his conclusions about the novel is that it 'can make the whole man alive tremble' (*Phx* 535), as he says so well in 'Why the Novel Matters', it is at least arguable he discovered that while writing *Kangaroo* and *The Plumed Serpent*.

The essays can help us understand why the novel form was something he found challenging throughout this period. 'The Novel' insists that a novel creates relatives, not absolutes: 'In a novel, everything is relative to everything else, if that novel is art at all' (*Phx II* 416). 'Why the Novel Matters' explains further: 'In the novel, the characters can do nothing but *live*. If they keep on being good, according to pattern, or bad, according to pattern, or even volatile, according to pattern, they cease to live, and the novel falls dead' (*Phx* 537). We can compare these attractive but assertive formulations of relativity with the actual behaviour of Richard Lovat Somers, the hero of *Kangaroo*. At the end of Chapter 13 we find him insisting, very movingly, that 'life makes no absolute statement. It is all Call and Answer.'

As soon as the Call ceases, the Answer is invalid. And till the Answer comes, a Call is but a crying in the wilderness. And every

Answer must wait until it hears the Call. Till the Call comes, the
Answer is but an unborn foetus.
   And so it is. Life is so wonderful and complex, and *always* relative.

(*K* 295–6)

Somers in the novel would appear to have reached the same point as
Lawrence in the essays. But the novel is much more problematical than
any of the essays, and its version of relativity far more subtle. Within
five pages, Somers is reading the *Sydney Bulletin*—something utterly
scrappy and unserious. 'Bits, bits, bits. Yet Richard Lovat read on. It
was not mere anecdotage. It was the sheer momentaneous life of the
continent. There was no consecutive thread. Only the laconic courage
of experience' (*K* 300). Not for the first time, the reader of the novel may
feel he is hearing something that reminds him of the novel he is actually
reading. But the point is that the *Bulletin* makes the soul-strugglings and
beautiful lucidity of the previous chapter look ridiculous; life may always
be relative, but not in the way propounded there! Somers

> kicked himself still harder thinking of his frantic struggles with the
> 'soul' and the 'dark god' and the 'listener' and the 'answerer.'
> Blarney—blarney—blarney! He was a preacher and a blatherer,
> and he hated himself for it. Damn the 'soul', damn the 'dark god',
> damn the 'listener' and the 'answerer', and above all, damn his own
> interfering, nosy self.

(*K* 300)

But even that reaction does not deny the genuineness of the experience
which called up the language of 'call' and 'answer'. Somers finds
himself silly and pretentious; but we readers, serious novel-readers,
know that the responsible, soulful, self-questioning stance of the
previous chapters had been that of the European still unable to escape
his self-responsibility; while the outrageous reaction is that of a man on
the loose who is trying (unsuccessfully) to rid himself of such
responsibility. 'In all this change, I maintain a certain integrity'
(*Phx* 537), says 'Why the Novel Matters'; the integrity here is not that
of the created character alone, but of the understanding reader. We do
not simply rejoice that a pretentious man has momentarily seen
through himself; Somers is as inevitably a preacher, even when reacting
against preaching, as a Lawrence novel is a vehicle for challenging its
readers; the novel's integrity is that of showing not only how a man
changes (as Somers so often changes in *Kangaroo*) but how he cannot
simply escape the man he has been in the past. Somers' past inevitably
exacts a kind of loyalty from him; he can never simply escape it,
however much he feels he can.

This kind of integrity is most important in *Kangaroo*; it is larger and more comprehensive than any of the characters individually can be. Even the existence in the novel of great chunks of the *Sydney Bulletin* for 22 June 1922, reproduced verbatim, should not make us feel that this is a novel where anything goes, where anything can be allowed to happen. The cuttings demonstrate 'the laconic courage of experience' (*K* 300); but there are clearly other kinds of experience for the once-responsible European—the novel offers them, and Somers cannot avoid them. The novel's version, that is, of 'everything is relative' is a sophisticated one which relies on our integrity as readers; it is not simply a matter of saying that sometimes Somers feels serious, sometimes ridiculous.

Another example of the novel working out vividly what is rather plainly stated in the essays comes in its insistence that experience is more than reaction, and novels more than sustained reactions. Lawrence's main target in 'Surgery for the Novel—or a Bomb' is the self-consciously serious modern novel, 'absorbedly, childishly concerned with *what I am*':

> '. . . oh, lord, if I liked to watch myself closely enough, if I liked to analyse my feelings minutely, as I unbutton my gloves, instead of saying crudely I unbuttoned them, then I could go on to a million pages instead of a thousand. In fact, the more I come to think of it, it is gross, it is uncivilised bluntly to say: I unbuttoned my gloves. After all, the absorbing adventure of it! Which button did I begin with?' etc.
>
> (*Phx* 518)

He was surely thinking of passages like this from Dorothy Richardson's novel *Pointed Roofs*—one of the three 'serious novels' the essay mentions:

> Unperceived, she eyed the tiny stiff plait of hair which stuck out almost horizontally from the nape of Harriet's neck, and watched her combing out the tightly-curled fringe standing stubbily out along her forehead and extending like a thickset hedge midway across the crown of her head, where it stopped abruptly against the sleekly brushed longer strands which strained over her poll and disappeared into the plait.[8]

'The absorbing adventure of it!' Dorothy Richardson is clearly trying to touch the very quick of immediate, reactive experience; her character is not thinking, feeling, understanding, but is effectively lost in what Lawrence calls 'the author's discoveries' (*Phx* 518). 'Surgery for the Novel—or a Bomb' sets this kind of self-conscious serious novel against the moralising popular novel, and finds both equally inadequate; what has so frequently been taken as a self-indulgent narrative chattiness in *Kangaroo* is, I suggest, a deliberate attempt to be honest and clear and truthful beyond the limitations of such self-consciousness and such moralising. *Kangaroo* offers more than reactions to experience; it suggests the kind of integrity I have already discussed. The narrative voice of *Kangaroo* aims to be both popular and serious, unpretentious and enquiring; and the fiction that results is not only consciously different from *Pointed Roofs* and *Ulysses* and *The Sheik*—it is, I think, experimental in its own way.

Early in *Kangaroo*, when Somers confesses that he is a writer, Jack Callcott wonders of what kind: "'Write about the bushrangers and the heroine lost in the bush and wandering into a camp of bullies?" "Maybe," said Somers' (*K* 36). But Somers is not really that kind of writer, and *Kangaroo* not that kind of popular fiction (although *The Boy in the Bush* could be said to be). Somers, indeed, finds that 'all the scruples and the emotions and the regrets in English novels do seem waste of time out here' (*K* 211); the reader of *Kangaroo* becomes very conscious that this novel, too, is picking its way over the debris of novels inadequate for the job of describing the cultural dislocation which Somers experiences. *Kangaroo* not only makes us aware of the kinds of novel it cannot be; it challenges us by describing itself as 'this gramophone of a novel' (*K* 309), and questions what kind of form its experience should take; for 'life doesn't *start* with a form. It starts with a new feeling, and ends with a form' (*K* 111). I suggest that *Kangaroo* is claiming to be more radically new, more adequate for coping with modern experience, than the modern novels discussed in 'Surgery for the Novel—or a Bomb'. It is not a novel of scruples, emotions and regrets, though such things play a part in it; it is not concerned with 'emotional adventures' except in so far as the characters are betrayed by such. 'We insist,' it says instead, 'that a novel is, or should be, also a thought-adventure, if it is to be anything at all complete' (*K* 308). It is well aware that 'chapter follows chapter, and nothing doing' (*K* 312), but the new form it finds for its own kind of adventuring (not the bushranging kind) is relaxed, provocative—and necessitated by leaving behind both the old world and the old-style (or even new-style) novel.

It is, in fact, very odd to find critics still objecting to a novel written in 1922 because it lacks a strong 'consecutive thread',[9] and because its apparent digressions are as important as its central narrative. No one says such things about a novel like *Ulysses* (published early in 1922); the comparison is in order because Lawrence made it himself. Throughout the composition of *Kangaroo*, he had been impressing his correspondents with its oddity; it was 'a mad novel' (09 vi 1922), 'a queer show' (13 vi 1922), 'funny sort of novel where nothing happens and such a lot of things *should* happen' (22 vi 1922). But when he finished the part he wrote in Australia, it was not only its peculiarity which he stressed: 'such a novel! Even the Ulysseans will spit at it' (09 vii 1922). That was a significant moment.

Ulysses had been published in Paris while Lawrence was in Sicily, but he knew at least some of it from reading Compton Mackenzie's copies of the *Little Review* (which printed extracts) in January and February 1920. Mackenzie remembered him saying that it was 'more disgusting than Casanova . . . I *must* show it can be done without muck'.[10] He probably first heard of its reception in Europe (and perhaps of Middleton Murry's review of it) from Koteliansky in a letter he received early in July 1922, and replied: 'I shall be able to read this famous *Ulysses* when I go to America. I doubt he's a trickster' (09 vii 1922). There can have been few if any copies in Australia at that date, but Lawrence was right about getting it in America; despite the seizure of copies by the US Post Office, some had got into the country, and it was one of the first things Lawrence asked for when he arrived. He wrote to Seltzer that 'I read it is the last thing in novels: I'd best look at it' (22 ix 1922). Seltzer managed to have a copy forwarded: 'Thank you so much for getting it me,' Lawrence replied. But it had 'wearied' him: 'so like a schoolmaster with dirt & stuff in his head: sometimes good, though: but too mental' (21 xi 1922). He used his reading of it, however, when he wrote 'Surgery for the Novel—or a Bomb' in February 1923; but both before he wrote that article, and indeed before he had read very much of the book itself, he took *Ulysses* to be the epitome of the advanced and sophisticated modern novel. And he felt that even the sophisticate, the Ulyssean, would find *Kangaroo* peculiar; and, for sure, would not like it. *Kangaroo* was modern in a way that would inevitably provoke resistance; as he wrote in 'Morality and the Novel', in 1925,

> Obviously, to read a really new novel will *always* hurt, to some extent. There will always be resistance. The same with new pictures, new music. You may judge of their reality by the fact that they do arouse a certain resistance, and compel, at length, a certain acquiescence.
>
> (*Phx* 531)

But he would not have been thinking of *Ulysses* when he wrote that; he would have been thinking of *The Plumed Serpent*, and *Kangaroo*, and perhaps *Women in Love*.

And there was undoubtedly resistance to *Kangaroo* when it came out, not only incomprehension. Even as perceptive and sympathetic a reviewer as Alyse Gregory could write despairingly of Lawrence that 'In spite of his vigorous honesty and his insight he has not the kind of background or information that could justify even so fragmentary a venture into the fields of sociology, economics or psychology.'[11] *Kangaroo*'s ranging over sociology, economics and psychology—we might add politics and history—is not simply amateurish ambition on Lawrence's part, but part of the novel's insistence that modern man necessarily lives through such involvements—through, indeed, such very fragmentariness. Miss Gregory's criticisms actually make us see how modern the novel is; Somers is a kind of culture-hero, going through the experiences of his age. It is significant, too, that the *TLS* reviewer actually pointed out that the book was 'experimental, masterful, challenging the rules and his readers'.[12] It is only surprising that so few critics, either today or in the twenties, have bothered to consider *Kangaroo* as experimental.

But in spite of novels like *The Rainbow*—'Tell Arnold Bennett that all rules of construction hold good only for novels which are copies of other novels. A book which is not a copy of other books has its own construction' (16 xii 1915)—Lawrence has not often been considered a technically innovative writer, nor one we would naturally call 'modernist'. And *Kangaroo*'s talk of itself as a novel, its references to form (and self-proclaimed idiosyncrasy of form), its suggestions of the kind of novel it could not be—all have been seen as obvious weaknesses. I suggest that, in conjunction with its determinedly serious *and* popular tone—popular without the excesses of *Mr Noon*—they act to make us aware of its very existence as a novel, and its very impossibility of being both honest and conventional. A straightforward narrative could not incorporate such convoluted thought-adventures as Somers engages in; but it is important, too, that Somers' experience also interferes with his thinking. It continually throws him back on himself and makes him question his loyalty to the very past for which he is nostalgic; it then pitches him headlong into experience which once more makes him change his mind. Considered realistically, even the narrative events which the novel does allow are rather odd. On no more evidence than a few essays and some rather unspectacular conversation, Somers is wooed by two conflicting political parties to be their spokesman and guide; he shows no aptitude for such a job, and they both show appalling political naivety in asking him to consider it. But Lawrence is concerned to have his hero faced by those two appeals, as any European in the twenties was faced by the rival claims of Socialists and *Fascisti* and an apparent need for political action. Lawrence makes the appeal of both Struthers and Kangaroo go very deep into Somers; they attack his very sense of loyalty to person, to class, to authority and to tradition; they force him, indeed, to enquire where his deepest loyalties lie. And that enquiry is at the heart of the book, and far outweighs any desire for fictional naturalism.

Again, it struck Lawrence's agent in 1922 that the chapter 'The

Nightmare' was out of place in *Kangaroo*; he suggested that it could be cut down to a couple of pages in the novel, and published complete somewhere else. Since then, innumerable critics have complained that the episode is only a digression. They have not realised its importance in demonstrating how Somers arrived at the state of isolation which the novel shows him (literally) suffering from; an isolation not only of class or country, but of loyalty and belief; it shows Somers' final progress to that position, 'broken off from his fellow men', 'broken off from the England he had belonged to'. 'Without a people, without a land. So be it. He was broken apart, apart he would remain' (*K* 287). *Kangaroo* is, I suggest, a modernist novel because it contains within itself an account of how its author came to be in a position to write it, and to want to write it, for all his feeling of being 'broken apart'. Somers' feeling of alienation finds countless parallels in the history and literature of the last hundred years; alienation which struggles against itself but does not wish to be relieved. The fact that such alienation in this case stemmed primarily from a reaction to the First World War is almost the only unusual thing about it. The novel sets itself to be honest about the individual's experience in the aftermath of a death in belief—in relationship, in community, in society. And it is significant that, having finally tracked down this death in belief to his experiences in the War, in the 'Nightmare' chapter, the novel should go on to the chapter ' "Revenge!" Timotheus Cries', with its demonstration of Somers' independence of other men and its haunting enquiry into the Call and the Answer; and that, in its turn, such a mellifluous and mystical enquiry should be succeeded by the chapter 'Bits'. Bits of newspaper, bits of isolated and malevolent people who lack 'central selves' (*K* 309), a lack of 'consecutive thread' (*K* 300)—such are the necessary consequences of Somers' experience, the necessary aftermath of 'The Nightmare'.

And, in its turn, 'Bits' is succeeded by 'Jack Slaps Back' and its questioning of the very truth of a novel. How can a novel be honest, it asks, when vital experience has been of the kind just suggested?

> To be brief, there was a Harriet, a Kangaroo, a Jack and a Jaz and a Vicky, let alone a number of mere Australians. But you know as well as I do that Harriet is quite happy rubbing her hair with hair-wash and brushing it over her forehead in the sun and looking at the threads of gold and gun-metal, and the few threads, alas, of silver and tin, with admiration. And Kangaroo has just got a very serious brief, with thousands and thousands of pounds at stake in it. Of course he is fully occupied keeping them at stake, till some of them wander into his pocket. And Jack and Vicky have gone down to her father's for the week-end, and he's out fishing, and has already landed a rock-cod, a leather-jacket, a large schnapper, a rainbow-fish, seven black-fish, and a cuttle fish. So what's wrong

with him? While she is trotting over on a pony to have a look at an old sweetheart who is much too young to be neglected. And Jaz is arguing with a man about the freight-rates. And all the scattered Australians are just having a bet on something or other. So what's wrong with Richard's climbing a mental minaret or two in the interim? Of course there isn't any interim. But you *know* that Harriet is brushing her hair in the sun, and Kangaroo looking at huge sums of money on paper, and Jack fishing, and Vicky flirting and Jaz bargaining, so what more do you want to know? We can't be at a stretch of tension *all* the time, like the E string on a fiddle. If you don't like the novel, don't read it.

(*K* 312–13)

The novel could obviously create such experience with the greatest ease—if it chose. But its real enquiry lies elsewhere, up those 'mental minarets'—'what more do you want to know?' The question is perfectly serious; what kind of knowledge about people—what kind of novel—will help us to understand the true dimensions of our experience? *Kangaroo* is extraordinarily good at describing the ordinary events of life; meeting neighbours, walking along a sea-shore, reading a newspaper. But it also has a strong sense of when to leave such things alone. It is doing, in fact, exactly what Lawrence described in his much-quoted description of the moral novel:

> The novel is the highest example of subtle inter-relatedness that man has discovered. Everything is true in its own time, place, circumstance, and untrue outside of its own place, time, circumstance. If you try to nail anything down, in the novel, either it kills the novel, or the novel gets up and walks away with the nail.
>
> (*Phx* 528)

Kangaroo challenges us with our own desire to nail things down and say what is really important in our experience. But every nail of authorial philosophy—and every truth of local experience—is tested both by the novel and by Somers; and every nail which Somers tries to drive into the novel as something sure and tested—his loyalty to the working class, for instance—is in its turn walked away with by his actual and contradictory experience. It is fair to say that this can be frustrating for the reader, and that Lawrence is writing a continually honest novel rather than a continually successful one; but that is the novel's only way of being true to what it sees as the real dimension of post-war experience. All the critical discussion of the artlessness of *Kangaroo* (and the saving grace of such marvellous descriptions) has disguised the way in which the novel is actually a rather desperate search for the honest realisation of position. *Kangaroo* uses almost every formal technique

available to the novelist to experiment with ways of realising Somers'
contradictions. It demonstrates how difficult it is to make a novel out of
such contradictions; but it also implicitly suggests that only in a novel
can the conflicts between experience lived and experience desired, the
interweaving of one isolated life inevitably with many, start to express
the situation of a man who is determined to cut himself off from his
fellows, and who is incapable of cutting himself off from his roots.

But why should such a novel emerge from a visit to Australia? Lawrence saw nothing in Australia directly comparable to the Socialist-
Digger confrontation of the novel; like so much else in the book,
that confrontation belongs to the consciousness of the European
(fresh, in Lawrence's case, from the Socialists and *Fascisti* of Italy)
rather than to Australia. It is clear, however, that the real Australia
was for both author and novel the occasion for a fortunate realisation of
an internal predicament. From the very first page, Somers is a stranger
and observer in a country we may well take to be more foreign than
Australia. He and Harriet are looking for a taxi; everything about them
separates them from the laconic casualness of the men at the roadside
who confront them, and they are instantly recognisable as European—from old countries, if not from the Old Country itself. The
isolation of people who have abandoned both a real and a symbolic Old
Country is the key to the whole book. *Kangaroo* is as much a journey
into the self as are those other famous travel works, *Heart of Darkness*
and 'Sailing to Byzantium'. Australia is the country you find when you
leave home and wander; somewhere both unknown and familiar; a
stage on a journey with an unknown direction, but one which may well
take you a full circle back to your old country (or your old life) again;
but never again can that old country be the same. Australia is explicitly
real and symbolic: 'Poor Richard Lovat wearied himself to death
struggling with the problem of himself, and calling it Australia' (*K* 33);
the country's very 'absence of control or will or form' (*K* 32) makes the
European continually conscious of what he has left, or lost—and conscious, too, that he is incapable of simply leaving his own past behind.
The 'Nightmare' chapter makes this clearest; at his furthest remove
from Europe, Somers has his most intense vision of how his feelings
over the past five years have isolated him. What died out of consciousness in those years was not just part of Richard Somers, or even of a
writer like Lawrence, but that responsible and didactic old-world
authoritarian self which reached its apex in the nineteenth century—and which has now to be cut free. The novel is an examination of
the way an individual's relationship with his own country has changed;
he can now no longer believe in it, in its progress or its good faith. 'He
had always *believed* so in everything—society, love, friends. This was
one of his serious deaths in belief (*K* 273–4). Somers would like, now,
to believe in Kangaroo, or in Willy Struthers; they both offer new ideas

of society, of love and of friends. Cannot 'mates', cannot active love, become the inspiriters of man's belief? But as Somers confronts his old-world self, and how it changed, he realises that for him they cannot; all he can do is hold himself back from both friendship and love for his fellow men, live his own life—and be unhappy about doing precisely that—and be the hero of a novel which inevitably implies a relationship with people, a community of understanding.

Lawrence makes Somers a writer, perhaps to point up that very peculiarity; but Somers is not a novelist—how could he be? He is a writer of poems and essays. It is as if Lawrence is himself conscious that his own biggest contradiction, given the power of Somers' realisations, lies in being a novelist; a writer about community, writing for some kind of audience. Somers feels that 'I write, but I write alone . . . I want to do something along with men' (*K* 79). Is writing a novel a way of doing, or not? For Somers, essayist, it is not. For D. H. Lawrence, novelist—it is the crux of the problem. Simply renaming a novel a 'thought-adventure' is not enough: is it the reader's adventure, too? Somers decides, before quite realising why, that after all he wants no more social involvement: 'It seems like a trap to me, all this social business and this saving mankind. Why can't mankind save itself? It can if it wants to. I'm a fool. I neither want love nor power. I like the world. And I like to be alone in it, by myself' (*K* 225–6). But such a paragraph is being written into a novel which a great many people are reading in the perfectly ordinary way of 'social business'; a novel is never 'alone' in the world; nor is a novelist; nor, for that matter, is a reader. Our adventure is not Somers', and it always runs the gamut of Somers' criticism of it. Can we, like him, continually realise our true relationship with the world? Somers is continually nostalgic for community, always wondering if he can ever be a social being again, in any meaningful way: caught uneasily between the times when he is assured that his own capacity for life is mysterious, in the fullest sense of the word; and those times when he feels simply alone. But at least he is shown with the courage of his loneliness.

What brings him to this position, and what brought Lawrence-the-man, if not Lawrence-the-novelist, is something naturally provoked by Australia. An actual democracy, a daily existence without reference to a cultural past—Australia feels like home for the European determined that Europe has become insignificant. While actually working on *Kangaroo*, Lawrence wrote to Koteliansky that 'One can be so absolutely indifferent to the world one has been previously condemned to. It is rather like falling out of a picture and finding oneself on the floor, with all the gods and men left behind in the picture' (09 vii 1922). But the art of gods and men was one which he also wanted to get back into; Lawrence as novelist could never get away for very long from his desire to say how people should live. He had always considered his novels as arenas in which his ideas could attack the world around them; this was the special value of the novel over the essay or the short-story or the poem. Back in 1913 he had been simply optimistic about what, as a novelist, he could do: 'I think, do you know, I have inside me a sort of answer to the *want* of today: to the real deep want of the English people, not to just what they fancy they want' (01 ii 1913). That kind of optimism had been akin to his hopefulness about marriage, about love, about sexual relationship, about the future of art and the novel, about the future of society itself. He was optimistic about people's capacity to change, and to realise a deeper sense of themselves than that to which they were accustomed. The early essay 'Art and the Individual' is full of the kind of confidence about the future of society which is implicit in Lawrence's early writing, and which he seems to have inherited from that tradition of nineteenth-century nonconformist liberalism in which he had been brought up. 'Art and the Individual' talks of the discussion of social problems 'with a view to advancing to a more perfect social state' (*Phx II* 221): 'To be in sympathy with things is to some extent to acquiesce in their purpose, to help on that purpose. We want, we are ever trying to unite ourselves with the whole universe, to carry out some ultimate purpose . . .' (*Phx II* 226). Such a sense of things progressing to an ideal is the very touchstone of what we might call the philosophy of liberalism; progress and purpose become synonymous; the individual looks for change and advance in himself, in his fellows, in his society. We see such an attitude in its most self-serving form in Mrs Lawrence's belief that her children should, above all, get on in life. She meant, advance economically, in class and professional expertise, to the respected status of professional men. But that was itself only a materialistic reflection of a belief in society and advance which lay, for instance, behind the 1870 Education Act—the Act to which Lawrence and so many of his contemporaries owed their chance of becoming pupil-teachers, teachers, and thus professional men. It is a belief which we can see directly behind Lawrence's lifelong ambition to change the world; sometimes to damn it, sometimes to save it—but, always, to reform it. At one stage Lawrence certainly considered the career of a minister of religion; but with his religious beliefs severely damaged by nineteenth-century rationalist philosophers—Mill, Huxley, Robertson—he could at least be the secular equivalent; the social critic, the advanced and revolutionary thinker, the articulate Socialist, the man who offered to change human consciousness. We can observe Lawrence being all these things between the years 1906 and 1912, but it was as a writer of fiction that he found his metier; his thinking and philosophising informed the pages of novels, stories and poems directed at people's capacity for belief. The role of writer, he later told Catherine

Carswell, was a matter of discovering 'whither the general run of man-kind, the great unconscious mass, was tending . . . those who sought the new must take their stand right in the flux'.[13]

That was the role which Lawrence consciously set himself in the years up to the war. But, in common with a number of other writers rooted in the nineteenth century, he found the war tore a gap in his optimism which never really healed. For Henry James, for instance, the war was

> a thing that so gives away the whole long age during which we have supposed the world to be, with whatever abatement, gradually bet-tering, that to have to take it all now for what the treacherous years were all the while really making for and *meaning* is too tragic for any words.[14]

Lawrence's reaction to the war, so strong right from the start, was the more extreme because of his former hopefulness— like Somers, 'He had always *believed* so in everything. . . .' (*K* 273). In 1922, Lawrence shows Somers still living the shadow of the death in belief which the war occasioned. Somers would like to believe in Kangaroo; and he finds that Willie Struthers' very different version of society and its conflicts also appeals deeply to him. Kangaroo and Struthers offer him more than political programmes, or even political philosophies; they offer him renewed versions of the self he has been and potentially still is. Struthers is the working man who wants to cut through the husk of social organisation to an egalitarian state, and who can use Somers' polemical gifts—just as Lawrence had for a time, in 1915, believed that he could use his writing to change society. Kangaroo is the man who believes in love, in aristocracy, and in a kind of wise, liberal advance, that works for the betterment of people—though not democratically. We can see exactly these things in Lawrence's own career as a writer; but after the death of his own belief, Somers ends up failing to do anything or join anything. He has discovered that what he wants is a new religious attitude to life, not a reshaping of society, and this is *Kangaroo*'s break-through as a novel; as so often in Lawrence's career, it succeeds in answering the unresolved problems of its predecessor. It confronts the potential Aaron and the potential Lilly with the actual leader and the led—and rejects both; the change *Kangaroo* ends up promoting is not the organisation of society, but the relationship of man to his universe.

And, as usual, that needed a wholly new novel (*The Plumed Serpent*) to work out. But the conclusion also meant a radical revision of Law-rence's old attitudes. In 1925 he republished the essay he had written for *The Signature* in 1915—'The Crown'—and remarked that he only altered it 'a very little' (*Phx II* 364); but that is not true at all, as a comparison of the original MS[15] and the printed text reveals. 'The Crown' had belonged to exactly that period when Lawrence hoped that his writing could have a political effect, and could be an instrument for direct change, and he prefaced its republication with a statement of exactly the opposite—which was the position he had reached by 1925. 'I knew then, and I know now, it is no use trying to do anything—I speak only for myself—publicly. It is no use trying merely to modify present forms' (*Phx II* 364). That is the authentic voice of the post-war Somers. It is, however, crucial that *Kangaroo* also makes clear the loneliness of a man who has adopted that position; his vulnerability, too. Harriet sees her husband, for a moment, as 'so isolated he was hardly a man at all, among men. He had absolutely nothing but her. Among men he was like some unbelievable creature—an emu, for example. Like an emu in the streets or in a railway carriage. He might well say phoenix' (*K* 195). Lawrence's critics have too often dismissed his ideas of man and society and isolation without realising the sadness and, in a way, the absurdity, of the man and thinker who reached such conclusions; they were *faute de mieux*. And in spite of his insistence on isolation, there is still in Somers a longing for a different way of life; his isolation gives birth to a novel, and the novel is, contradictorily, a paean to human isolation and, like any novel by Lawrence, a book insistently aware of its readers and their capacity to change.

After the War, a strange mixture of didacticism, prophecy, common sense and idealistic isolation directed the course of Lawrence's writing; the preacher no longer believed in preaching, and the liberal idealist no longer believed in the idealism. But the writer, and in particular the novelist, was never simply the preacher or the idealist; he knew his contradictions, and his best work was written out of them, as I have suggested that *Kangaroo* was written out of them. Lawrence continued to believe in his writing long after he declared himself no longer concerned with society; his writing remained a link with the people of his old world and his own past, though it was also a link he instinctively felt rather than one he understood. His relation with the England he knew best, as I have pointed out in earlier chapters, was always problematical: England was, in the fullest sense, 'his own and not his own'. Writing in general, but in particular the writing of a novel, with its creation of an alternative world, kept open for Lawrence communication with a world beyond himself. His writing in the twenties sometimes suffered from his position as a prophet who no longer believed in social change, and as idealist who preferred to be as far removed as possible from most human affairs. A short novel like *St Mawr* actually flaunts its belief in isolation rather than realising the danger. But in a novel like *Kangaroo* Lawrence could still live out the

fuller implications of his isolation; and if the resulting fiction is more
inconsequential and less poignant than a novel like *Women in Love*, it can
still be a true kind of fiction. *Kangaroo* was perhaps the only novel
Lawrence wrote in the twenties which did not wrench its fiction to
support an idea, but (instead) showed why that was such a temptation.
Lady Chatterley would be a novel which insisted that people can be
different, and, simultaneously, that they can't be and won't be. *The
Plumed Serpent* would argue that people can be different if clocks can be
put back (or forward), and if a certain vitalism can be taken with blind
seriousness, and if religion can again become a dominant force in society. But the dangerous shallowness of most of the lives actually lived in
those two last novels shows the price Lawrence had to pay for his
last-ditch idealism. Only the quality of doubt in Kate Leslie, in *The
Plumed Serpent*, reaches out to claim our attention; not the quality of her
faith. The seriousness at which the two last novels aimed was that of
ideas sustained, not of lives lived.

Kangaroo, however, is an extremely honest living-through of the problems Lawrence carried within himself; of his twenties novels, it is the
least damaged by the straining of insistent belief against persistent
pessimism. It is the creation of the European Lawrence caught literally
mid-way between his old world of hope and progress and an unknown
new world; it had to be a peculiar and experimental novel because the
novel form itself is a form of the old world. Narrative implies progression, and the most important things in *Kangaroo* do not progress but are
realised slowly, from inside. *Kangaroo* is a novel which insists that
Europe should no longer have any claim on a man's loyalty and his
sympathies; but it is also true to the fact that nostalgia for belief in
human beings and human community is something that cannot simply
be put aside, however insistent on his singleness and isolation a man
may become. This aspect of the book emerges very clearly in its final
pages, as Harriet and Somers hold streamers which link them with
their Australian friends standing on the quay; as the ship moves out, so
the streamers break and fall—'blowing away, like broken attachments,
broken heartstrings'. They move out into the harbour, with 'Sydney
rather inconspicuous on the south hills, with its one or two sky-
scrapers. And already the blue water all round, and a thing of the past'
(*K* 394). The very last lines run: 'It was only four days to New Zealand,
over a cold, dark, inhospitable sea' (*K* 394). We get very strongly the
sense of a journey not only to, or from, Australia, but into realisation
and homelessness and loss. 'Leaving his own British connection' is for
Somers such a loss: 'The darkness that comes over the heart at the
moment of departure darkens the eyes too, and the last scene is remote,
remote, detached inside a darkness' (*K* 393). The appealing past is left
behind; but, in another way, detaches itself and becomes a clearer-cut
remoteness. *Kangaroo* is irritating, beautiful, quirky, honest, by

turns—precisely because its problems with honesty are so great, and are allowed to over-ride any other considerations; the form of the novel has to take the shape of the search, the realisation, the nostalgia, the renewed search, and the final detachment which is both necessary and poignant.

9 *The Plumed Serpent*

For all the fervour of self-exploration apparent in *Kangaroo*, Lawrence's novels were never simply 'thought-adventures'; for most of his life they were a major source of his income. So we find him in Australia during July 1922 writing to his American publisher Seltzer: 'Depressing to have such petty sales always.—I must come to America & try & do a novel there, that's all' (18 vii 1922). By 1922 he had suspected for years that his publishing future, so far as it might make him money to live and to travel as he wished, lay in America; and of course, his journey half the way round the world in 1922, on his way there, was the most expensive thing he had ever done. I think we can assume that an American novel was implicit in the very idea of going to America; and, indeed, the novel Lawrence wrote on his first visit there was the only original piece of fiction he wrote between September 1922 and January 1924.

There was also the matter of Mabel Luhan's invitation. She it was who had originally asked Lawrence to Taos, in New Mexico, hoping he 'could penetrate and define that magic, in which we moved';[1] as Lawrence put it, just after he arrived, 'she wants me to *write* this country up' (18 ix 1922). He had told her while he was still in Australia that 'I shall be so glad if I can write an American novel from that centre. It's what I want to do' (09 vi 1922), and no sooner had he arrived than he was wondering, to Seltzer, 'if I'll get a novel out of here? It would be interesting if I could' (19 ix 1922). His first reaction was that 'one's heart is never touched at all—neither by landscape, Indians or Americans' (27 ix 1922), though he wrote the essay 'Indians and an Englishman' within a few days of arriving. But within a month of arriving he was at work on a novel—after all, he had begun *Kangaroo* within a month of landing in Australia.

The American project, however, was not planned as a stage in the kind of self-understanding which *Kangaroo* had been. He told Mabel Luhan that 'he wanted to write an American novel that would express the life, the spirit, of America and he wanted to write it around me—my life' (*Nehls* ii 180). Notes for this survive, as does the beginning of a draft; it describes how an American woman arrives in Taos, realises her dissatisfaction with her marriage, and eventually finds a satisfactory relationship with an Indian. It seems to have been started shortly after Lawrence's return from a visit to an Apache reservation; and it is striking how it immediately lays down the structure of nearly all the fiction he was to write in America: dissatisfaction with both European and North American consciousness, a realisation of the 'spirit of place', and a rejection of the White husband by the passionately seeking woman—to be succeeded by her new experience with the Indian. That new experience came into every work of the imagination Lawrence began in the Americas apart from 'The Flying Fish', which is about a European called back in spirit to Europe. Mabel Luhan was certain that this novel-project came to an end because of Frieda Lawrence's jealous opposition to it; this is unlikely, given that Lawrence used precisely the same material in both 'The Woman Who Rode Away' and 'The Princess', in 1924. But it is hard to imagine Lawrence being able to write a full-length novel based on Mabel Luhan which would not eventually have become satirical; the 'spirit of America' which he saw in her, as opposed to what he saw in the place and the Indian, was exactly the spirit he found he could not stand. He did not believe in her attraction to the Indian: 'I tell you, leave the Indians to their own dark destiny. And leave *yourself* to the same' (08 xi 1923). Such a woman's experience of the Indian would inevitably have come to resemble Mrs Witt's attraction to Phoenix in *St Mawr*, and that was not what he wanted for his new novel's heroine.

His own doubts about his role as a novelist of America—and even *in* America—were also coming to a head at the start of the winter of 1922:

> It seems to me, in America, for the inside life, there is just blank nothing. All this outside life—and marvellous country—and it all means so little to one . . . I know now I don't want to live anywhere very long. But I belong to Europe. Though not to England.

> (17 xii 1922)

Even in Australia, he had been most deeply concerned with the links between the European and his past; Somers' problems come from Europe, and he carries them round with him. In America, Lawrence obviously had great difficulty creating an *American* experience; and the best thing in the novel he did write there, for most readers, is the internal struggle of the European Kate Leslie. But Lawrence was getting into a position where he no longer wanted to describe the typical experience of the European; he wanted his writing, and in particular his novels, to take a step forward into another world altogether. As he put it after writing the first version of his American novel, England has 'got to pick up a lost trail. And the end of the lost trail is here in Mexico. . . . The Englishman, *per se*, is not enough. He has to modify himself to a distant end. He has to balance with something that is not himself' (25 x 1923). And Lawrence felt that his role as a novelist had come to be the creation of that 'something that is not himself'; his imaginative writing in America was practically all devoted to that purpose.

But 'in the U.S. I could do nothing' (31 v 1923): and the idea of going down to old Mexico to try a novel was perhaps suggested by the Lawrences' first hosts in America, Witter Bynner and Willard Johnson. Frieda told Seltzer that 'Lawr wants to go to Mexico, he thinks he might write his American novel there—You know he would like to write a novel of each continent—if possible.'[2] As Lawrence put it, more prosaically, to Bynner, 'I can't continue doing nothing. We must go somewhere and settle. I must write. I want to write, and we've a living to make' (*Nehls* ii 226). And in Mexico he hoped to find that challenging sense of opposition to the European he was, which he had had a taste of in the Apache reservation; he now wanted to go somewhere where the Indian population was indigenous.

The party of four went down to Mexico at the start of April 1923; after a few weeks based in Mexico City and spent travelling to Indian and Aztec sites in the neighbourhood, Lawrence reaffirmed his desire to 'settle down & do a novel here' (09 iv 1923); when they moved to Chapala, he began. In less than six weeks, in one of those outpourings of energy which created *Kangaroo* and the final *Lady Chatterley*, he completed the first draft of the novel he was to call 'Quetzalcoatl'. It suffered two false starts, for all Lawrence's feeling that 'I wanted to do a novel. I sort of wanted to do a novel here. I could never begin in Mexico [City]' (26 v 1923). But it took its opening sequence from the Lawrences' experience in Mexico City at the start of April, and that set a pattern for its development; away from modern, Europeanised Mexico, away from the American influence, towards something indigenous: something that looked forward and not back. By mid-June it was 'two thirds done,' and we hear the first note of that significant confidence that 'Quetzalcoatl' was not only a good novel, but that it was more *important* than his other novels had been. 'It interests me, means more to me than any other novel of mine' (15 vi 1923).

But it was more than fifteen months before he could start work on it again. It is possible that he did not actually complete it, but left it *'nearly* finished—near enough to leave' (27 vi 1923), as he told Mrs Freeman, something borne out by the abruptness of its ending. But he regarded 'Quetzalcoatl', anyway, only as a first draft. *Kangaroo* had been written just as fast, in another foreign country, but for all the heavy correction which Lawrence gave it in October 1922, it was only written once. I do not think, however, that we need share L. D. Clark's idea of why Lawrence rewrote 'Quetzalcoatl': 'He was apparently concerned about the accuracy of what he was writing, uncertain, perhaps, of his anthropological knowledge'.[3] It is true that Lawrence did attempt to meet the anthropologist Manuel Gamio in 1924, and that he asked a friend in Mexico City to read the final MS before it went to the publisher. But 'Quetzalcoatl' was a novel he had come to believe in as intensely important, and he wanted (as with all his novels except *The Lost Girl*, *Aaron's Rod* and *Kangaroo*) to have the chance of coping with the problems which had only become clear during the writing of the first version. If 'Quetzalcoatl' as its stands[4] really is unfinished, with Kate just packing her trunks before leaving for Europe, we can be sure that Lawrence had come to find that was not the ending he really wanted: in the final version, her struggle against leaving is far longer, and in the end she stays. The book had to be rewritten to ensure that it progressed to such a conclusion; it had to make a world Kate could not, after all, turn her back on.

In September 1923, Lawrence went back into Mexico, but not to work on 'Quetzalcoatl'; before restarting that, he worked on Mollie Skinner's Australian novel and turned it into *The Boy in the Bush*. His reasons were, again, significant: 'I think I shall go ahead with that, the Boy, to finish it before I try Quetzalcoatl again, because this is much more important to me, my Quetzalcoatl' (18 x 1923). He wanted to rewrite 'Quetzalcoatl' without any pressure on him from other projects; and again he stressed its *importance*. After wintering in Europe, and being back in New Mexico for the spring and summer of 1924, he wrote three stories which have very properly been seen as preparations for the novel: *St Mawr*, 'The Woman who Rode Away' and 'The Princess'. And though the novel's setting remained the shore of Lake Chapala, he had long planned to go to quite another part of Mexico to rewrite it: 'particularly I want to go to Oaxaca' (03 iii 1924) he had told Bynner. He had never been there, but he must have heard about its isolation and its totally Indian population. It was, however, well south of the Tropic of Cancer, and would have been unbearably hot in the summer; he planned to go there in the autumn. Before he went, though, he saw the Hopi Snake Dance in Arizona, which provoked his longest account of Indian religion so far; the experience was crucial for the rewriting of the novel, as it suggested what was currently happening to the 'Indian with his own religion inside him'—how he had had to 'adjust himself to circumstances which really are mechanical',[5] and how he had failed. The novel would, instead, show the Indian living out his religion; and between 19 November 1924 and 1 February 1925 Lawrence rewrote 'Quetzalcoatl' into the novel we know as *The Plumed Serpent*.

Of all the novels he ever wrote, it took most out of him. In mid-January it was still going well—'it is good, but scares me a bit, also' (12 i 1925)—but the day he finished it, Lawrence went down with malaria. Influenza, tuberculosis and an earthquake added to his miseries; he nearly died, and only just managed to get back into New Mexico in April. There is hardly a comment on the novel in his letters for months except anguished relief that it was finished: 'I daren't even look at the outside of the MS. It cost one so much. . .' (06 iv 1925). In mid-May, 'I feel still that I can't look at it' (21 v 1925). But at the start of June he began to revise it, and knew again how important it was to him: 'my Quetzalcoatl novel lies nearer my heart than any other work of mine' (10 vi 1925). From then until its publication he struck one particular note when referring to it: 'in my opinion it is my most important thing so far' (18 vi 1925); 'I consider this my most important novel, so far' (23 vi 1925); 'I still say, this is the most important of my novels' (16 x 1925); 'I still think it is my most important novel' (20 x 1925); 'Nobody will like it, but I think it's my most important' (26 x 1925). We need to understand why he so insistently used the word 'important' to describe it.

'I have been thinking lately, the time has come to read Dostoevsky again: not as fiction, but as life. I am so weary of the English way of reading nothing but fiction in everything' (11 i 1926). Lawrence wrote that just before *The Plumed Serpent* was published. If we put the remark beside the essays on the novel which he wrote during the summer of 1925, we can see them expressing the same demand: that fiction be more than romance, and that the novel at its best should *do* things to people. It can work on them as life, rather than as fiction: 'The novel as a tremulation can make the whole man alive tremble' (*Phx* 535). 'It can help you not to be dead man in life' (*Phx* 538). All the essays insist on the essential morality of the novel, and on its power to evade the morality (or purpose) of its author; but the morality of the novel is educative. The novels we value 'educate' us 'in the feelings' (*Phx* 759), 'set the whole tree trembling with a new access of life' (*Phx* 536)—Lawrence's language for the effect of the novel is always dynamic: helping, demanding, educating. His finest expression of this idea of the novel comes in a letter he wrote to Carlo Linati just before finishing *The Plumed Serpent*; it sums up his later philosophy of the novel, as he actually felt himself to be practising it:

> I can't bear art that you can walk around and admire. A book should be either a bandit or a rebel or a man in a crowd. People should either run for their lives, or come under the colours, or say *how do you do*? I hate the actor-and-the-audience business. An author should be in among the crowd, kicking their shins or cheering on to some mischief or merriment . . . whoever reads me will be in the thick of the scrimmage, and if he doesn't like it—if he wants a safe seat in the audience—let him read somebody else.
>
> (22 i 1925)

A novel is to be read 'not as fiction, but as life'.

This is an aspect of Lawrence as a novelist to which far too little attention has been paid. In the extant discussion of *The Plumed Serpent* there is a great deal of confusion about what it means to call the novel a work of art. Its detractors tend to say that though parts of it may be interesting, it is indefensible as a work of art because it preaches at us.

Its defenders tend to say that, although there may be flaws in it, it should be defended *as* a work of art; Kessler points to its 'monomythic structure' with its 'hidden primal myth adventure',[6] Vickery instances the fact that Ramon's quest is symbolic rather than ideological.[7] The idea of art is, in both cases, opposed to the idea of preaching; it is assumed that works of art enact and do not state their meanings; they lead us into delight, not into conviction; their qualities are formal, not dynamic. The book's main defender in the last fifteen years, L. D. Clark, writes confidently that the novel 'confuses practical with artistic ends . . . but two things save the book from the author: Lawrence's profound sympathy with the land he was writing about, and his uncanny skill at synthesising form and setting and symbol'.[8] But what *are* such book's 'artistic ends'? If being practical is not an artistic end, why should 'sympathy with the land' be, or uncannily synthesised symbols? *The Plumed Serpent* raises the whole problem of that conveniently manufactured division between art and prophecy which confuses so many writers about Lawrence; and itself makes clear that, by 1925, a good deal of Lawrence's art was—whether we like it or not—a prophetic art. By 1925, a kind of preaching was, for Lawrence, a novel's function—or it had no function; a novel was the construction of a 'scrimmage' in which the reader was to be involved; a novel should not be walked around and admired, but had to *involve* its reader—in choices, rebellion, realisation, commitment. If we choose, like L. D. Clark, to save the novel from its author by enjoying its descriptions of flowers and lakes, that is up to us; but it is simply self-congratulatory to declare such enjoyment the artistic point of the novel. Admiration has also been shown for the 'open-ended' ending as characteristic of 'almost all his major work';[9] Moore writes of it as yet another example of Lawrence's 'deliberately inconclusive conclusions'.[10] Kate ends up saying to Cipriano, 'You won't let me go!' (*PS* 462). But that means that Kate is staying in Mexico with Cipriano and Ramón; either because Cipriano stops her going, or because she insists that he stop her going. *The Plumed Serpent* is not a book to offer us ambiguities, and it is critically perverse to find one here; it simply shows what we want 'art' to offer us.

Again, after Kate's expressions of dislike for the Quetzalcoatl religion, the novel forces her to realise that 'as an isolated individual, she had little or no significance' (*PS* 403); 'Poor Kate, it was hard to have to reflect this. It meant a submission she had never made. . . . For she had believed truly that every man and every woman alike was founded on the individual' (*PS* 405). 'Poor Kate'—we can sympathise with her, but not condone her errors. With her author's hand on her, driving her forward into realisation, she has no choice; and the prose suffers one of those imperceptible shifts from free indirect speech to the prose of the implied author: 'The individual, like the perfect being, does not and cannot exist, in the vivid world. We are all fragments. And at the best, halves. The only whole thing is the Morning Star' (*PS* 405). Kate, as a European of her generation, finds it almost inexpressibly hard to submit to such ideas, and Lawrence knows that his representative European 'could not submit, off-hand. It had to be a slow, organic process' (*PS* 433). But she can take a few steps in the right direction: 'Now she understood Ramón's assertion: Man is a column of blood: Woman is a valley of blood. It was the primeval oneness of mankind, the opposite of the oneness of the spirit' (*PS* 433). The book's art is devoted to establishing the power of such an assertion, and to show it working out in a society as well as in an individual. Kate struggles against it; but at the end, as she clings to Cipriano and stays in Mexico, we see her doing what a European can and should do. Against the odds created by her own culture, she forces herself to submit to the new. And the reader, down there in the arena, probably protesting against what he is experiencing, should feel his own resistance being whittled away as well.

The art of *The Plumed Serpent* has come a long way from the struggles of isolation which gave *Kangaroo* its peculiar kind of honesty; its problems are set in the public arena and presented as the concerns of a whole society. One critic's resistance to this idea has led him to assert that *The Plumed Serpent* is not a realistic novel at all, 'but a psychodrama set in the country of the mind'; its characters and events 'are not apprehended by Lawrence as real or autonomous, but as mere shadows of the struggle in his own psyche'.[11] That is what comes of any attempt to see the novel's art conventionally; of all Lawrence's novels *The Plumed Serpent* is the most concerned to set its drama in a real world of social events and politics—in a world where a national religion can be created. It demonstrates Lawrence saying, in effect: 'In the event of the kind of changes I would like to see in the world, these kinds of things may be expected to happen.' The events of the novel are the realisation, the manifestation, of its vision; and it is clear that Lawrence did a good deal of background reading into the ways of the Aztec religion and the Mexican inheritance, to give his novel roots in the history of a people, and a realistic kind of religion. He did his best to create a necessary solidity of event and religion to make the vision fully manifest. And his concern with that marvellously created place to which Clark addresses himself so eagerly is to create the sight, sound and smell of a country from which religious awareness arises naturally; we feel its magic, and can know its otherness. Lawrence transposed the Indian dances and rituals he had seen in the southern United States into his revival of the Aztec religion of Old Mexico, because these Indians had shown him the activity of 'a vast old religion, greater than anything we know: more starkly and nakedly religious' (*Phx* 146); and he wanted his new novel to confront both Mexican and European with that naked religion. It was, in fact, to be a novel showing not simply survivors (like the North American Indians), but a genuinely primitive people coming together under the sway of an old religion; a novel showing a community, 'a tribal integrity and a living tradition' (*Phx* 145). Lawrence used his book-knowledge and his own experience to demonstrate the rebirth of a religion in a country genuinely torn between the old world and the new—but, here, turned back in its tracks to show how 'the oldest religion, which comes down to us from man's pre-war days, will start again' (*Phx* 147).

But however much the novel needed its realistic Mexican setting, it also needed the experience of the foreigner; primarily in Kate Leslie, but at the start of the book in Owen and Villiers as well, and to some extent in Ramón. Owen and Villiers drop out of the novel because their unchangingly North American response to Mexico means they can respond to neither new nor old. But the novel needs Kate, to confront the European with what is most lacking in her culture. Kate, as a Celt, in fact belongs to a 'primitive' European race which is at least a step away from the 'finished' (*PS* 446) pattern in England or North America; Ramón says to her, about the Irish, 'Let them find themselves again, and their own universe, and their own gods. Let them substanti-ate their own mysteries . . . as we have tried to substantiate Quetzal-coatl and Huitzilopochtli' (*PS* 443). The Germans are to think once more 'in terms of Thor and Wotan, and the tree Igdrasil', the Druidic world is to see 'that they themselves are the Tuatha De Danaan, alive, but submerged' (*PS* 261). 'We must begin with a religion',[12] as Ramón says in the rather simpler 'Quetzalcoatl'.

But Kate also puts her finger on the real problem, both for herself and for the novel. She will tell the Irish to substantiate their gods and find themselves 'if there is anybody to listen' (*PS* 443). In 1915, Law-rence himself had rented a room in High Holborn in which to preach the terms of the new life; as he wrote to William Hopkin, 'art after all is indirect' (14 ix 1915). But no one listened in 1915. It was only as a novelist that Lawrence could speak to his generation, and it was not as a conventional novelist that he wanted to speak. Setting his religious novel in Mexico at least gave it a coherence, an unchallengeable quality that he could not have given such a novel with a European set-ting—though it also gave it an alien quality which allowed two genera-tions of readers to escape its message and discuss it, instead, as a work of art damaged by metaphysic. But the conditions of economic and social need in Mexico, a society in the grip of change with a strong religious culture in the not too distant past—these allowed a fictional Mexico to be a model society for religious change; and, for the novelist, a demonstration model.

And the book is designed not simply to show us Kate's confrontation with that world, but to bring *us*—European and American readers—to such a confrontation. It has been complained that 'what weakens the book is not the inclusion of this fictive religion itself but the spurious rhetoric which attends it'.[13] But that is to miss the point; the rhetoric is necessary precisely because, like Kate, we are not confronted only with ideas of change but with the actual change itself. The Quetzalcoatl hymns, prayers and chants have no meaning and no function except that of confronting us with a religious revival as it happens. They are, in the novel's own language, a *manifestation* of doctrine. Like Ramón, we know that the trappings of the Aztec pantheon are, in themselves, unimportant: 'Quetzalcoatl is to me only the symbol of the best a man may be, in the next days' (*PS* 285). But the religion must be made manifest. Clark, too, suggests that the book's rhetoric is regrettable: 'the worst side of Lawrence was never more evident than it is in this novel: the careless language, the wearisome repetitions'.[14] But the language of a novel is a chosen language, not simply an unwitting 'worst side'. In the case of *The Plumed Serpent* we can, fortunately, compare its language with that of the first four essays of *Mornings in Mexico*, which Lawrence actually wrote while working on the novel during December 1924; they confirm that he was perfectly capable of writing differently about Mexico, if he chose. Like his best travel-writing, the essays are both realistic and speculative, working from beautifully created situations and characters towards the particular idea which Lawrence finds interesting. The essay 'Market Day', for instance, ends with a speculation about the contact between people at the market, and what they actually come for: 'It is fulfilled, what they came to market for. They have sold and bought. But more than that, they have had their moment of contact and centripetal flow.'[15] Without announcing its concern as religious, the essay creates a sense of the 'spark of exchange' which has occurred between people—something 'utterly intangible':

> Like the evening star, when it is neither night nor day. Like the evening star, between the sun and the moon, and swayed by neither of them. The flashing intermediary, the evening star that is seen only at the dividing of the day and night, but then is more wonderful than either.[16]

When, in the novel, Kate is being rowed down the lake of Sayula, she looks at the man rowing and sees

> the abstracted, transfigured look of a man perfectly suspended between the world's two strenuous wings of energy . . . a gleam that hung unwavering in his black eyes, and which suddenly reminded Kate of the morning star, or the evening star, hanging perfect between night and the sun.
>
> (*PS* 100)

But while 'Market Day' develops the idea from the immediate contact between people—the literal contact of barter and exchange—the novel uses the metaphor far more abstractly and didactically. What Kate sees in the eye of the man rowing is not her contact with him, but something he possesses because of his mediation between the actual and the spiritual. It is her job to come to terms with it—and ours. The metaphor of the Morning Star later becomes encased in Ramón's rhetoric as a Lord of Quetzalcoatl; and it is, again, clear that Lawrence is using language very differently from anything that appears in the essay.

> 'But I am the Morning and the Evening Star, and lord of the day and the night. By the power that is put in my left hand, and the power that I grasp in my right, I am lord of the two ways.
>
> 'And my flower on earth is the jasmine flower, and in heaven the flower Hesperus.
>
> 'I will not command you, nor serve you, for the snake goes crooked to his own house.
>
> 'Yet I will be with you, so you depart not from yourselves.'
>
> (*PS* 190–1)

A kind of manufactured proverbalism—'the snake goes crooked to his own house'—is mixed with prose redolent in language, cadence and structure of the Authorised Version, and particularly of the Book of Revelation. 'I am the Morning and the Evening Star,' says Ramón: Jesus says 'I am the root and offspring of David, and the bright and morning star'.[17] 'And he that overcometh and keepeth my works unto the end, to him will I give power over the nations. . . . And I will give him the morning star.'[18] 'Yet I will be with you,' says Ramón: 'I am with you alway,'[19] says Jesus. Not only here, but throughout the hymns and prayers of the Quetzalcoatl religion, we find the strangest mixture of Aztec hymns (which Lawrence knew from Spence's *Gods of Mexico*), scraps of Eastern religion, and the language of the Bible—the latter often transmuted through those hymns Lawrence knew from the Congregational chapel. Roger Dataller has pointed out the direct borrowing from 'Someone will enter the Pearlygate',[20] but traces of many other hymns are suffused into the hymns of Quetzalcoatl. The repeated refrain 'Quetzalcoatl has come!' (*PS* 365) draws on the refrain 'Deliverance will come!'—in the last verse, 'Deliverance has come!'—from the hymn 'I saw a way-torn traveller'.[21] 'My name is Jesus, I am Mary's Son. I am coming home' (*PS* 128) suggests 'My soul is sick, my heart is sore: Now I'm coming home' in 'I've wandered far away from God'.[22] The language of Revelation pervades both novel and nonconformist hymns; 'Jesus the Saviour, bright Morning Star' begins the last verse of

'Over the river faces I see'.[23] It is impossible to say whether Lawrence
knew he was quoting so extensively; by his own account, the hymns he
knew as a child were 'woven so deep in me' that they were 'the same to
my man's experience as they were to me nearly forty years ago'
(*Phx II* 597). The real problem is, however, not the source of the imag-
ery but the use to which it is put. It creates a very soft, flaccid kind of
poetry (or poetic prose); the ritual chants and hymns read as if they
wrote themselves.

But their function is to subdue our conscious minds. In the words of
a letter Lawrence wrote to Rolf Gardiner a few months before the final
version of the novel, 'I know there has to be a return to the older vision
of life. . . . It needs some welling up of religious sources that have been
shut down in us: a great *yielding* rather than an act of will' (04 vii 1924).
How is such a *yielding* to be dramatised? A novel creates its own fictive
world; *The Plumed Serpent* has to create a world which will subdue us to
itself, compel us to accept its direction of our religious sense. F. R.
Leavis suggests that 'It is by a kind of incantation . . . that Lawrence
tries to generate conviction'.[24] The point surely is that incantation
never tries to convince us but to charm us, subdue us to its magic. If the
hymns and chants read like automatic writing, that is perhaps
because Lawrence is offering to subdue our conscious minds to the
extent to which his own is subdued; the mixture of faiths and languages
is not to be analysed, but accepted; not queried as to its meaning, but
allowed to *be* its meaning.

That the attempt is a failure, then, is not to be ascribed simply to
'bad writing', but to a failure with what the novel is trying to do; and
the corresponding passages of *Mornings in Mexico* work better not only
because Lawrence was not, in them, trying to convince his readers of
anything, but because their function is different. They do not show up
that cruel gap between what a writer wishes his readers to be, and what
they are; the gap between belief that people in general and *en masse* can
be different, and belief that isolation (like the writer's own) prevents
them from being any kind of community, or any real kind of audience.
Kate is the only audience in the novel who reacts to the Quetzalcoatl
religion, and her hesitations, isolation and assertive individuality in the
face of it suggest what Lawrence feared his novel's audience would be
like. Kate may be 'blenched with disillusion' (*PS* 136), but Quetzalcoatl offers her little she can believe in. Nevertheless, Lawrence constructed his religion, and invented its manifestations; and felt it to be
the most 'important' thing he had ever done, even though 'important'
itself suggests exactly his distrust of his audience. They ought to
respond more than, probably, they would; Lawrence did not call it his
'best' novel.

A similar problem with the novel's language and purpose is created
for us in the much discussed passage of the execution of the prisoners in

'Huitzilopochtli's Night'. At the vital moments, the dialogue is printed in dramatic form:

> Cipriano: 'The grey dog, and the grey bitch, we kill, for their mouths are yellow with poison? Is it well. men of Huitzilopochtli?'
> Guards: 'It is very well, my Lord.'

(*PS* 393)

Lawrence certainly knew what risks he was running in such a passage; that much is clear from Kate's reaction at the start of the next chapter, when she feels 'shocked and depressed' (*PS* 401). But like the dances and incantations, these dramatic passages suggest men under the sway of ritual; they cannot turn round and say 'this is execution without trial—I won't take part.' The ritual (as ritual should) robs them of individuality or choice; their words are only formulae. Strictly speaking, they *have* no feelings about what they are doing, and narrative which might highlight the existence of individual human beings is, therefore, abandoned. General Cipriano is given a logic which would not defeat the weakest waking mind, and which comes particularly oddly from a soldier: '"When many men come against one, what is the name of the many?" Guards: "Cowards, my Lord"' (*PS* 394). But the dramatic exchanges are designed to carry us over such objections; they are designed to subdue individual consciousness to mass unconsciousness. The exchanges sound rehearsed because they are hypnotic, unthinking; the repetition of 'men' in Cipriano's reply relieves the actual men who respond from all individual responsibility:

> Cipriano: 'Cowards it is. They are less than men. Men that are less than men are not good enough for the light of the sun. If men that are men will live, men that are less than men must be put away, lest they multiply too much. Men that are more than men have the judgment of men that are less than men. Shall they die?'
> Guards: 'They shall surely die, my Lord.'

(*PS* 394)

And although Kate is shocked by the executions, she too feels that, 'as men', Ramón and Cipriano are probably right. Her conscious, 'European' objections are quickly overcome, and her hesitations have less force than we would expect. They are only steps on the road of her own self-realisation, and are presented as weaknesses in her, not as saving strengths. Her objections come from that part of her which belongs to 'her mother, her children, England, her whole past' (*PS* 446), and are presented simply as aspects of her 'egoistic will':

> She was aware of a duality in herself, and she suffered from it. She could not definitely commit herself, either to the old way of life, or to

the new. She reacted from both. The old was a prison, and she loathed it. But in the new way she was not her own mistress at all, and her egoistic will recoiled.

(*PS* 446)

In the novel's terms, the men at the execution, by giving themselves up to powers beyond them, have gone further in the right direction than Kate has. And the novel as a whole does not apologise to us for saying such things, or for offending our sensibilities; it does not offer to conciliate us for the behaviour of the executioners, or for the doctrine of male superiority it also professes.

Lawrence knew that this was not the kind of novel his contemporaries liked; in the words of the essay he wrote just before starting 'Quetzalcoatl', readers like to be able to say: 'That's me! That's exactly it! I'm just finding myself in this book!' (*Phx* 518). But the novel he wanted to write has 'got to have the courage to tackle new propositions without using abstractions; it's got to present us with new, really new feelings, a whole line of new emotion, which will get us out of the emotional rut' (*Phx* 520). *The Plumed Serpent* offers almost no scope for identification with character; we certainly cannot find ourselves in men like Ramón or Cipriano, or in women like Carlota and Teresa. They keep their distance from us. The satisfaction this novel offers is to find ourselves in the 'new emotion' of an abnegation of self, and an awareness of our circumambient universe.

The Plumed Serpent offers itself, then, as the religious novel for its generation. It is an extraordinary ambition. But a number of things work against it; the main one, perhaps, being the radical division between its treatment of the individual and its presentation of the mass. On one level, *The Plumed Serpent* has no time for individuals, and calls their individuality 'egoistic will'; individuals should be absorbed into the unknowing but responsive current of mankind, and readers too should be prepared to give up their expectations of what a novel should be, so as to respond directly to the ritual and the chants. On another level, however, the novel's finest passages are always of the individual becoming aware of a place—of a group—of an animal—and of his, or her, final loneliness; and such an individual hates, fears and distrusts all masses, finding them emanating evil. And it is only with the individually responsive reader that such a novel can be sure of communicating. The novel apparently leads people forward, *en masse*, to confront them with 'new, really new feelings': it also presents the isolated individual's feelings as the only source of honesty and truth. What are the reasons for this division?

By 1924, Lawrence was prepared to devote a major work not just to the expression of ideas about a radically changed human society, but to the actual creation of that society, that alternative world, as a novel; it would be a place to answer Kate's cry *'Give me the mystery and let the world live again for me!'* (*PS* 114). It would be a world apprehended dynamically, in the process of change—not just an old world made new and discovered by accident, as in the 'Autobiographical Fragment' of 1927, where a surviving Lawrence wakes to Eastwood in the year 2927. *The Plumed Serpent* shows a new world being fashioned out of a society as unpromising as that revealed in its first two chapters. Twentieth-century Mexico is American, European and Indian in a mutually destructive mixture; but by the end of the book, even a dyed-in-the-wool European self is shown starting to accept the newly revealed mystery; and the country itself is in the process of being shaped into a genuinely New World. Such a novel should be the kind of thing Lawrence had always wanted his novels to be—an actual revelation of the life men could live. As he put it in 1923, about what we should expect of our modern novels,

> Supposing a bomb were put under the whole scheme of things, what would we be after? What feelings do we want to carry through into the next epoch? What feelings will carry us through? . . . *What next?* That's what interests me. 'What now?' is no fun any more.
>
> (*Phx* 520)

The Plumed Serpent, of all Lawrence's novels, is the one which takes the question 'What next?' most seriously; it is not a novel like *Women in Love*, which says how two people manage, after all, to survive in an alien world. *The Plumed Serpent* says how the world can be changed so that it will no longer be alien. In short, it is doing what Lawrence felt a novel should be doing, in the middle twenties; it was his most 'important book, so far' because it said what should come next. As such, it constitutes a direct challenge to our sense of what a novel should be; it occupies that uneasy and uneven ground between what we have chosen to call art and what we have been too ready to call propaganda. It is certainly a flawed and obsessive novel, but it has not, I think, been taken seriously for what it *is*; a serious suggestion of how men should live, in 'the next epoch'. It was not latent Fascism in its author which made him turn his back on the democratic forms evolved by Western society; it was a thorough-going attempt to say what a religious society would be like. Lawrence did not, somehow, forget to be an artist when he showed himself so little concerned with the psychology of everyday life in characters like Ramón and Cipriano; he was making a serious attempt to write a new kind of novel.

But we do not, after all, read novels in terms solely of their intentions; and *The Plumed Serpent* has generally alienated its readers fully and fatally. It is, to be sure, melodramatic as romance, inadequate in its version of the everyday and necessary life of ordinary people, crude in its versions of political events, vicious in its version of political retribution, insistently religious. But what is equally clear, and rather more important, is that Lawrence failed to create the new kind of novel, the new genre, he was aiming for; and we should ask why he should so much have wanted to do what he did, and why he was so out of touch with his readers as not to realise the effect of such a novel.

The Plumed Serpent is a book written with such grandiose ambition that it seems to address itself to a whole generation. In fact, it is one of Lawrence's most private books, not his most public; it tells us so much more about Lawrence, his feelings and ambitions and concerns and hopes, than it does about ourselves or our future. It polarises Lawrence's own division between the novelist who felt himself intensely English, the novelist who felt attached to the fate of a community—and the man and artist who, like Richard Lovat Somers, felt 'without a people, without a land' (*K* 287). *The Plumed Serpent* shows the chasm— which had been growing in his novels for years—between the artist whose idea of community was vital to him, whose idea of his novels was that they could change people—and the artist whose ultimate belief in any community he actually knew was nil, and whose novels had been in danger of turning into the monologues of a man alone in a wilderness of his own seeking. *The Plumed Serpent* hurls itself towards the ideals of a life based once again on a communal religion, sustaining and integrating; but, significantly, it is almost unconcerned with the actual lives of the people in the grip of that new religion. Only Juana is a character with a life undeniably her own, and also an adherent of the new religion. In the worst sense, the novel has done what Ramón says *he* has done: 'broken the cords of the world' (*PS* 181). It does not work out the results of its religious revival in the lives of the people of Mexico; there is a brief note that Prime Minister Montes makes the new religion the national religion of Mexco—and that is all. A new situation has developed, as the Quetzalcoatl religion actually begins to affect the lives of the mass of the people. But, in the end, as every reader probably feels, Lawrence is only concerned with the choice and dilemma of Kate Leslie; only her objections to the course she is actually taking keep the book alive during its last few chapters. This interest is natural for a writer who had put in his 'Epilogue' to *Movements in European History* at the end of September 1924—shortly before starting *The Plumed Serpent*—that 'there is nothing to be done, *en masse*'.[25] That suggests how caught Lawrence was, as an artist, between the individual whose life he followed with such concern, and the community he wanted to write for. In that same 'Epilogue' he wanted 'every youth, every girl . . . to follow only the leader who is a star of the new, *natural Noblesse*'.[26] The Novel shows how concerned he still was with that leader, how little with the community as it changes or could change. After the isolated individualism demonstrated by Somers in *Kangaroo*, *The Plumed Serpent* shows Lawrence going back to the idea of the leader and the led; change as this novel envisages it can only be promoted by a leader. Lawrence had written in July 1924, while planning his return to Mexico to write the novel, that there is 'no more unison among man than among the wild animals—coyotes and chipmunks and porcupines and deer and rattlesnakes. They all live in these hills—in the unison of avoiding one another' (04 vii 1924). And yet, in the same letter, he declared 'I know there has to be a return to the older vision of life', and described that 'great *yielding*', that 'welling up of religous sources' which I quoted above. *The Plumed Serpent* is designed to create such a welling up (and to provoke it, in its reader), and to find unison between men; it promotes a yielding, insists upon an unknown, demands a unison and hates a mass. Lawrence was caught exactly where his career as a novelist for the past twelve years had brought him; as a responsive individual who desired to be a novelist for his society. That final collapse into illness which nearly killed him, the moment he finished *The Plumed Serpent*, looks very like his other dramatic and nearly fatal collapse, in the winter of 1911; a total physical breakdown under the pressure of intolerable divisions in his own nature, which *The Plumed Serpent* had not only failed to reconcile, but had actually created in their intensest form.

10 *Lady Chatterley's Lover*

The Plumed Serpent, unlike most of Lawrence's later novels, contains few seeds which could germinate in another novel; it is not a work which discovers a new subject as it goes along. It does, however, seem to have immediately provoked a piece of writing which is, in part, a commentary upon it; while still ill in Mexico, in March and April 1925—he was to write no other fiction at all for eight months—Lawrence began a story he called 'The Flying Fish', which he felt so important that, being unable to write himself, he dictated its first few pages to Frieda (*Tedlock* 55). 'The Flying Fish' shows Gethin Day, sick with malaria, stuck in Mexico, with his 'old connections and his accustomed world' broken from him, wanting to go back to the family home 'among the hills in the middle of England' (*Phx* 781–2). 'Now he was sick from the soul outwards, and the common day had cracked for him, and the uncommon day was showing him its immensity, he felt that home was the place' (*Phx* 783). The relevance of such a conclusion for the author of *The Plumed Serpent* is clear. Lawrence never finished 'The Flying Fish': but the fiction he wrote in the next three years of his life was extraordinarily concerned with England; the vision of the 'greater day' would not be as alien as it is in *The Plumed Serpent*, but would be located among those hills 'in the middle of England'.

His first step on the road to *Lady Chatterley's Lover* was, perhaps, *The Virgin and the Gypsy*,, which he wrote in January 1926. He had been back in England in the late summer of 1925, and visits from Frieda's daughter Barby in the winter finally provoked him to create his first fable of post-war England. Yvette, the virgin of the title, finds herself drawn to sensual experience of a kind utterly alien to the middle-class mores of her marvellously created (and hated) family. There is no possibility that she might have a lasting relationship with the gypsy; but at least she is saved from the Leo Wetheralls of her world, and she has realised the 'greater day' of passion when the gypsy looks at her 'as if he really, but *really, desired* me.'[1]

Perhaps significantly, although finished and typed, the story was not published; publishers may have baulked, Lawrence himself may have had second thoughts. At all events, in spite of requests from both Secker and Knopf for another novel, Lawrence resisted the idea for a good deal of 1926—'I'm not going to lay myself waste again in such a hurry' (07 vii 1926), he told Dorothy Brett. But in the summer of 1926 he went back to England again, just when he was feeling that 'I shall have to do something or other, soon' (26 viii 1926). The colliery strike which succeeded the General Strike was still continuing, and although Lawrence hated it, he did find 'a queer, odd sort of potentiality in the people, especially the common people' (30 viii 1926). He obviously contemplated a novel about England—though 'I'd have to come to England to do it' (02 ix 1926)—but the most important thing to stem from his visit was a renewed sense of how much he belonged to the place and its people. 'It is they who are, in some peculiar way, "home" to me . . . I am very much like them,' as he wrote after the visit; but, too, 'I feel I hardly know any more the people I come from . . . I shrink away from them, and I have an acute nostalgia for them' (*Phx II* 264). In that mood, in Italy at the end of October, he began what Frieda described (with Lawrence's comment) as 'a short long story, always breaking new ground, the curious class feeling this time or rather the soul against the body; no I don't explain it well, the *animal* part [Ooray!!! Eureka. D.H.L.]' (*Frieda* 233). She saw one thing clearly, for all her muddle: the power and subtlety of the presentation of that 'curious class feeling', as well as the book's sexuality. The barriers between Constance and the gamekeeper Parkin exist both inside and outside them; but particularly inside her. She is shown as necessarily and in the end fatally ignorant of Parkin and his world. It has been argued that the main difference between the first and the later versions of the novel consists in 'jacking Parkin a few notches higher on the social scale':[2] but the changes made to Constance are perhaps even greater.

This can be seen in one of the finest episodes in the first version—her visit to Sheffield—which also appears in the second version of the novel (published as *John Thomas and Lady Jane*) but not in the final version. Constance goes to the Tewsons to see Parkin and, in both versions, goes to the front door. She doesn't know they don't use it. In the first version: ' "You've come to th' front door," he said. "Yes," she replied, not knowing what he meant. "Shan't you come in?" ' (*FLC* 186). In the second version: ' "You come to th' front door!" were his first words to her, as if in reproof. "And oughtn't I?" she said, as she climbed the step. "Ay! If you like! Only everybody goes to th' back" ' (*JTLJ* 349). It is a typical change; in the second version she asks what he means, Parkin explains, and their relationship continues as before. In the first version, she does not enquire, he does not explain, and he formally invites her in; the distance between them is maintained and (indeed) reinforced. As with so much of their relationship in the first version of the novel, the visit shows them in a state of mutual embarrassment; to counter this, Parkin emphasises his real sense of distance; and Constance, both consciously and unconsciously, responds in kind. When she leaves after tea, it is with relief at getting back to a world she knows, and with some complacency that she has made her visit to the working class: 'Her heart was sad for him and for herself. But also, she was rather pleased with herself. And she drew a sigh of relief when she was in the modest luxury of her own car, driving away from it all' (*FCL* 200). Her feelings of superiority inevitably include her response to his need of her; when she and Parkin clasp hands in Duncan Forbes's car, even the handclasp is not simply mutual:

> Secretly she took his hand and held it hidden between them. She felt his fingers close convulsively over her own with the sudden, unconscious, possessive clasp. And she exulted a little in the convulsive nervous clasp. It was really in spite of himself. His hands, his body, betrayed his will. They would not let him resist her.
>
> (*FLC* 220)

She cannot help holding herself apart. The equivalent moment in the second version of the novel comes in Hucknall Torkard church:

> She herself felt a little raw and lost. She groped for his hand, and it closed over hers for a moment with that sudden soft, strong grasp of trust, then relaxed and lay still, while she held it in both her hands, clinging to it for safety.
>
> (*JTLJ* 372)

It is a moment of perfectly mutual need.

In such ways Lawrence changed the wilful, upper-class woman of the first version to the warmer and more sympathetic woman of the second; and in so doing he gave up the peculiar realism about England with which the first version had created the social divisions between the lovers. In the first version, Constance recognises that she finds Parkin attractive partly because he *is* working-class; she is eager for 'the vulgar healthiness and the warm passion of a common man like Parkin' (*FLC* 204). 'But,' it goes on, 'she dared not tell him so. She dared never let him see the sickness that was in her soul. She must always play the lady, the donor, she who gives the gift.' Her role is something she cannot escape, and it leads directly to their climactic quarrel towards the end of the novel. Parkin's fear that, inevitably, and in spite of her denials, she will want her own way and will try to put it over him, is something we must feel, too. 'You're top dog as regards yourself,' he tells her:

> She was breathless with indignation and anger. Her blue eyes blazed with angry contempt.
>
> 'Well, if you won't come into *my* house for fear of being under dog,' she said scathingly, 'what *would* you do? Would you let me come into *your* house and *me* be the under dog, and you be the top

dog—live like Bill Tewson and his wife and brats, all in one heap?
Would you like me to do that?'
   'You'd never do it, so what's the talk?' he said.

(FLC 225)

He is right: she never would. Nor could she even try, for reasons
implicit in her tone. Parkin, too, is more obstinate and more bitter in
this first version, which succeeds in creating a real sense of both class
divisions and of human need.

But there are, all the same, signs at the close of the book that Lawrence's shrewd analysis of class and role is being overtaken by an even
greater desire to bring Parkin and Constance together, against the
odds. She feels, rather inconsistently, 'how good it would be to be
merely Mrs Parkin!' (*FLC* 252)—but immediately compromises her
sense of what that would be like:

> No, she needn't go into a workman's dwelling! But some farm-
> house, or some suburban villa with nine or ten rooms—she didn't
> care! Anything, to be in contact with life. And if she could possibly
> be in *contact* with the working people, well and good. It would be
> nonsense to try and pretend to be one of them.

(FLC 252)

She confronts her future with that curious mixture of insight and blind-
ness—and, as the book's last line reminds us, 'Ah well! The future was
still to hand!' (*FLC* 253). She is still thinking of Parkin—'he was a
man, if he wasn't a gentleman' (a distinction that can have no meaning
in terms of the person we have seen her to be); the book's conclusions
about her relationship with him are being stretched to the limit.

Another curious thing at the end of the book is Duncan Forbes's
sudden acquisition of the role of Lawrentian spokesman. 'I've hated
democracy since the war. But now I see I'm wrong calling for an
aristocracy. What we want is a flow of life from one to another'
(*FLC* 243)—but Forbes has not called for an aristocracy. The author of
The Plumed Serpent had, however, and Forbes's remark sounds like an
author jotting down a recantation towards the end of a draft, so as to
cope with it properly in a rewritten version.

The same is most certainly true of the language of the last paragraph,
when Constance is thinking about Parkin: 'My lady's fucker, as he
called himself so savagely! How he had hated her for not taking him
fully seriously in his manly fucking! Ah well. . .' (*FLC* 253). This is not
how Constance has ever thought. The obscene words have not entered
the novel since the half-way point—and Parkin uses them to challenge
her. 'What do you call me, in *your* sort of talk?' he asks her, angrily. 'My
lover!' she stammers—and he forces his language on her. ' "Fucker!"

he said, and his eyes darted a flash at her, as if he shot her.' And, for a moment, she uses the word because it is *his* word and she refuses to be intimidated: 'my "fucker" as you call it' (*FLC* 127). The point is a vital one, considering what Lawrence does with the language os sexuality in the second and third versions of the book. The first version is entirely experimental in its use of the obscene words—they only appear on three occasions. Parkin uses the obscene vocabulary primarily to emphasise his class distinction from Constance; it makes her feel that he is 'more alien than a foreigner, as if he belonged to a bygone race of men!' (*FLC* 96). He makes her say 'fucker' for the sake of hearing her use language so much *below* her; but then realises that, in fact, 'there's nawt even to lauch at in itÆ' (*FLC* 128). He does not thereafter use the language at all, and it does not reappear in the novel until that last paragraph. In Constance's mouth, it is quite unrealistic; it reads like Lawrence's reminder to himself that this language for sexuality is worth developing.

Again, there is nothing in this version comparable to the sexual explicitness of the second and third versions; there is, indeed, some utterly conventional silence as the novel moves from Constance saying 'Yes! I will yield to him' to the sentence which starts: 'Afterwards, he was gloomy. . .' (*FLC* 51). There is, however, an unconventional insistence on touch and on warmth; as the novel goes on, there are striking, half-sensual moments (as in the scene in the moonlight when they wreathe each other in flowers) which might make us wonder why the earlier scenes were so conventional; and there are moments of authorial commentary, in the second half, which undoubtedly account for Lawrence's remark to Secker that the novel was 'very improper' (23 xi 1926). 'She knew, as every woman knows, that the penis is the column of blood, the living fountain of fullness in life' (*FLC* 156); there is a distinct development from the language used in *The Plumed Serpent* (see above, p. 158). The novel enquires, briefly, into the 'mystery of the phallus'; but it is not a novel which *shows* us that phallus.

As if realising that this first writing of the novel had only begun to realise the potential of the subject, Lawrence seems to have rewritten it immediately. I have already suggested how Constance becomes warmer and Parkin less bitter; there is far less of a gap between them, and the second version ends with the relationship confirmed. There is no quarrel of the kind which is so important in the first version. The second version, however, uses the obscene vocabulary much as the first version had, with some refinements. 'Cunt' remains 'one of the indefinable sexual words of the dialect', and after using the word Parkin 'returned back to the man of her own day, but not of her own class' (*JTLJ* 175); but he does not challenge her in the same way with it. On the contrary, he now uses 'his' language cautiously, even deferentially. As a young man, he says, he wanted 'a woman—you know—as wanted me as well' (*JTLJ* 232); and continues, carefully, 'I'd rather have a woman an'—what should I say?—good fuckin' . . . than not have a woman' (*JTLJ* 234). When Connie (as she now becomes) tries to get through to him in what she takes to be 'his' language, she simply shows her ignorance of it—'Tell me it isn't only fucking' (*JTLJ* 236)—and baffles him. But after that episode, as in the first version, the obscene vocabulary is dropped, and there is no reminder of it at the end. Lawrence is careful to integrate it with class and character; it is in the fullest sense a realistic language; but because Parkin is no longer quite so hostile to Connie, and because they are both starting to be seen in terms of the flow between them rather than as inhabitants of a particular class, the language is starting to lose the particular point of the first version.

There is, however, a far greater sexual explicitness in this version, which is its most striking development. It depicts literally the 'flow of life' which had been purely metaphorical in the first version. The descriptions of sexual activity are less frequent than in the third version, and rather less detailed; they are not, in fact, descriptions from which morals can be drawn, as those in the third version tend to be. They present, rather, something necessary to the new-found subject of the novel. Having chosen to root its subject in a sexual relationship which transcends class and conventional modes of feeling, Lawrence makes his novel perfectly honest about sex. He had started, in October 1926, writing a story about post-war England, its classes and its barriers—and its sensuality, or lack of it; he found himself beginning to suggest what could bridge the gulfs he had detected, and in what sense there *was* an England which he valued, and to which he could address himself. But in the first version he could find very little to bridge the social gulfs he depicted so well. One of the few qualities unequivocally asserted by that first version had been the 'good-heartedness' never forgotten by Mrs Bolton after the death of her husband: 'That's how it feels. Once a wife, *in your heart*, always a wife, I say . . . having a man goes to the heart with very few, as far as I can see' (*FLC* 88).

Significantly, the second version repeats the episode but alters the key word to *touch*. ' "Can a man's touch on a woman last so long?" "Eh, my lady, what else is there to last, if it's the right man?" ' (*JTLJ* 179). The second version shows touch, and physical love, making their way round the barriers that at the same time it is making less important. By the end of the second version, indeed, Connie is saying 'there was no longer any such thing as class' (*JTLJ* 293), and the novel agrees with her: 'Class is an anachronism. It finished in 1914' (*JTLJ* 294). The novel divides people, instead, into warm-blooded and cold-blooded; only the latter are 'the proletariat, the world over, from colliers to kings' (*JTLJ* 295). And the only democracy that matters is 'the democracy of touch' (*JTLJ* 65), as Tommy Dukes puts it. The centre of the novel is shifted away from the realities of life in England; and its lovers are liberated from their bonds. Its last scene, for which there is no equivalent (nor could there be) in either of the other versions, is appropriately one in which Connie and Parkin go back to the wood and, simply, touch one another: ' "I must touch you! I must touch you, or I shall die!" she said. "Ay! Touch me then!" ' (*JTLJ* 374). The lovers end the novel destined for each other, simply remaining apart while Parkin gets his divorce—though even that may not be an insuperable barrier. If Connie cannot bear life on her own, Parkin promises to come to her, and they can go abroad—' "to Italy if you like." "If you feel it's the best, I will. I'll do anything you like, for the best" ' (*JTLJ* 376). They can be together, on her money and with England forgotten; the first version's concern with England is ignored, together with its concern for an industrial population. The mill-ponds at Felley seem 'abandoned like everything that is not coal and iron, away below. The dead countryside! and the grisly live spots, the mining settlements!' (*JTLJ* 376). The extant world is shrinking to insignificance; the romance, however, is fulfilled, and the lovers exist independently of any real world.

But Lawrence was left with the problem of what to do with the novel. Censorship had interfered with six of his previous novels;[3] but this time he had written a book which not only ran counter to the conventions of its day, but chose deliberately to oppose them. No longer would a cut here or there make it publishable. Lawrence later told David Garnett that 'In my early days your father said to me, "I should welcome a description of the whole act"—which has stayed in my mind till I wrote this book' (24 viii 1928); so the idea of the sexually explicit novel had been in his mind for around fifteen years. And the new subject of this book demanded that it should be written 'so differently from the way I have written before!' (10 i 1927), as he told Else Jaffe. But there was, too, I suggest, another impulse at work. All his life he had painted or made copies of paintings; but the paintings he began to do exactly at the time he started the first version of the novel were something quite new for him; and his delight in them was enhanced by their outrageousness. They were not posed, Academy style figures; they were nudes insisting on their sexual nature. Lawrence told Earl Brewster in February 1927—just as he was ending the second version of the novel—how he put a phallus 'in each one of my pictures somewhere. And I paint no picture that won't shock people's castrated social spiritually (27 ii 1927). 'Boccaccio Story' and 'Fight with an Amazon', for instance, both painted during December 1926 and January 1927,[4] not only *did* shock people's 'castrated social spirituality' when they were exhibited in London in 1929 (both were among the thirteen pictures impounded)—they were surely designed to do so. We find the same attitude to the public in a letter Lawrence wrote to Secker shortly before finishing the second version of the novel: 'It's what they'll call *very* improper—in fact, impossible to print. But they'll have to take it or leave it, I don't care. It's really, of course, very "pure in heart". But the *words* are all used! Damn them anyhow' (08 ii 1927). He could move directly from the sexuality of the novel to that of the paintings: the novel was

> so improper, according to the poor conventional fools, that it'll never be printed. And I will *not* cut it. Even my pictures, which seem to me absolutely innocent, I feel people *can't even look* at them. They glance, and look quickly away. I wish I could paint a picture that would just *kill* every cowardly and ill-minded person that looked at it. My word, what a slaughter!
>
> (08 iii 1927)

The combination of unholy glee and moral fervour which accompanied the printing and distribution of the third version of the novel is clearly foreshadowed here; the novel is becoming primarily a means of challenging its readers.

But Lawrence had already decided to make no move towards publication of the second version, despite the protestations of his English and American publishers. It was not as if he were making very much money by his writing, just then, and he was increasingly troubled by illness: 'it is not cheap, being ill and doing cures' (18 xi 1927). But any attempt to publish the book in the normal way would have led him into a tremendous amount of work, hostility and concern—if indeed anything at all could be done with it. It also seems plain that he was himself a little astonished at what he had produced, and wanted to 'let it lie and settle down a bit before I think of having it typed' (09 ii 1927). He was also, according to Frieda, dissatisfied with it, remarking 'that the second version was not strong enough' (*Tedlock* 283). With the example of his paintings before him, he must have wondered how far he could go in a novel, both in sexual explicitness and in aiming at his English audience—two things becoming linked in his mind.

Lady Chatterley's Lover, the third version, only took shape after he had discovered a way of publishing it; I would suggest that the mode of its production was a final and decisive influence on the kind of novel it became. The idea of private publication which, over the years, he had considered several times, finally crystallised during a visit to Florence on 16 November 1927, when he lunched with Reggie Turner and probably saw Pino Orioli—friends of Norman Douglas. Douglas' current private publication of his books in Florence[5] must have struck Lawrence as the perfect solution of his own dilemma; and as soon as he had a way of publishing it, the book stopped being 'a young woman' who 'may still go in the fire' (06 vi 1927). It became, instead, 'a tender and sensitive work, and I think, proper and necessary, and I have it, so to speak, in my arms' (18 xi 1927). The word 'necessary' should catch our attention; it suggests both the challenge and the attack of the third version. Within three weeks he was rewriting the book, and did the final version with amazing speed, in exactly five weeks.

The second version set itself to overcome problems raised by the first version—but in so doing, had changed the very situation which provoked the problems. The third version was different again, because it challenged its reader—it could, now, be sure of a reader—directly. The use of the obscene words, again, distinguishes this version from its predecessors. Up to the half-way point, there is little to choose between them, barring a couple of emancipated remarks by Tommy Dukes and Charlie May. But the difference can be felt when Mellors (the Parkin of the third version) tells Connie, as he had in the second version, 'Th'art good cunt, though aren't ter?' (*LCL* 185). Previously she had responded 'What is that?' (*JTLJ* 175), and in telling her, Parkin had realised his distance from her—and that was the end of the matter. But in *Lady Chatterley* she cheerfully asks 'What is cunt?' and he tells her, ending up ' "it's a' as it is, all on't." "All on't," she teased. "Cunt! It's like fuck then." ' Mellors misses no chance to instruct her: 'Nay nay! Fuck's only what you do. Animals fuck. But cunt's a lot more than that. . .' (*LCL* 185). He is not only initiating her into a language of sexuality; he is becoming strangely expository—and we inevitably feel that it is for our benefit. His prescriptions for behaviour begin to dominate the action: 'I believe if men could fuck with warm hearts, and women take it warm-heartedly, everything would come all right. It's all this cold-hearted fucking that is death and idiocy' (*LCL* 215). A letter from Mellors ends the novel—a device which allows him to be more than usually didactic, and which shows what a distance the idea of such a character had come since the gypsy's letter which ended *The Virgin and the Gypsy*; in his letter, Mellors uses the language of sexuality with extraordinary deliberation.

> My soul softly flaps in the little Pentecost flame with you, like the peace of fucking. We fucked a flame into being. Even the flowers are fucked into being between the sun and the earth . . . when the real spring comes, when the drawing together comes, then we can fuck the little flame brilliant and yellow, brilliant.
>
> (*LCL* 316–17)

Such language is being pushed to the very limits of its usefulness; the four-letter words have lost their roots in the language of a class, and are being aimed instead at the wondering heads of their readers. The passage, for instance, in which Mellors tells Connie that 'I don't want a woman as couldna shit nor piss' (*LCL* 232) is perfectly functional; as 'A Propos of *Lady Chatterley's Lover*' puts it, 'the mind has an old grovelling fear of the body and the body's potencies. It is the mind we have to liberate, to civilise on these points' (*Phx II* 491). A letter Lawrence wrote to Ottoline Morrell offered her the same doctrine, and confirms that it *is* a doctrine; I do not know of another case where Lawrence extracted (or indeed could have extracted) so particular a point from one of his novels: 'If a man had been able to say to you when you were young and in love: an' if tha shits, an' if tha pisses, I'm glad, I shouldna want a woman who couldna shit nor piss—surely it would have been a liberation to you. . . (28 xii 1928).' We are fortunate in possessing her reaction to this: 'Ottoline handed me the letter . . . "I don't think it would," she said seriously; and then, shaking her head and with a great burst of laughter, "in fact, I'm quite *sure* it wouldn't." '[6]

What is true of the obscene language of the novel is also true of the novel as a whole; in particular, the realism of the earlier versions is given up for the sake of a more pointed presentation of theme and idea. Even so striking and successful a scene (in all three) as that in which Connie and Parkin/Mellors make love for the first time is subtly changed in the third version. The second version had very carefully established the growth of her relationship with Parkin, during successive visits to the wood, and we begin to understand Parkin's own feeling about what he knows is happening: 'He always looked for her to be there, and wanted her to be there, and dreaded it. . . . With his whole soul he wanted *not* to start an intrigue with her, not to involve the two of them in the inevitable horrible later complications' (*JTLJ* 118). There is nothing like this in the third version, where the strangeness is maintained until the last minute, and the sexual relationship comes as an answer and a revelation, not as a culmination. It is in fact particularly stressed how little Connie and Mellors relate to each other; where the second version shows Connie intensely aware of Parkin—'she quivered, he stood so near to her' (*JTLJ* 119)—in the final version, at the identical moment, we find Connie 'glancing shyly at the keeper, almost unaware of him' (*LCL* 118). In the second version, when she starts crying, Parkin asks her 'There's nothing amiss, is there?' It is not the question he wants to ask, or that she wants to be asked; but it is natural to ask it. The third version, instead, shows Connie crying 'in all the anguish of her generation's forlornness' (*LCL* 119–20); her symbolic role is clear, and neither she nor Mellors uses words at all. The sexual meeting is the sudden, inarticulate and symbolic conclusion to the way 'she was to be had for the taking. To be had for the taking' (*LCL* 121). Parkin's splendidly rueful remark in the second version, when it is all over—' "Ah well!" he said to himself. "It had to come!" ' (*JTLJ* 121)—is alien to the spirit of the third version, where 'The man lay in a mysterious stillness. What was he feeling? What was he thinking? She did not know. He was a strange man to her, she did not know him. She must only wait, for she did not dare to break his mysterious stillness' (*LCL* 121). The stillness, the strangeness and the woman's submission are offered, I think, as examples, not just as occurrences; the scene is moving away from realism towards symbolic demonstration.

In the course of writing this final version of the novel Lawrence created something which has been widely recognised as reading more like a fable than a novel. But this was not because *Lady Chatterley* had been conceived as a fable; the very naturalism of the sexual descriptions—more detailed, more demonstrative than those in the second version—works against our reading the novel as a fable, as Scott Sanders has pointed out.[7] It is, rather, because with the opportunity of private publication which Lawrence had chosen in November 1927, he was making the book his strongest possible attack on 'the lily-livered host' (10 i 1928): 'I do want to publish 1000 copies of the unexpurgated edition, and fling it in the face of the world . . . it's got to be done' (12 ii 1928), as he told Dorothy Brett. Frieda Lawrence summed up the development by suggesting that the first version 'he wrote as she came out of him, out of his own immediate self. In the third version he was also aware of his contemporaries' minds' (*FLC* 10). Such a distinction very properly stresses the public quality of the third version. Things which had been realistic in the early versions were now given an attacking edge. The realism and pathos of Clifford as a cripple are ignored almost completely. Instead, he is made to stand for things, one after the other; the modern intellectual; the writer of probing and analytical short stories; the industrialist with a dream of machine power; the modern male fixated on the mother-figure of Mrs Bolton; the blustering, self-righteous husband confronted with his wife's taking a lover. He is, in a special sense, the novel's *creature*: his eyes bulge with disaster, he goes 'yellow at the gills with anger' (*LCL* 80), he sits intoning to himself the fact that 'this is the old England . . . and I intend to keep it intact'—but he fails to hear the 'eleven-o'clock hooters at Stacks Gate colliery' (*LCL* 44). When his motorised chair breaks down, Lawrence inserts passages of pure cartoon humour: 'They waited, among the mashed flowers under a sky softly curdling with cloud. In the silence a wood-pigeon began to coo roo-hoo hoo! roo-hoo hoo! Clifford shut her up with a blast on the horn' (*LCL* 195). There is, naturally, no equivalent for that in the second version. Clifford then loses his temper thoroughly; but in the second version apologises to Parkin, at first indirectly—'I'm afraid I rather lost my temper with the infernal thing!'—and then directly: ' "excuse anything I said," he added rather offhand' (*JTLJ* 216). In the final version his only apology to Mellors is 'I hope I have said nothing to offend you' (*LCL* 198). There is a continual hardening of the case against Clifford, but not simply because Lawrence hates him (the usual judgement); what is obvious in the third version is not what Clifford is *like*, but what Lawrence wants to do with him, and demonstrate through him. He reads Racine to Connie:

'After all,' he said in a declamatory voice, 'one gets all one wants out of Racine. Emotions that are ordered and given shape are more

important than disorderly emotions. . . . The modern world has only
vulgarised emotion by letting it loose. What we need is classic control.'

(*LCL* 144)

The changes from the second version have made Clifford more lucid, a
clearer example, a better chopping-block—but less interesting:

'After all,' he said, 'you've got all the important feeling there in
Racine. The feelings modern novelists and people pretend to feel are
only vulgarisations of the classic emotions, just as the curves of the
art nouveau furniture are vulgarisations from the true line of the
curve. . . . The modern world has worked emotions up to such a
false vulgarity,' he said, 'the only way is to have as few emotions as
possible: none, for preference.'

(*JTLJ* 140)

Clifford is just as hateful in the earlier version—and more dangerous,
because partly right. The final version is crisper, utterly un-
sympathetic, more economical, more useful to the novel's polemic.
For the final *Lady Chatterley* is a crusading novel, with a crusading
idea of the novel behind it. 'From my point of view, it is an assertion of
sound truth and healthy reaction against all this decay and sneaking
perversity which fills most of the books today' (18 xii 1927), he told
Harold Mason as he was writing it. It was 'a kind of bomb: but a
beneficial one, very necessary' (09 iii 1928), he told Secker; it tells people
what 'I believe is necessary for us to become' (12 iii 1928); it is 'phallic,
& intentionally so' (15 iii 1928). It is still not sufficiently recognised
how often the main ambition of Lawrence's writing in his last years
was to make people think more clearly, rather than to appeal to their
emotions. I suspect that this was a discovery he only came to slowly,
himself, and the conscious realisation of it may well post-date *Lady
Chatterley*; but the idea certainly grew as the novel changed. In the
words of his letter to Morris Ernst of November 1928, 'I believe in the
living extending consciousness of man. I believe the consciousness of
man has now to embrace the emotions and passions of sex, and the
deep effects of human physical contact' (10 xi 1928). The third version
of the novel cuts a direct road through to making its reader 'embrace
the emotions and passions of sex'; it confronts him directly with them,
so that—in the words of 'A Propos of *Lady Chatterley's Lover*'—he can
'think sex, fully, completely, honestly and cleanly. Even if we can't act
sexually to our complete satisfaction, let us at least think sexually,
complete and clear' (*Phx II* 489–90). The novel actually shows us a

man who cannot act sexually to his complete satisfaction—Tommy Dukes—who decides to 'remain as I am, and lead the mental life. It's the only honest thing I can do' (*LCL* 42). And he says things which correspond directly to thoughts Lawrence himself expressed in *Pansies*.[8] (Clifford, who one might have thought would be a much clearer case of someone for whom sex has gone wrong, is not allowed to talk like that; his incapacity is simply symbolic.) The novel is ambitious enough, however, to conjure us, its readers, to embrace the deepest and closest experience of which human beings are capable, and not simply to 'lead the mental life': Dukes does not have the advantage of being able to read *Lady Chatterley's Lover*, and to learn from it.

The novel also attacks us for not being adequate for the experience which, simultaneously, it presents to us. That is the extent of its double-sidedness. It sets Connie and Mellors in a world of their own even more completely than does the second version; they inhabit a world which is little more than a wood polarised against an industrial landscape. England, the land towards which all of Lawrence's fiction is utlimately addressed, is formally addressed in this novel: 'England, my England! But which is *my* England?' And the novel concludes that 'The new England blots out the old England' (*LCL* 162–3); old England shrinks to the dimensions of two people, one wood, one crocus, and the hope of a little farm; while 'the mass-will of people, wanting money and hating life' (*LCL* 315) is for Mellors and, I suggest, for the novel, an adequate dismissal of the rest of its inhabitants. The people of Clifford's world are ineffectual and self-conscious; 'the common people were so many, and really so terrible' (*LCL* 165). *Lady Chatterley* celebrates the aloneness of two people, and their passion: isolated, ecstatic beings, 'in the formal scheme of a pastoral idyll',[9] waiting for the spring. It is a novel which isolates us, too, both by its insistent challenging of us, and by making its romance occupy so lonely a refuge from the world we inhabit. How did the novelist who created the worlds of *Sons and Lovers*, of *The Rainbow*, of *Women in Love*, come to the point of *Lady Chatterley's Lover*? It is my final question.

In the summer of 1928, a few months after finishing the novel, Lawrence wrote an outline autobiography for a publisher which, together with the 'Autobiographical Sketch' he probably wrote sometime earlier that year, and the essay 'Nottingham and the Mining Countryside' of 1929, concludes his own account of his relationship with the country of his youth and upbringing. After some detail about his childhood, the outline 'Autobiography' summarises his adult life in two paragraphs; but it stresses two things—travel and isolation. 'In England during the period of the war—pretty well isolated. . . . Henceforth he put away any idea of "success," of succeeding with the British bourgeois public, and stayed apart' (*Phx II* 302). It is important that this should have been his summary, in the year of *Lady Chatterley*, of his relationship with England. In the 'Autobiographical Sketch' he also asks, rather less brusquely, 'why is there so little vital contact between myself and the people whom I know? Why has the contact no vital meaning?' (*Phx II* 595). It is a matter he continually returned to, in the last years of his life; as in his letters to Trigant Burrow. 'What ails me is the absolute frustration of my primeval societal instinct' (13 vii 1927); 'Myself, I suffer badly from being so cut off. But what is one to do?' (03 viii 1927). *Lady Chatterley's Lover* represents the final position he had reached as a novelist, with a desire to attack, to change, to purify and to regenerate an England he still somehow belonged to; and it constructs a romance cut off from England and the English. Lawrence creates a character who speaks as if what he said (and the novel in which he says it) might itself be part of a movement towards regeneration: 'We've got to come alive and aware. Especially the English have got to get into touch with one another, a bit delicate and a bit tender. It's our crying need' (*LCL* 290). But at other times Mellors speaks as if the people of the English Midlands were quite hopeless: 'They're a sad lot, a deadened lot of men: dead to their women, dead to life. The young ones scoot about on motor bikes with girls, and jazz when they get a chance. But they're very dead' (*LCL* 315). In the end, Mellors turns to the one woman he knows, and the little farm where he can be alone with her; the 'crying need' of the English people goes unanswered. The extending of consciousness, the getting into touch with one another, are things impossible in the created world of the book; Clifford will never change, nor will Mrs Bolton; nor will any of the 'cronies' except perhaps Tommy Dukes; nor will Bertha Coutts, nor Hilda, nor Duncan Forbes. Connie's father, Sir Malcolm, is the only person even capable of relationship, apart from the two lovers; and his moments of contact with Mellors are laughable. The book is a heartfelt appeal to the people of England; but it also mourns the passage of the England in which it can no longer believe. Rhys Davies heard Lawrence say, sometime in the winter of 1928, that 'you young don't know what England could mean . . . the old England is gone and you've let her slip away' (*Nehls* iii 275–6. He also heard Lawrence say that *Lady Chatterley's Lover* was 'his last long work of fiction, the last large attempt to tell men and women how to live' (*Nehls* iii 274). If those remarks are reported correctly, they are a good example of the kind of contradiction in Lawrence as a novelist with which I am concerned. The book is an attempt to tell people how to live; but it does not believe in them enough to allow them to exist except as examples of depravity.

In spite of some marvellous creation of tender feeling between the two lovers, *Lady Chatterley* suggests that by 1928 Lawrence was in the position of not knowing what he wanted a novel to be, because he did not know who it was for; he no longer had any sense of that relationship with his audience which had sustained even the loneliest of his previous novels. The book's final revelation is of its author trying to speak for, and to, England, his England; but for Lawrence in 1928 there was no longer any such place. It had dissolved into the isolation that as a novelist had become his only real habitation; the community he knew, and could never forget, was not one that in the end he could speak for.

11 *Lawrence, England and the Novel*

Lawrence's early life demonstrated to him the divisions of the community in which he grew up; besides having a miner for a father and a woman who had been a school-teacher for a mother, he was himself a scholarship boy, encouraged to 'get on' in life and to free himself from the economic constrictions of his parents' life; but he knew the life of the miner's kitchen better than any other, and seemed to be, of Eastwood people, 'bone of their bone' (*Delavenay* ii 665). His attachment to that community as he grew up was, however, as divided as the community itself. He felt strongly drawn to it, and as violently repelled; he carried the memory of it round the world with him, and recreated its whole detailed life in novel after novel written in places as far apart as Cornwall, Sicily, and the woods around the Villa Mirenda near Florence. In that last case, it was a life he had not known personally for nearly twenty years. It was also true that he could not bear to live in England, nor to visit it for very long.

But not only do his novels demonstrate their attachment to England by returning time after time to the life of that Midlands community—they also reproduce that search for an *ideal* community, not Eastwood at all, which concerned Lawrence all his life. Their heroes and heroines, however, tend to settle for a final isolation away from both England and the ideal which has tempted them. Lawrence himself knew, as an imaginative writer as well as an ordinary man, that someone of his own upbringing was almost inevitably caught between a social isolation created by an uneasily divided upbringing (with its attendant success in the world and upwards class movement)—and an often nostalgic attachment to the very idea of a community whose life he could wholeheartedly share. *Lady Chatterley's Lover*, his most schematic novel, actually shows a man from the working class and a woman from the gentility coming together in a symbolic union. But that same novel also creates the isolation of two souls, forever set apart, forever rejecting the world around them, escaping the roar of the industrial world which lies just beyond the wood of all their dreams.

Lawrence's novels have mostly been discussed in terms of their theories and their creation of realistic life; they also, very clearly, bring to a head his own contradictions, between that sense of isolation and that dream of community; but, too, they reach out for an audience of the people of England. At the time of *Sons and Lovers*, he could quite simply assert that 'I do write because I want folk— English folk—to alter and have more sense' (23 iv 1913); *The Rainbow* offered its readers a vision of a new society; *Women in Love* insists that there *can* be another world. Lawrence's concern for England in the twenties became, perhaps, the necessarily limited concern of the exile and the *déclassé*; but it was also that of a writer who had learned to write directly out of his own self-divisions, and who by the very writing of novels was asserting a link with a community of readers stronger than any attachment felt by his heroes and heroines. The novels demonstrate a continual care and concern which the characters—not being novelists—might well find foolish. Taken in the context of Lawrence's life as a writer, as I have tried to take them, his novels dramatise the development of his idea of the novel as a means of challenging his readers—but, above all, as a way that only *Lady Chatterley's Lover* really fails in, of asserting community even while preaching isolation.

Notes

PREFACE

1. *Mr Noon* MS is in the Humanities Research Center, University of Texas. It is scheduled for publication in the forthcoming edition of Lawrence's works to be published by C.U.P.
2. Terry Eagleton, *Criticism and Ideology* (London: NLB, 1976), p. 43.

CHAPTER 1 *The White Peacock*

1. *Eastwood & Kimberley Advertiser*, 18 October 1901, p. 6.
2. Although Ford Madox Hueffer only changed his surname to Ford in 1919, I have used his later and better-known name throughout.
3. 'The White Peacock' MS (*Roberts* E 430a), in the library of the University of California at Berkeley.
4. *English Review*, 8 (May 1911), 356.
5. A. M. [Allan Monkhouse], *Manchester Guardian*, 8 February 1911, p. 5.

CHAPTER 2 *The Trespasser*

1. Graham Hough, *The Dark Sun* (1956; rpt. Harmondsworth: Penguin Books, 1961), p. 49.
2. Kenneth Alldritt, *The Visual Imagination of D. H. Lawrence* (London: Edward Arnold, 1971), p. 10.
3. William York Tindall, *D. H. Lawrence and Susan his Cow* (Columbia: Columbia Univ. Press, 1939), p. 206.
4. Helen Corke, 'The Writing of The Trespasser', *D. H. Lawrence Review*, 7 (Fall 1974), 232–3.
5. Helen Corke and Malcolm Muggeridge, 'The Dreaming Woman', *The Listener*, 80 (25 July 1968), 104.
6. Corke, 'The Writing of *The Trespasser*,' p. 230.
7. Helen Corke, *In Our Infancy* (Cambridge: Cambridge Univ. Press, 1975), p. 225.
8. *Ibid.*, p. 227.
9. *Nation* (London), 12 (19 October 1912), 154.
10. *Standard*, 21 June 1912, p. 5.
11. *Manchester Guardian*, 5 June 1912, p. 5.
12. *English Review*, 12 (July 1912), 661.
13. *Westminster Gazette*, 8 June 1912, p. 18.

14. H. A. Mason, 'D. H. Lawrence and *The White Peacock*', *The Cambridge Quarterly*, 7, No. 3 (1977), 225.
15. Corke, 'The Writing of *The Trespasser*', p. 236.
16. *Ibid.*, p. 235.
17. Edward Garnett, *Friday Nights* (1916; rpt. London: Duckworth, 1932), p. 154.
18. D. H. Lawrence, *The Mortal Coil and Other Stories* (Harmondsworth: Penguin Books, 1971), pp. 104–5.

CHAPTER 3 *Sons and Lovers*

1. Louie Burrows appears to have collaborated with Lawrence on 'Goose Fair'. See his letters to her of 20 xi 1909 and 09 iii 1910.
2. See Lawrence's letter to Louie Burrows of 06 xii 1910.
3. Corke, *In Our Infancy*, p. 200.
4. 'Paul Morel' MS (*Roberts* E 373b—but 271 pp., not 260 pp.) in the Humanities Research Center, University of Texas.
5. *Ibid.*, p. 173.
6. *The Complete Plays of D. H. Lawrence* (London: Heinemann, 1965), pp. 526–7.
7. *Ibid.*, p. 530.
8. *Athenaeum*, No 4469 (21 June 1913), p. 668.
9. D. H. Lawrence, 'Foreword to *Sons and Lovers*', in *The Letters of D. H. Lawrence*, ed. Aldous Huxley (London: Heinemann, 1932), p. 100.
10. *Ibid.*, p. 102.
11. *Ibid.*, p. 101.

CHAPTER 4 *The Rainbow*

1. The MS of the 'Burns Novel' (*Nehls* i 184–195) is in the Humanities Research Center, University of Texas.
2. James Lockhart, *Life of Burns* (1828; rpt. London: Dent, 1907), p. 31.
3. Lawrence also used the name Burns for the autobiographical sketch of Kate's first husband in the early version of *The Plumed Serpent*, 'Quetzalcoatl'; see Chapter 9, note 4.
4. 'Elsa Culverwell'; see Chapter 6, note 1.
5. Frank Kermode, *Modern Essays* (London: Fontana, 1971), p. 163.
6. See Mark Kinkead-Weekes, 'The Marble and the Statue', in *Imagined Worlds*, ed. M. Mack and I. Gregor (London: Methuen, 1968), p. 414.
   'The Sisters' MS (*Roberts* E 44lb, pp. 291–6) is in the Humanities Research Center, University of Texas.
7. 'The Sisters', p. 293.
8. *Ibid.*, p. 293.
9. *Ibid.*, p. 294.
10. *Ibid.*, p. 296.
11. Identified by Mark Kinkead-Weekes; see note 6 above. 'The Wedding Ring' MS (*Roberts* E 44lb, pp. 373–80) is in the Humanities Research Center, University of Texas.

12. 'The Wedding Ring', p. 375.
13. *Ibid.*, p. 375.
14. *Ibid.*, p. 375.
15. *Ibid.*, p. 377.
16. Kinkead-Weekes, 'The Marble and the Statue', p. 377.
17. 'The Wedding Ring', p. 377.
18. *Ibid.*, p. 378.
19. *Ibid.*, p. 379.
20. *Ibid.*, p. 380.
21. As Kinkead-Weekes has pointed out, although we cannot know very much about the 'Sisters', 'The Wedding Ring' and the first 'Rainbow' individually, we can tell roughly how their proportions changed. Thus, the surviving fragment of 'The Sisters', very near the end and perhaps the end itself, is numbered pp. 291–6; so the whole of the story of Ella and Gudrun is told in about 300 pages. The 'Wedding Ring' fragment comes fairly near the start of Ella's relationship with Birkin, but it is numbered pp. 373–80; so obviously the affair with Ben Templeman was given more space, and it is a fair assumption that Gudrun's relationship with Gerald was also developed at greater length. The first 'Rainbow' was even longer; the episode of Ursula teaching (which Lawrence used in the final MS of the novel) took place over 200 pp. of folio TS into the book. This means that over 200 pp. were taken up with the childhood of the two girls and Ursula's meeting with Ben Templeman. The first 'Rainbow' probably described Ursula's parents in some detail, and perhaps her grandparents too. When Ivy Low visited the Lawrences in February-March 1914, she read part of the 'Rainbow' MS describing Sunday at the Brangwen home when Ursula and Gudrun were children (*Nehls* i 219).
22. Walter Pater, *The Renaissance* (1873; rpt. London: Fontana, 1961), p. 205.
23. *Ibid.*, pp. 207—8.
24. *Ibid.*, p. 209.
25. In fact, it was the Assyrian and Egyptian sculpture there which impressed him most (21 ix 1914), and the Egyptian eventually found its way into *Women in Love* (*WL* 358).
26. It is not quite clear whether Methuen actually rejected the first 'Rainbow' in August 1914. At the prosecution of the later version in November 1915, they claimed to have done so; but they also admitted having failed to read the novel carefully enough, in its final form—something they would certainly have done in the case of a novel they had previously rejected on the grounds of its immorality. Their claim to have rejected the novel in August 1914 was almost certainly based on its *technical* rejection (along with a great many other books) because of the outbreak of war.
27. Kinkead-Weekes, 'The Marble and the Statue', p. 385.
28. *Ibid.*, p. 385.
29. James Joyce to Harriet Shaw Weaver, 17 iii 1931; in *Selected Letters of James Joyce* (London: Faber & Faber, 1975), p. 359.
30. R. E. Pritchard, *D. H. Lawrence: Body of Darkness* (London: Hutchinson, 1971), p. 67.
31. H. M. Daleski, *The Forked Flame* (London: Faber & Faber, 1965), p. 79.
32. Frank Kermode, *Lawrence* (London: Fontana, 1973), p. 47.

33. F. R. Leavis, *D. H. Lawrence: Novelist* (London: Chatto & Windus, 1955), p. 170.
34. S. Miko, *Towards Women in Love* (New Haven: Yale Univ. Press, 1971), p. 183.
35. The Penguin text prints 'are': MS, TS and first edition agree on 'were'.
36. *The Rainbow* TS (*Roberts* E 33lb), in the Humanities Research Center, University of Texas, p. 743.
37. J. M. Murry, *Reminiscences of D. H. Lawrence* (London: Cape, 1933), p. 48.
38. Kinkead-Weekes, 'The Marble and the Statue', p. 384.
39. I am indebted to Lesley Brooksmith for this sentence from an unpublished essay.
40. *The Autobiography of Bertrand Russell* (London: Allen & Unwin, 1968), II, 53.
41. J. M. Murry, *Between Two Worlds* (London: Cape, 1935), p. 337.
42. *The Autobiography of Bertrand Russell*, II, 53.
43. *Ibid.*, II, 53.
44. *Ibid.*, II, 21.
45. Bertrand Russell, *Principles of Social Reconstruction* (London: Allen & Unwin, 1916).
46. Murry, *Between Two Worlds*, pp. 335–6. (The text of Murry's diary printed in *Reminiscences of D. H. Lawrence* is modified and revised.)
47. Murry, *Reminiscences of D. H. Lawrence*, p. 65.
48. The novel's internal time-scale would put Ursula's encounter with the horses in the autumn; the passage was, of course, written in February.
49. *The Rainbow* MS (*Roberts* E 331a), in the Humanities Research Center, University of Texas, p. 707.
50. *The Rainbow* MS.
51. D. H. Lawrence, *Letters to Bertrand Russell*, ed. H. T. Moore (New York: Gotham Book Mart, 1948), pp. 81–2.
52. Colin Clarke, *River of Dissolution* (London: Routledge & Kegan Paul, 1969), p. 52.
53. *The Rainbow* TS.
54. *The Rainbow* MS.
55. *The Rainbow* TS.

CHAPTER 5 *Women in Love*

1. Murry, *Between Two Worlds*, p. 336.
2. Cynthia Asquith, *Diaries 1915–1918* (London: Hutchinson, 1968), p. 89.
3. *Ibid.*, p. 424.
4. F. R. Leavis, *D. H. Lawrence* (Cambridge: Gordon Fraser, 1930), reprinted in *For Continuity* (Cambridge: Minority Press, 1933), pp. 120–3.
5. George Orwell, *The Collected Essays, Journalism and Letters*, 4 vols. (1968; rpt. Harmondsworth: Penguin Books, 1970), IV, 52.
6. *Observer*, 26 June 1921, p. 4.
7. Rebecca West, *New Statesman*, 17 (9 July 1921), 388.
8. W. Charles Pilley, *John Bull*, 17 September 1921, p. 4.
9. Edward Shanks, *London Mercury*, 4 (August 1921), 433.
10. J. M. Murry, *Nation and Athenaeum*, 29 (13 August 1921), 713.

11. David Cavitch, *D. H. Lawrence and the New World* (New York: Oxford Univ. Press, 1969), p. 62.
12. West, *New Statesman* (9 July 1921), p. 390.
13 Murry, *Nation and Athenaeum* (13 August 1921), pp. 713–14.
14. *Saturday Westminster Gazette*, 58 (2 July 1921), 15.
15. D. H. Lawrence, *St Mawr & The Virgin and the Gypsy* (1925 and 1930; rpt. Harmondsworth: Penguin Books, 1950), p. 79.
16. Scott Sanders, *D. H. Lawrence: The World of the Major Novels* (London: Vision Press, 1973), pp. 123–32.
17. Daleski, *The Forked Flame*, p. 147.
18. Pritchard, *D. H. Lawrence: Body of Darkness*, p. 105.
19. Keith Sagar, *The Art of D. H. Lawrence* (Cambridge: Cambridge Univ. Press, 1966), p. 96.
20. *Ibid.*, p. 97.
21. *Ibid.*, p. 103.

CHAPTER 6 *The Lost Girl*

1. 'Elsa Culverwell' is my name for the unpublished MS described in *Tedlock* 44–6 under the title 'My mother made a failure. . .', and now in the Morris Library of the University of Southern Illinois at Carbondale.
2. Carl Hovey to Robert Mountsier, 17 ix 1920; letter in the collection of Mountsier's papers in the Humanities Research Center, University of Texas.
3. H. L. Mencken to Fanny Butcher, 23 iv 1921; in *New Mencken Letters*, ed. C. Bode (New York: Dial Press, 1977), p. 141.
4. Despite at least three request by Lawrence to Martin Secker for the spelling 'Ciccio' (24 vi 1920, 18 ix 1920, 08 ii 1927), the spelling 'Cicio' of the *Lost Girl* MS (*Roberts* E 209, in the Humanities Research Center, University of Texas) was retained in Secker's edition and subsequent reprint, and is current in the present-day editions of Penguin Books and Heinemann. The spelling 'Ciccio' will be restored in the forthcoming edition published by C.U.P.
5. James Joyce, *Ulysses* (1922; rpt. London: The Bodley Head, 1960), p. 933.
6. Leavis, *D. H. Lawrence* (1930), p. 123.
7. Hovey to Mountsier, 17 ix 1920.

CHAPTER 7 *Aaron's Rod*

1. Daleski, *The Forked Flame*, p. 190.
2. John Alcorn, *The Nature Novel from Hardy to Lawrence* (London: Macmillan, 1977), p. 100.
3. Daleski, *The Forked Flame*, p. 211.
4. Eliseo Vivas, *D. H. Lawrence: The Failure and the Triumph of Art* (Bloomington: Indiana Univ. Press, 1960), p. 22.
5. Sagar, *The Art of D. H. Lawrence*, p. 114.
6. Lawrence habitually sent copies of his books to his two married sisters; it says something, perhaps, about Aaron's treatment of his family that, to begin with, Lawrence particularly asked Secker not to send them *Aaron's*

Rod (11 vi 1922). The sheer perversity of Aaron abandoning his family was perhaps more than Lawrence wanted to send members of his own family, who had small children of their own.

7. D. H. Lawrence, *Sea and Sardinia* (1921; rpt. Harmondsworth: Penguin Books, 1968), p. 207.
8. Vivas, *D. H. Lawrence: The Failure and the Triumph of Art*, p. 22.
9. Sagar, *The Art of D. H. Lawrence*, p. 113.
10. Daleski, *The Forked Flame*, p. 212.
11. Leavis, *D. H. Lawrence: Novelist*, p. 32.
12. D. H. Lawrence, *Apocalypse* (1931; rpt. Harmondsworth: Penguin Books, 1974), p. 126.

CHAPTER 8 *Kangaroo*

1. Richard Aldington, *D. H. Lawrence: Portrait of a Genius, But . . .* (1950; rpt. New York: Collier Books, 1961), p. 243.
2. H. T. Moore, *The Priest of Love* (London: Heinemann, 1974), p. 351.
3. Sagar, *The Art of D. H. Lawrence*, p. 136.
4. Pritchard, *D. H. Lawrence: Body of Darkness*, p. 150.
5. *Kangaroo* MS (*Roberts* E 182), in the Humanities Research Center, University of Texas.
6. Martin Secker to Curtis Brown, 01 xi 1923; in M. Secker, *Letters from a Publisher* (London: Enitharmon Press, 1970), p. 17.
7. Moore, *The Priest of Love*, p. 349.
8. Dorothy Richardson, *Pointed Roofs* (London: Duckworth, 1915), p. 16.
9. Cavitch, *D. H. Lawrence and the New World*, p. 133.
10. Compton Mackenzie, *Octave Five* (London: Chatto & Windus, 1966), p. 167.
11. Alyse Gregory, *Dial*, 76 (January 1924), 71.
12. Anon, *TLS*, 13 December 1923, p. 864.
13. Catherine Carswell, *The Savage Pilgrimage*, 1st ed. (London: Chatto & Windus, 1932), pp. 38–9.
14. Henry James to Howard Sturgis, 05 viii 1914; in *The Letters of Henry James*, ed. P. Lubbock, 2 vols. (London: Macmillan, 1920), II, 398.
15. MS of 'The Crown' (*Roberts* E 80a and b) in the Humanities Research Center, University of Texas. The fourth section, for instance, is largely rewritten in the 1925 version.

CHAPTER 9 *The Plumed Serpent*

1. Mabel Luhan, *Lorenzo in Taos* (New York: Knopf, 1932), p. 12.
2. Frieda Lawrence to Thomas Seltzer, 10 ii 1923; in D. H. Lawrence, *Letters to Thomas & Adele Seltzer*, ed. G. M. Lacy (Santa Barbara: Black Sparrow Press, 1976), p. 68.
3. L. D. Clark, *Dark Night of the Body* (Austin: Univ. of Texas Press, 1964), p. 36.
4. 'Quetzalcoatl' TS (*Roberts* E 313b), in the Houghton Library, University of Harvard.

5. D. H. Lawrence, *Mornings in Mexico & Etruscan Places* (1927 & 1932; rpt. Harmondsworth: Penguin Books, 1960), pp. 89–90.
6. J. Kessler, 'Descent in Darkness: the Myth of *The Plumed Serpent*', in *A D. H. Lawrence Miscellany*, ed. H. T. Moore (Carbondale: Southern Illinois Univ. Press, 1959), p. 258.
7. John Vickery, '*The Plumed Serpent* and the Eternal Paradox', *Criticism*, 5 (1963), 119–34.
8. Clark, *Dark Night of the Body*, p. 73.
9. Alastair Niven, *D. H. Lawrence: The Novels* (Cambridge: Cambridge Univ. Press, 1978), p. 170.
10. Moore, *The Priest of Love*, p. 399.
11. Pritchard, *D. H. Lawrence: Body of Darkness*, p. 171.
12. 'Quetzalcoatl' TS, p. 272.
13. Kermode, *Lawrence*, p. 110.
14. Clark, *Dark Night of the Body*, p. 13.
15. Lawrence, *Mornings in Mexico*, p. 51.
16. *Ibid.*, p. 52.
17. *Revelation* xxii. 16.
18. *Revelation* ii. 26-8.
19. *Matthew* xxviii. 20.
20. Moore, *The Priest of Love*, pp. 371–2.
21. Ira D. Sankey, *Sacred Songs and Solos—1200 Hymns* (London: Marshall, Morgan & Scott, n. d.), No 1014.
22. *Ibid.*, No 471.
23. *Ibid.*, No 1017.
24. Leavis, *D. H. Lawrence: Novelist*, p. 68.
25. D. H. Lawrence, *Movements in European History*, ed. J. T. Boulton (Oxford: Oxford Univ. Press, 1971), p. 321.
26. *Ibid.*, p. 321.

CHAPTER 10 *Lady Chatterley's Lover*

1. Lawrence, *St Mawr*, p. 228.
2. Sanders, *D. H. Lawrence: The World of the Major Novels*, p. 179.
3. Viz., *The White Peacock, Sons and Lovers, The Rainbow, Women in Love, The Lost Girl, Aaron's Rod*.
4. See *Paintings of D. H. Lawrence*, ed. M. Levy (London: Cory, Adams & Mackay, 1964), pp. 75, 91.
5. E.g., *Birds and Beasts of the Greek Anthology* (September 1927) and *In the Beginning* (December 1927), both printed by the Tipografia Giuntina—the press Lawrence was to employ.
6. *Ottoline*, ed. R. Gathorne-Hardy (London: Faber & Faber, 1963), p. 55.
7. Sanders, *D. H. Lawrence: The World of the Major Novels*, p. 195.
8. E.g., 'Leave Sex Alone', 'Let us Talk, Let us Laugh', 'The Effort of Love' (*Poems* i 470, 471, 506).
9. Cavitch, *D. H. Lawrence and the New World*, p. 197.

Index

Page numbers in **bold** type indicate major references.